Early Childhood Education & Play

Level 5

Early Childhood Education & Play

Level 5

Eilis Flood

and

Catriona Hardy

Gill & Macmillan

Gill & Macmillan
Hume Avenue
Park West
Dublin 12
with associated companies throughout the world
www.gillmacmillan.ie

© 2013 Eilis Flood and Catriona Hardy

978 07171 5716 7

Index compiled by Cliff Murphy
Design and print origination by O'K Graphic Design, Dublin
Printed by Printer Trento Srl, Italy

The paper used in this book comes from the wood pulp of managed forests. For every tree felled, at least one tree is planted, thereby renewing natural resources.

For permission to reproduce photographs, the author and publisher gratefully acknowledge the following:

© Alamy: 25, 40, 89, 104, 109, 138, 156, 192; © Getty Images: 3, 134; © Shutterstock: 118; Courtesy of Glen Outdoor School, 'Ireland's First Outdoor Daycare': 176; Courtesy of HighScope Educational Research Foundation: 55; Courtesy of Open Clip Art Library: 158, 183, 191; Courtesy of The Park Academy Childcare: 174; Courtesy of Storysack: 124.

The author and publisher have made every effort to trace all copyright holders, but if any has been inadvertently overlooked we would be pleased to make the necessary arrangement at the first opportunity.

Contents

Section 1

APPROACHES TO EARLY
CHILDHOOD EDUCATION

The Montessori Approach

Maria Montessori was the founder of the Montessori approach to education. Montessori promoted the idea that children have a greater ability to learn when they are taught via a practical approach in a carefully formulated environment. Before Montessori's time many educators simply passed on as much information as possible to children, so the Montessori methods were a significant turning point in early childhood education and care (ECEC). The Montessori approach remains popular in many countries. There are many Montessori training courses and purpose-built Montessori schools in Ireland, catering particularly for children aged 3–6. A smaller number of Montessori schools for children aged 6–12 are also in operation.

Maria Montessori

Maria Montessori was born on 31 August 1870 in Chiaravalle, Italy. Both of her parents – her father Alessandro and her mother Renilde – were well educated for people of their time. Her father was an old-fashioned, conservative gentleman who worked as a civil servant. Her mother, who was some years younger than her husband, was an avid reader. In 1875, Montessori and her parents moved to Rome and she was enrolled in a local school there. As a young child, Montessori learned easily and did exceptionally well in exams. Her intentions were to become an engineer. This was deemed an unusual choice for a woman, as engineering was considered to be a typical male career. Montessori was encouraged by her parents to become a teacher. She was adamant, however, that she would not take up a traditional female career, so she decided to become a doctor. Her father was opposed to this and she suffered a further setback when she was refused entry to medical school.

In 1890, Montessori enrolled at the University of Rome to study physics, maths and natural science. She received her diploma some time later. She eventually succeeded in becoming the first woman to enter medical school in Italy. She won a series of scholarships which, together with the money she earned through giving some private tuition, enabled her to pay for most of her medical education herself. The time that she spent at medical school was not easy. As she was the only woman on the course, she had to cope with a lot of jealousy and prejudice from her male peers. She spent most of her time working alone on college projects, while the men studied and worked as a team. She was a dedicated and conscientious student, however, and in July 1896 she became the first woman to graduate from the University of Rome Medical School and qualify as a doctor. She subsequently became widely known because of this historical title.

Also in 1896, Montessori spent a significant amount of time visiting and working in a psychiatric clinic in Rome. Here she treated vulnerable children who were lacking in care and education. As a result of this neglect, they were unable to function in normal life. It was from this experience that Montessori realised the importance of providing children with the appropriate stimulation needed to function and thrive as human beings. It was here that Montessori met and worked alongside Giuseppe Montesano, with whom she later had a love affair.

In 1898, Montessori gave birth to a son, whom she named Mario. She did not raise Mario herself, however; he was cared for by a family near Rome. Montessori visited him on a regular basis and they had a good relationship, particularly later on in life. Mario continued his mother's work after her death. It is not fully understood why Montessori and Montesano did not marry. There has been much speculation and it is thought that neither of them believed in the idea of marriage. Also, it was a crucial time in Montessori's career, when her work was becoming increasingly well known. She was busy lecturing on the lack of resources for children with special needs and, as a result of her successful work, she was appointed co-director with Montesano at an orthophrenic school. At this school, she was able to introduce many of her innovative ideas regarding the education of young children. She spent two years working here designing new materials, teaching and observing children by day and writing up her notes by night.

In 1904, Montessori was appointed Professor of Anthropology at the University of Rome.

She also spent time at a day care centre in the slums of San Lorenzo in Italy. Here she cared for children aged 3–7, while their parents were working. She observed the positive reactions of children when they were given the opportunity to work with real materials. She also observed the differences between these children and those she had worked with previously. She saw the great potential that children had when they were provided with an environment equipped with appropriate learning apparatus to suit their developmental needs.

Montessori established her first *Casa dei Bambini* (literally 'children's house') in January 1907. There was a small opening ceremony conducted to mark the occasion, but some people did not think it would be very successful. Montessori felt differently, however, and she was confident that the new environment she had created would give children the opportunity to learn to the best of their ability. She also felt that it would be a place where children were treated equally and with respect, an approach they had never experienced before. Montessori believed that this was the most successful way to teach children.

During her research, Montessori came across the work of two French educators from the nineteenth century: Jean Marc Gaspard Itard and his student, Edouard Seguin. Itard supported education through the senses, while Seguin created practical materials to help the development of a child's sensory perceptions and motor skills. These men were influential figures and Montessori incorporated elements of their work into her curriculum for education. At this time, Montessori also broadened her knowledge by exploring the works of Jean-Jacques Rousseau, Johann Heinrich Pestalozzi and Friedrich Froebel. The news of Montessori's approach to education was spreading quickly and fascinating people around the world. By the end of 1908, there were five 'children's houses' in operation: four in Rome and one in Milan. Young children now had the ability to read and write.

In 1909, Montessori gave the first training course in her approach to education. Her notes from this became her first book, *The Montessori Method*, which was published that same year in Italian. It became a book of high demand and was soon translated into 20 different languages. Montessori societies, training courses and schools were now being established all over the world. Montessori gave lectures in many countries across Europe and in America. Montessori now devoted all her time to educating people about her approach to education. Montessori's other books include *The Absorbent Mind* and *The Discovery of the Child*.

In 1949, Montessori received the first of three nominations for the Nobel Peace Prize. She attended her final formal engagement in 1951, which took place in London. She died on 6 May 1952 in the Netherlands, with her son Mario by her side.

Core Concepts of the Montessori Approach

This section provides detailed information on the core concepts of Maria Montessori's approach to ECEC, including:

- Developmental planes
- Sensitive periods
- Prepared environment
- Materials
- Curriculum
- Work cycle
- Three-period lesson
- The role of the teacher.

Developmental Planes

Montessori believed that human development does not occur in a steady routine but rather in a series of developmental planes. She identified four planes of development from child to adult:

- 0–6 years
- 6–12 years
- 12–18 years
- 18–24 years.

The First Plane: 0–6 years (The Absorbent Mind)

Montessori described the child aged 0–3 as the *spiritual embryo*. During the first six years of life, the child goes through a lot of physical and psychological growth, exploration and development. This growth and development occurs without the child being aware that it is happening. The child is developing in all areas of their body.

  The child is always absorbing their surroundings. Montessori called this the *absorbent mind*. Montessori believed that this time is a very crucial time, since so much learning is taking place for the child. The child begins to talk, walk and socialise with others. They begin to establish limitations and expectations. The child needs love, stability, patience and understanding. The child should be allowed the freedom and independence to do tasks for themselves and be allowed to make mistakes. The child must be placed in an environment in which they can develop and become *normalised*. (Normalisation occurs in all children – it means that development is proceeding normally.) Montessori developed a specific curriculum for children aged 3–6.

The Second Plane: 6–12 years (Childhood)

The child has the capacity to explore a wide range of tasks and opportunities, provided they are readily available to them. Montessori designed a specific curriculum for children aged 6–12 years. It is similar to the curriculum for children aged 3–6 years, but with a wider and more challenging range of exercises. It is at this stage that the child now has the ability to use their imagination.

The Third Plane: 12–18 years (Adolescence)

The adolescence plane involves the creation of the adult. It is the progression from childhood to adulthood. There is still important development yet to come during the final plane.

The Fourth Plane: 18–24 years (Maturity)

The child has now become a grown adult and has developed independence and responsibility. The adult has developed spiritual strength and can work for the good of society. All previous planes are in preparation for this final plane.

Sensitive Periods

The term 'sensitive periods' was introduced by a Dutch biologist, Hugo De Vries, who analysed the development of animals and insects. Montessori applied this theory of sensitive periods to education. She observed the behaviour and movements of children and, after careful analysis, established a schedule of sensitive periods. These sensitive periods suggest that there are different areas of the environment to which children are particularly attracted at specific stages of their development. Learning and development occur in unison with these attractions or interests. Montessori discovered that children have a great capacity to develop by themselves. Sensitive periods occur during the first six years of life, at certain ages. Montessori believed that this is a crucial time for children, since these experiences shape their personalities. Sensitive periods are at the centre of the Montessori approach to ECEC. They form the basis of planning and implementation and they are one of Montessori's most identifiable concepts.

Order

Order is one of the first sensitive periods to appear. It appears in the first few months of life and continues until approximately 4 or 5 years of age. Children's love of order is based on their need for a precise and organised environment so that they can begin to understand their surroundings. Children in the Montessori classroom respond positively when materials are put in their correct place; often, children will insist on returning materials to their correct location in the classroom. Young children are often aware of irregularities in their environment. They notice if things are out of place and they can become quite upset as a result. The teacher can help the children achieve order in the environment by offering guidance in the completion of exercises where children are shown and reminded where materials should be placed.

Montessori observed that 'order is one of the needs of life which, when it is satisfied, produces a real happiness' (Montessori 1972: 52).

Movement

Children aged 0–4 possess sensitivity to movement. They have to move around in order to learn. The sensitive period for movement is most intense during the first year of life. Montessori highlighted the fact that humans are the only mammal that has to learn how to walk. Young babies are unable to control any of their own movements. Babies do not even know they have hands and feet. Around the age of 12 months, however, babies take their first steps. Walking develops without children ever being taught how to do it. Motor co-ordination, hand–eye co-ordination and refinement of the movements of the hand are the main tasks for children at this stage of development. The environment must be well prepared in order to give children opportunities to crawl and walk safely. Children's need to walk is so strong that they will be determined to figure out the skill and perfect it.

Language

Language is one of the longer-lasting sensitive periods. There are many different auditory stimulations in children's environment and yet babies are inevitably attracted to the human voice. It is from this that they learn to speak their native language. Children then progress to the sensitivity of the construction of language. During the first few years of life, learning to talk and understand others can be an intense but also an enjoyable time for young children. No one teaches children to talk: language develops naturally. By the age of 6 months, children say their first syllables. By the age of 12 months, children say a few intentional words. At 21 months, children can say a few phrases. At the age of 2, children have a variety of words and sentences. Around the age of 3, children speak in sentences and paragraphs; now they are able to express themselves in order to have their needs met.

Minute Objects

Children are aware of (and can be fascinated by) tiny objects in their environment. These objects are so small that they can go unnoticed by adults. This particular sensitive period peaks for children around the age of 2.

Refinement of the Senses

Refinement of the senses occurs as children spontaneously investigate and reach out to their surroundings. They see, touch, feel, smell, taste and hear. Children explore objects that are alike and different in their environment. Montessori developed *sensorial activities*, which are always popular in the classroom. During these activities children are free to work with a variety of materials to help refine the senses.

Social Aspects

When children become relatively stable in their general environment, they begin to attend to the social environment. During this time, children attend closely to the observed and expected behaviour of individuals or groups. Children who have been deprived of social interaction (for whatever reason) are less likely to feel comfortable around others. This feeling can take a long time to overcome.

Prepared Environment

Montessori proposed that in order to fulfil the various needs of children it is necessary for them to be educated in a suitable environment. This environment will result in a far greater capacity to learn. Montessori created such a place and called it the *prepared environment*. The Montessori classroom is generally known as the prepared environment. The prepared environment is very attractive to children. It is bright and welcoming and is equipped with many Montessori materials set on low-level shelves. Montessori was a believer of innovation in the classroom. The prepared environment is the ideal place where children can be innovative and explore a wide range of materials. The special materials in this environment will increase children's independence and self-esteem. The prepared environment is not necessarily a silent environment. Actually, the aim is to have an environment filled with the sounds of children busily working with various materials.

Montessori intended the prepared environment to be a nourishing and enjoyable place in which children can learn. When children reach the age of 3, they are ready to learn and explore independently. This makes a nourishing environment all the more important at this key stage. The Montessori prepared environment is specifically designed for children aged 3–6. Within the prepared environment, there is always a great sense of community. Children of many different ages work together in an atmosphere of co-operation and friendship, rather than competitiveness. The prepared environment supports equality and diversity. Children are all given equal opportunities and are educated about different cultures, especially through the cultural materials.

According to Montessori there are several principles of the prepared environment:

- Structure and order
- Freedom
- Reality and nature
- Beauty
- Social environment
- Intellectual environment.

Structure and Order

It is the responsibility of both the teacher and the children to create order in the Montessori classroom. They must ensure that every exercise has its correct place on the shelf and they must ensure that it is replaced after use. This helps the children to know exactly where to find each exercise. This also gives children a sense of responsibility. Children learn to be responsible for the particular exercise they are working with and they ensure that it is tidied away neatly with no pieces missing after use. Within the prepared environment, the teacher will have the materials arranged on low shelving according to their place in the Montessori curriculum. Each curriculum area has a separate shelf. The materials are presented in a hierarchy: from simple to complex, and concrete to abstract. Through observation, the teacher may notice that there is an item that the children overlook. Perhaps the teacher observes that the item needs replacing. If this is the case, the teacher may draw the children's attention to the fact that the item may have been moved to another location. The teacher will ensure that the environment is ready for use each day and that everything is as it should be.

Freedom

Freedom is vital in the Montessori classroom. Children must be free to choose the particular exercise they wish to work with, providing they have been introduced to it by the teacher. If a child has not been introduced to an exercise but they are eager to do it, the teacher may present the lesson if they think the child is ready. No child should ever be forced to partake in an exercise or group activity in which they do not wish to partake, nor should the teacher give any child an exercise to complete just for the sake of doing something. Montessori believed that freedom of choice at an early age helps children to become automatically attracted to other materials that are good for their educational needs in the future. Children choosing their own work and being taught things they *want* to learn enhances their concentration and confidence.

Children must have the freedom to work at their own pace: they should not be hurried to complete an exercise by the teacher or by other children. Each child should be free to repeat an activity as many times as they wish. The focus is not the quantity of exercises completed in one day: it is the enjoyment and satisfaction that the children receive from doing an activity correctly.

Children are given the freedom to sort out for themselves any issues that arise in the classroom. The teacher is there to observe and to step in if necessary. The multiple-age grouping in the Montessori classroom is important: children of various ages all work together and the younger children learn from the other children (and vice versa).

Children in the prepared environment also have freedom of movement: they can sit at whatever table they wish and they can do an activity at the table or on the floor. Montessori explained: 'There is respect for the environment and for the individuals within it, which comes through experience of freedom within the community' (Hainstock 1986).

Reality and Nature

In the Montessori classroom, everything is real: real furniture, a real mirror to polish, glass bowls and jugs that are used in real life. There is only ever one of each exercise. Children learn to wait their turn if there is another child using materials that they wish to use.

Children in the Montessori classroom must have access to nature of some kind. Children must have opportunities spend time outdoors, e.g. for caring for plants. Ideally, a Montessori school would have a small garden attached where children could visit regularly. Children should have the opportunity to gather objects for a nature table and to go on nature walks. The teacher will introduce magnifying glasses and other tools to help the children experience nature.

The prepared environment should be large, bright and airy. It should be eye-catching, with plenty of work space and space to walk around. The classroom should be child friendly, with child-sized furniture that allows the children to do things and get things for themselves without having to rely on the teacher.

Beauty

The Montessori classroom does not need to be lavish or expensive. It is better if it is realistic and furnished with good-quality materials. The colour of the walls should not be overpowering: colours should be attractive and bright, but soft. There must be a warm and welcoming atmosphere.

Social Environment

Through working in the prepared environment, children learn to encourage and help each other. As children get older they become more socially aware. Social interaction is encouraged in the classroom and children often work in groups. There is a great sense of community in the classroom. All children work together and co-operate, rather than being competitive. The older children especially guide the younger children in the classroom. Children regularly engage with each other during *circle time*.

Intellectual Environment

The purpose of the Montessori environment is not only to develop children intellectually but also to develop their personalities. Children learn creatively through developmentally appropriate materials within five curriculum areas:

- Practical life
- Sensorial
- Language
- Maths
- Culture/Science.

Some of these activities may be child or teacher initiated. Mostly, it is up to the children to decide what to work with. The teacher may initiate a new activity the child has not completed before. The following activities may be completed on a daily basis:

- Settling in time: jigsaws, play-dough, straws
- Work time: work with Montessori materials, typically in the first hour
- Circle time: a new lesson – songs, stories, poems, etc.
- Outdoor/art time: playing outdoors, art activity
- Story time.

Materials

Montessori experimented with many different activities and materials throughout her time working with children. She kept only those that the children used and enjoyed the most. Through observation, Montessori realised that it is important for children to be placed in an environment where activities are designed to support their development and where they have a choice of materials to use. This gives them the power to teach themselves. Montessori called this *auto education*.

Children aged 0–6 are at a stage of life where they possess their greatest ability to learn. Therefore, they can never have enough stimulating materials. Just as the Montessori curriculum has a number of curriculum areas, the Montessori classroom has a number of shelves to cater for these areas. One shelf is provided for each of the following: practical life, sensorial, maths, language and culture.

Each area of the curriculum has its own area or particular shelf in the classroom. Each piece of material has been designed to draw the children's attention, so there should be no real need for an adult to intervene. The materials should be cared for, all their original form, complete and with no pieces missing. Each piece of material should serve a purpose and should not be found in the Montessori class unless it does so.

The materials must be real and breakable: children will know that glass might break if it is dropped. There is a built-in control of error in the materials. This means that the children themselves will know during (or at the end of) an exercise if they have made a mistake. For example, if a child has made a mistake in the sensorial knobbed cylinder exercise, the child will discover this for themselves when they go to put each cylinder back in its place – the last cylinder will not fit. The child will know instantly that they must go back over their work.

Many materials can be used in different ways for different exercises, e.g. there are four exercises and two games that can be completed with Sensorial Colour Box 3. Materials must be presented in isolation and at the right time for each individual child, since the children will be at different stages of development. The teacher will observe children closely to ensure that they are ready to be introduced to a new exercise. Each child is introduced to simple and concrete exercises first, before moving on to more complex and abstract exercises. Every piece of material indirectly prepares children for future activities. For example, in mathematics the child uses spindles to help practise their numbers before progressing to the golden bead material.

> An interesting piece of work, freely chosen, which has the virtue of inducing concentration rather than fatigue, adds to the child's energies and mental capabilities and leads to self mastery. (M. Montessori, *The Absorbent Mind*)

Montessori Curriculum

Practical Life

It is usually the *practical life* exercises with which children will first experiment in the classroom. These are simple and relevant activities that children will recognise, perhaps because they have seen their parents do them at home, e.g. polishing a shoe or pouring water. Children have an innate desire to imitate exercises they have seen someone else perform. The practical life activities are very attractive exercises. They involve child-sized materials from real life. The materials are laid within easy reach on trays or shelving and they are displayed as they would be at home.

In doing these everyday tasks, children build on important skills, such as independence, co-ordination, concentration and self-esteem. Children find great joy in practical life exercises and will often repeat them several times.

Generally speaking, there is no particular prescribed list of materials involved in Montessori practical life curriculum. It is up to the individual teacher to arrange their own exercises, using materials based on the important Montessori principles of beauty, simplicity, isolation of difficulty, and progression (from simple to complex). Some of the most popular practical life exercises are listed on p. 14.

Independence

Through practical life exercises, children learn the skills that enable them to become independent. Children strive for independence. Teachers must show them the skill and then give them the opportunity and time to practise and perfect it without feeling rushed or hurried in any way. The experience of practising such exercises will stay with the children throughout life. This will help them to become independent and to learn social skills. Children can learn how to pour their own juice or button or zip up their own coat.

Co-ordination

Through practical life exercises, children's gross-motor movements will be enhanced. Gross-motor skills involve movement of the large muscles of the arms, legs and torso. Fine-motor skills will also be enhanced – these will involve the small muscles of the body that enable functions such as writing, grasping small objects and fastening clothing. In addition, hand–eye co-ordination is enhanced. This is the co-ordinated control of eye movement together with hand movement in order to execute a task.

Concentration

One of the most calming activities for children is concentration. The practical life exercises inspire children to develop concentration, since the exercises are designed in such a way that children must focus on the exactness of the action. The actions are controlled by the children, so children can repeat them as often as necessary. The exercises challenge the body as well as the mind. Practical life exercises will lay the foundation for work in other curriculum areas in the classroom.

Confidence and Self-esteem

As children perform and perfect practical life exercises, they feel a sense of achievement and pride. Therefore, self-esteem and self-respect develop. In addition, since a Montessori classroom involves children of mixed ages, children learn from each other without competition. They are given the opportunity to work independently and correct their own mistakes. They develop at their own pace.

Examples of Practical Life Exercises

Introductory activities	Manipulative skills	Care of the self	Care of the environment	Grace and courtesy
Talking in the classroom	Pouring rice from jug to jug	Button frame	Caring for books	Interrupting a conversation
Walking in the classroom	Spooning rice	Snap frame	Sweeping the floor	Saying please and thank you
Carrying a chair	Pouring rice into three containers	Velcro frame	Polishing a mirror	Introducing oneself as Gaeilge (in Irish)
Rolling/unrolling a mat	Squeezing water with a sponge	Buckle frame	Preparing fruit	Greeting people
Carrying a tray	Using tongs	Zip frame	Setting a tray	Offering food
Carrying objects on a tray	Using tweezers	Hook and eye frame	Cleaning up after meals	Asking politely for something
Fire drill	Opening and closing bottles	Bow frame	Washing dishes	Table manners
Handling scissors correctly	Opening and closing locks	Lacing frame	Washing clothes	Saying excuse me
The mystery bag	Folding cloths	Washing hands	Gardening	Coughing/sneezing politely
Opening and closing a door	The silence game	Polishing a shoe	Dusting	Expressing admiration
Carrying a sharp object	Cutting exercise	Brushing teeth	Arranging flowers in a vase	Offering help
Standing and pushing in a chair	Exercises while walking on the line	Combing hair	Caring for animals	Introducing a friend

Sensorial

The *sensorial* curriculum relates to the senses. Montessori believed that the senses are a starting point to intellectual growth and that sensorial exercises help to mature the eyes, ears, nose, tongue and skin. Children pass through a sensitive period for refinement of the senses, during which they become more interested in and aware of their surroundings.

Each sensorial exercise isolates one specific sense at a time – this is done in order to maximise the refinement of the particular sense. Montessori expanded on the known five senses. She included chromatic/colour, baric/weight, thermic/temperature and tactile/muscular.

Sensorial exercises are usually introduced to the children after they have completed several of the practical life exercises. Montessori stated: 'The senses, being explorers of the world, open the way to knowledge. Our apparatus for educating the senses offers the child a key to guide his explorations of the world' (Montessori 1988: 167).

Sensorial materials help children to:

- **Develop:** Activities develop children's senses. Exercises gradually build from simple and concrete to complex and abstract.
- **Order:** Exercises develop children's sense of order. This is because the activities identify a single perceptual quality, e.g. colour. As children progress, they are given examples of differences so that they can explore those patterns.
- **Broaden:** Children's experience of the world is broadened when the sensorial exercises awaken certain sense experiences that were previously unexplored, e.g. shapes, smells and textures.
- **Refine:** Exercises refine children's sense perception. Exercises allow children to experience and concentrate on particular qualities in perfect clarity and isolation.

Examples of Sensorial Exercises

Sense	What the sense perceives	Examples of sensorial material
Visual	Pattern	Knobbed cylinders, pink tower, broad stair, long rods, knobless cylinders
Chromatic	Colour grades	Colour Box 1, Colour Box 2, Colour Box 3
Auditory	Loudness and pitch	Sound boxes
Tactile	Texture	Touch boards, touch tablets, touch fabrics
Baric	Weight	Baric tablets
Thermic	Temperature	Thermic bottles
Gustatory	Taste and odours	Tasting bottles
Olfactory	Smells and odours	Smell jars
Stereognostic	Tactile and muscular impressions	The mystery bag

Language

Children have many requirements when it comes to language. They need a broad exposure to language, with correct articulation and punctuation. Children need to experience different modes of language, to hear and tell stories and to have freedom of conversation. Children need encouragement to communicate with others.

The Montessori language curriculum is based on phonics. Children also have experience with forming letters and they become familiar with sounds, thus becoming able to create words and sentences. Children work on vocabulary development, communication skills and reading and writing. The language shelf in the Montessori classroom will be equipped with metal insets, sandpaper letters and reading material in different colours. For more discussion on literacy, see Chapter 10.

Examples of Language Exercises

Introductory	Pink reading material	Blue reading material	Green reading material	Grammar
Eye-spy game	Object box	Object box	Picture and word cards	Noun box
Classified pictures	Picture box	Picture box	Phonogram booklet	The noun game
Exercises with the farm	Object and word box	Object and word box	Phonogram wordlist	Verb box
Insets for design	Picture and word box	Picture and word box	Phonogram sentence strips	The verb game
Sandpaper letters	Large picture card	Large picture card	Phonogram story books	Adjective box
	Secret box	Secret box		
Alphabet exercise strips	Reading lists	Reading lists	Phonogram lists in a folder	Singular and plural
Large, moveable alphabet	Puzzle words	Puzzle words	Word building with small moveable alphabet	
	Phrase strips	Phrase strips		
	Sentence strips	Sentence strips		

Maths

As with all Montessori materials, the maths curriculum is performed by children, using self-correcting materials. The exercises move from concrete to increasingly abstract as children progress through the curriculum. The exercises are sequential: each one builds upon the previous one. The maths shelf in the classroom will help children to differentiate concrete and abstract. Each exercise contains many similar elements (e.g. golden bead material) so that the child will find it easier to master.

The maths materials are presented to children when interest is expressed or when the teacher observes that an individual child is ready. When the child has been successful in completing the exercise, the teacher takes a passive role in order to allow exploration until the concept is mastered. Therefore, each child has the opportunity to develop a mathematical mind at their own pace.

Maths is a subject that is feared, since many people do not have good childhood experiences of maths. Montessori believed that a strong foundation of maths during the pre-school years would help children to succeed in maths in later life. For more discussion on numeracy, see Chapter 10.

Examples of Maths Exercises

Numbers 1–10	Golden bead material	Teens and tens	Linear counting	Introduction to addition	Introduction to subtraction	Introduction to multiplication	Introduction to division
Number rods	Teaching names of the quantities	Introduction to short bead stair	Hundred chain	Addition with snake game 1	Subtraction with small number rods	Multiplication with short bead stair	Division board and beads
Sandpaper numbers	Counting through 1–1000	Seguin Board A Exercise 1 11–19: beads	Thousand chain	Addition with snake game 2	Subtraction with short bead stair	Multiplication with board and beads	Division chart A
Number rods and cards	Beads practice	Seguin Board A Exercise 2 11–19: boards	Skip counting	Addition with small number rods	Subtraction strip board	Multiplication chart A	Division chart B
Spindle box	Naming the cards	Seguin Board A Exercise 3 11–19: beads and boards		Addition with short bead stair	Stages of recording	Multiplication chart B	
Zero games	Cards in sequence	Seguin Board B Exercise 1 10–90: beads		Addition strip board			
Cards and counters	Cards practice	Seguin Board B Exercise 2 10–90: boards		Stages of recording			
	Combining quantity and symbol	Seguin Board B Exercise 3: 10–90 beads and boards					
	Bird's eye view	Seguin Board B Exercise 4 11–99: beads and boards		Addition tables	Subtraction tables		
	Formation of numbers						
	Group/ individual operations with golden beads						

Culture/Science

The culture curriculum represents various ways of life. It gives children an introduction to geography, history, botany, zoology and science. Its aim is to promote a lifelong interest in nature and the world. All of the subjects are introduced from age 3 onwards. Children will be introduced to different maps, continents, plants, animals, history timelines and science experiments. All areas of culture should be accessible to the children. Children are then able to take their work from the shelves by themselves, perhaps to look at the pictures and go over what they have learned. Children should not have to ask permission to view this material. Some items will be colour coded (e.g. a matching exercise) and this acts as a control of error for the children.

The culture exercises allow the teacher to be innovative and to introduce other exercises that are related to children's culture. For more discussion on culture, see Chapter 10.

Examples of Culture/Science Exercises

Geography	History	Biology and science
Sandpaper globe	Calendars	Nature table
Coloured globe	Birthdays	Plastic animals
Jigsaw map of the world	The sandpaper clock	Pictures of plants and animals
Continent folders	Time	Life cycle of plants and animals
Introduction to land, air and water: jars and cards	A day in the life of a child	Parts of plants and animals
Introduction to landforms	Black and white timeline	Living and non-living
European maps: countries, capitals and flags		Simple science experiments: sink and float, magnets

Work Cycle

Every new exercise will be presented to the children by the teacher. The teacher uses a method called the *work cycle* to introduce the exercises. The same process is followed for the introduction of each new exercise. It is important that the teacher is consistent every time they use the work cycle. The teacher, having observed that the child is ready to do a new exercise, will introduce it as follows.

Example of a Work Cycle

- Invite the child to do an exercise with you.
- Explain to them that today you are going to show them how to do an exercise, e.g. Colour Box 1 (sensorial exercise).
- Invite them to accompany you to the sensorial shelf.
- Show them where the materials are kept on the shelf.
- Show them how to carry the material and invite them to find a free work space at the table or on a mat on the floor – in this case, at the table.
- Seat them on your non-dominant side (the side you don't write with – less movement, so the child can see better).
- Explain to them that you are going to show them how to do the exercise.
- Ask them to watch you. Explain that when you are finished, they can have a turn.
- Without too much talking, show them how to complete the exercise. Use slow, clear, methodical movements.
- Ask them if they would like to do the exercise.
- If they have been reasonably successful, ask them if they would like to repeat the exercise.
- If they say no, explain to them that they have been introduced to the activity and that now they can now do it whenever they wish.
- Ask them if they would like to help you to carry the exercise back to its correct place on the shelf.
- Record this presentation in the child's progress folder.
- End the work cycle.

Remember: if the child did not repeat the exercise correctly, they will need to be reintroduced to the exercise at a later date.

Note: Keep talking to a minimum. In some exercises, more talking is needed than others.

Three-period Lesson

The purpose of the *three-period lesson* is to give the child the correct language associated with a material. In many cases the child should have experience working with the particular material *before* they engage in a three-period lesson. The purpose of the lesson may be to teach the child the names of objects, quantities or colours. The three-period lesson is divided into three steps. Each step is isolated and it will help the child to absorb the language easily. These three steps are very important and they should be completed in this order:

1   This is…
2   Show me…
3   What is this?

Example of a Three-period Lesson: Golden Beads

Materials

1 × wooden tray
Units of golden beads:
- 1 × single bead
- 1 × ten-bead bar
- 1 × hundred square
- 1 × thousand cube
- 1 × felt mat

Presentation

- Begin the work cycle and then proceed to the three-period lesson.

1   This is…
- Isolate the single bead from the other beads.
- Place the single bead on the mat in front of the child, who is seated at your non-dominant side.
- Clearly name the single bead. Reiterate the name: 'This is a unit bead. We call it one. One.'
- Repeat the process with the ten-bead bar. (Isolate the bar, place it on the mat in front of the child, name it and reiterate the name.)
- Repeat the process with the hundred square.
- Repeat the process with the thousand cube.

2   Show me…
- Place all four units in front of the child, to see if the child is familiar with the name associated with each unit.
- Ask the child to show you a unit: 'Show me one unit.'
- Repeat this with all the units: 'Show me one ten. Show me one hundred.'
- You can move the units around at this stage.
- If the child answers correctly, move on to the next period of the lesson.

■ If they are unable to answer correctly, explain to them that together you have looked at golden beads today – and tomorrow you will look at them again. (Perhaps the child is not ready to complete the exercise.)

3   What is this?

■ Place all four units in front of the child again.

■ Ask the child to name each unit. Point to the single bead and say: 'What is this?'

■ Do this with each unit. You can move the beads around at this stage.

■ If the child names all of the beads correctly, invite them to repeat the exercise.

■ When the exercise is completed, invite the child to place the beads in the box and return the box to its shelf.

Link with Aistear

This lesson is suitable for children aged 4 and upwards. It links with the following themes, aims and learning goals of Aistear.

■ Wellbeing
  Aim 2, Learning Goal 1: Children will gain increasing control and co-ordination of body movements.

■ Identity and Belonging
  Aim 4, Learning Goal 4: Children will demonstrate dispositions like curiosity, persistence and responsibility.

■ Communicating
  Aim 1, Learning Goal 3: Children will interpret and respond to non-verbal communication by others.

  Aim 1, Learning Goal 5: Children will combine non-verbal and verbal communication to get their point across.

■ Exploring and Thinking
  Aim 1, Learning Goal 6: Children will come to understand concepts such as matching, comparing, ordering, sorting, size, weight, height, length, capacity and money in an enjoyable and meaningful way.

  Aim 2, Learning Goal 4: Children will demonstrate their ability to reason, negotiate and think logically.

Example of a Group Lesson (Practical Life): Washing Hands

Materials
1 × basin of clean warm water
Antibacterial soap
Paper towels
Pictures of germs under the microscope (optional)

Presentation

- Invite the children to sit around the table.
- Explain to them that today you are going to show them how to wash their hands.
- Ask the children to list times when we should wash our hands, e.g. after stroking a pet, after sneezing, etc. Invite a short discussion on this.
- Explain what germs are and how they can come to be on our hands. Help the children to understand that we cannot see germs but that they can make us sick. (Show the children pictures of germs under a microscope, if available.)
- Explain that careful washing of hands helps to prevent the spread of germs.
- Introduce the children to the items needed for washing hands.
- Ask the children to watch you as you do a dry demonstration of hand washing.
- Show the children what movements are needed for thorough hand washing: palm to palm; rub in between fingers; rotate fingers in opposing palm, etc.
- Use slow, clear, methodical movements. Ask the children to copy these movements.
- Introduce the basin of water and invite the children to watch as you now practise the hand washing movements in the water, using soap.
- When your hands are thoroughly washed, dry them with paper towels.
- Throughout the day, invite individual children to practise washing their hands in the sinks in the classroom.
- Record your observations in each child's progress folder.

Link with Aistear
This lesson links with the following themes, aims and learning goals of Aistear.

- Wellbeing
   Aim 2, Learning Goal 6: Children will make healthy choices and demonstrate positive attitudes to nutrition, hygiene, exercise and routine.

- Identity and Belonging
  Aim 3, Learning Goal 3: Children will interact, work co-operatively and help others.

- Communicating
  Aim 2, Learning Goal 1: Children will interact with other children and adults by listening, discussing and taking turns in conversation.

- Exploring and Thinking
  Aim 1, Learning Goal 1: Children will engage, explore and experiment in their environment and use new skills to manipulate objects and materials.

The Role of the Montessori Teacher

The prepared environment would not be complete without the Montessori teacher, who is the keeper of this environment. The Montessori teacher, however, is not the centre of attention in the classroom. They do not have a desk like traditional teachers; instead, they sit in among the children at circle time and throughout lessons.

The Montessori teacher's role centres on the preparation and organisation of materials in order to meet the needs and interests of the children. Teachers keep the classroom in meticulous order: all materials are complete and on their correct shelf in the correct order. The focus must always be children's learning. The teacher plans daily lessons and is always alert to changes in the children's interests, progress, moods and behaviour. The teacher will also create IEPs (Individual Education Plans) for each child.

The Montessori teacher must be a qualified professional who has been exclusively trained in the Montessori method of education. The teacher must be familiar with Montessori vocabulary (e.g. auto education) and also with the presentation of Montessori materials (practical life, sensorial, maths, language and culture exercises). The teacher must also be knowledgeable in child pedagogy and child development and they must be able to facilitate the children's needs accordingly.

Montessori teachers must never criticise or interfere with a child's work. Children must have the freedom to choose their own activities and learn without restriction. However, the teacher can offer help and encouragement when necessary. The teacher must never initiate any types of rewards or competitions. This will ensure that children are free to work at a pace that suits them.

Teacher as Guide and Facilitator

The Montessori teacher takes on many roles within the classroom environment. One of these is the role of guide and facilitator. They guide each child, introducing materials and assisting where needed. They carefully plan and create a well-prepared Montessori environment and atmosphere of learning. They do not intervene too often; instead, they will often step back while the children are working, allowing the children to learn by themselves. Children will gain satisfaction from their own discoveries and they will be able to draw their own conclusions. Rather than supplying children with answers all of the time, the Montessori teacher will ask the children for their opinion on solving various issues. The teacher will actively engage the children in the learning process, thus enhancing the children's ability to think for themselves. In many cases, children learn directly from the environment and from other children, rather than from a teacher.

Teacher as Observer

The Montessori teacher should be a patient and meticulous observer. They must engage in careful observation on a regular basis. They must document what they observe about each child, e.g. their interests, repetition with materials and social interaction. This helps the teacher to prepare the environment with the children's interests as the main priority. The teacher can share observations with parents. It is important that they are in regular correspondence with parents and maintain a good relationship.

Teacher as Reflective Practitioner

The teacher must reflect regularly on their own performance, especially during and after completing an exercise. They must carefully establish the elements of the lesson that worked and the elements that didn't work, and they must reflect on the reasons for this. They must consider whether there is anything they could change to make the lesson more successful or enjoyable for the children in the future. Simple changes can often make a big difference, e.g. timing issues or the addition of extra resources.

Montessori referred to the Montessori teacher as a 'directress'. However, the term 'teacher' is most commonly used in Ireland today.

The Froebel Approach

- **Friedrich Froebel**
- **Core concepts of the Froebel approach**

Friedrich Froebel

Friedrich Wilhelm August Froebel was born in Thuringia, south of Berlin, on 21 April 1782. He was the youngest son of Johann Jacob Froebel, a Lutheran pastor. Friedrich Froebel's mother died when he was an infant aged 9 months. His father remarried some years later and had another son. Friedrich Froebel experienced an unhappy childhood as a result of feeling neglected by his father and stepmother. He spent much of his upbringing living with his bachelor uncle, Herr Hoffman, who was left in charge of Froebel's early life and education. Froebel attended the local school close to where his uncle lived. As a child, Froebel excelled at subjects such as geometry and mapmaking and he displayed a true love of nature.

When Froebel was 15 years old, he was offered a two-year apprenticeship with a forester and surveyor in Neuhaus, Germany. He also began to study maths and botany. He classified groups of plants and read a range of books on the subjects. As a young adult, Froebel spent a period of time studying architecture in college in Frankfurt. At this stage of his life, he believed that this would be his main career. It was in Frankfurt, however, that he encountered Dr Anton Gruner – the principal of a new progressive model school in Frankfurt. Gruner was impressed by Froebel and he urged him to rethink his career as an architect and consider taking up a teaching position at the school. Froebel hastily switched career paths and accepted this opportunity. He spent two years assisting Gruner at the school.

Froebel then moved to Yverdon in Switzerland, where he spent two years observing and teaching under Johann Heinrich Pestalozzi at Pestalozzi's progressive model school. This was a great learning experience for Froebel and it shaped his life as a teacher. Pestalozzi perceived children as having a built-in desire to learn. Teachers at this type of school encouraged children's natural curiosity and exploration. There was a big emphasis on nature and exploring the outdoors. The school also welcomed the poorest of children to attend. This democratic school atmosphere was a pivotal change in pedagogy for Europe: previously, young children were expected to listen to lectures and learn through the rote method.

During his time at the Pestalozzi school, Froebel also began working with a wealthy family and he spent time each day tutoring the family's three children. The children's parents offered Froebel a small patch of their property to use as a garden. He used a very practical, hands-on approach to teaching. He was intrigued by the children; he enjoyed answering their questions and being part of their development. These experiences convinced Froebel that the best way to teach children was through action and observation. He was an astute observer, ever curious about children and their development.

In 1811, Froebel began studying at the University of Gottingen. His studies were interrupted for a time when he had to join the military during the Napoleonic Wars. When his time in the military was over, Froebel returned to educational work. He began to put his educational theories into practice in schools and his ideas were becoming increasingly popular and well known.

In 1816, Froebel founded the Universal German Educational Institute at Griesheim. It was here that other teachers came to study his methods. In 1826, Froebel published his famous book, *The Education of Man*, which gave a detailed account of his philosophy of education. Froebel accepted and followed the ideas and principles of Pestalozzi and was influenced by his knowledge and practice. He had great respect and appreciation for the learning environment created by Pestalozzi as well as the lessons that Pestalozzi devised. By now, however, he was beginning to form his own understanding of child development and early childhood education. He could see areas of Pestalozzi's approach that could be improved upon. Froebel's aim was to develop a clearer philosophical base and organisation to early childhood education and to incorporate some of his beliefs into the teaching of young children. He saw that the spiritual element of education was missing from Pestalozzi's theory and he believed that the spiritual elements of education are a crucial part of early learning.

Froebel returned to Germany in 1837, where he established the first kindergarten in Blankenburg in Thuringia, Germany. He coined the term 'kindergarten', which literally means 'garden of the children'. The kindergarten was a new institution for the education of young children. This new approach to early childhood education was the first of its kind and it was centred on the education of children aged 3–7. It recognised that young children had the necessary capabilities of learning social and intellectual skills. The kindergarten soon had a teacher training school attached. Froebel's kindergarten attracted widespread interest and other kindergartens soon developed. At this time Froebel was continuing to teach, refine and document his beliefs of early childhood education.

Froebel died on 21 June 1852. After his death, his reputation grew as an early childhood educator. Kindergartens were established throughout Germany. It wasn't until after Froebel's death that the kindergarten phenomenon moved worldwide. The first US kindergarten was opened for German immigrant children. Froebel did not live to see his kindergartens emerge on an international scale.

Core Concepts of the Froebel Approach

This section provides detailed information on the core concepts of Friedrich Froebel's approach to ECEC, including:

- Stages of development
- Environment
- Curriculum
- Categories of play
- The role of the teacher.

According to Froebel, childhood is a very special phase of a person's life. Froebel perceived the first seven years of life to be the most meaningful. He described children as being born good people, with a creative side and the potential to be successful in life. Froebel focused on the needs of children prior to them entering school. Children should be provided with the necessary knowledge and skills to facilitate them to become responsible members of society. Froebel saw a need to provide an environment where children could be nurtured, protected and provided with appropriate educational stimulation through worthwhile materials. The correct educational environment encourages children to grow and develop in their own ways. Froebel's love of nature, along with his strong Christian faith, led him to believe that every person had a spiritual worth and dignity, and that education is necessary to develop this spirituality.

Froebel based his philosophy of ECEC on a number of key concepts:

- Self activity
- Creativity
- Social participation
- Family involvement
- Motor expression.

Self Activity

Free self activity is a key concept of the kindergarten programme and can involve either work or play. Children become aware of their surroundings and this provides freedom and peace of mind. In order to ensure that free self activity is as effective as it can be, purposeful activities must be created in a child-centred environment. Any activity forced upon children is not going to be a valid learning experience. Children are given the opportunity to think for themselves. There is little time for interference from others, such as the teacher or other children.

Creativity

According to Froebel, every child has a creative side. Children express this creativity through various media, e.g. physical activities, gestures and expressions. Through education, this creativity becomes visible. When children are presented with materials with which they enjoy experimenting, they create new forms and alternative uses for the material, often without even realising it. Children must always be encouraged to be creative. For example, during art activities, the children are allowed to do things for themselves without instruction from the teacher. They can make their own discoveries and gain inspiration from their peers.

Social Participation

Children strive when they are in the company of other children. To facilitate children's learning, adults must provide them with the opportunity to interact socially. This can be done through participating in group activities and games. This interaction helps children's development in many areas, e.g. moral and intellectual development.

Family Involvement

Froebel advocated the need for regular and positive interaction between young children and their family. Very closely related to the child are parents, siblings, grandparents, extended family and educators. Froebel felt strongly that parents and educators work together to ensure the best education for their child. Parents require guidance from educators and vice versa. Both parties should respect each other and maintain regular correspondence with each other. Educators may offer an open door policy for parents and encourage them to call regularly.

Motor Expression

The explanation of motor expression is that of experiential learning. This means learning through doing, i.e. learning through hands-on experience rather than just verbal communication. Froebel designed a curriculum where children are constantly involved in practical activities, rather than listening to the teacher for the entire work period. The child is not forced to fit into a normal development pattern. The teacher allows the child to develop at their own pace through meaningful experiences.

Froebel's Stages of Development

Froebel identified a number of specific stages relating to children's educational development:

- Infancy
- Childhood
- Boyhood
- Youth.

Infancy

Infancy is a time of extreme dependence on adults. Language, sensory and motor co-ordination and development are just beginning at this time. Froebel emphasised the importance of sensory development at this stage. Children are heavily reliant on their senses to experience and learn through.

Childhood

This stage is a crucial stage for the development of language. It is at this time that children should be shown objects and adults should name these objects clearly for them. Play is also emphasised at this stage, but only if it is purposeful activity with appropriate materials. Children will also need direction and guidance from adults regarding play. This is an important role of the teacher at this time. Children who are provided with the best early years education will have the potential to continue this success in later years.

Boyhood

Children's education at this stage is determined by their environment. The education process has moved from being child centred to curriculum centred. In the previous stage, one of the main activities of children is play. In this stage, however, the main activity is work. The children's environment widens at this point, thus providing them with a greater selection of activities. Froebel was a believer in manual work. According to him, children aged 6–12 require manual work on a regular basis. The core subjects of Froebel's boyhood stage include religion, nature, maths and language. There is an emphasis on subjects that help children to express themselves, e.g. drawing, painting and gardening.

Youth

This stage lasts right through to adulthood. Children become more mature and are able to learn much more about themselves and the environment.

Kindergarten Environment

One of Froebel's most respected concepts is that of the kindergarten. Froebel put his deepest reflections into practice in this unique environment. He proposed a holistic approach to learning, which recognises children as active human beings who see patterns and make connections in their own lives.

Froebel viewed the kindergarten classroom as an extension of the home. Therefore, it must be a physically safe yet intellectually stimulating place, where materials promote children's curiosity and interest. The kindergarten environment is a functional place where learning occurs for children. It is not merely a place where children are amused for a period of time. The envitronment is bright, with plenty of natural light.

The environment gives children free access to a wide variety of materials that promote opportunities for learning and creativity. Froebel identified the fact that children are a part of nature. A successful prepared environment such as the kindergarten must, therefore, combine indoors and outdoors. Each kindergarten has a natural physical environment (e.g. an outside garden area) where children can grow plants and flowers and interact socially with nature.

The kindergarten environment promotes a range of characteristics in children, e.g. independence, individuality and responsibility. These characteristics are fostered through the use of experiences, play and a variety of materials.

Froebel recognised that parents are children's primary educators and that they provide the most consistent and influential educational experiences for children. A child's first educational experiences will most likely occur within their family. Therefore, as well as providing a home-like environment in the kindergarten, the Froebel approach involves teachers working closely with parents. As mentioned earlier, Froebel encouraged parents to become involved in the kindergarten environment and for both parents and educators to work in partnership together. Parents can share with teachers the expectations they have for their children. Parents can become involved in school trips or events. Teachers can provide ways for children to learn about themselves and their relationships with family and friends. Froebel's kindergarten facilitates diversity and allows children of different nationalities, ethnic groups, etc. to be welcomed and treated equally. Children work together in harmony.

Kindergarten Curriculum

Froebel favoured a child-centred curriculum in his kindergarten, with an emphasis on nature in the classroom. This is known as a naturalistic form of education. Children need real, hands-on experience and opportunities for play in order for learning to be effective.

In the kindergarten environment, children are given freedom and encouragement to develop at their own pace. They are allowed to rest if they wish; there is no emphasis on intellectual tasks or a hectic, routine schooling. Children are not forced to learn a curriculum that the teacher or another body decides is appropriate for them. Instead, they themselves choose what to learn and what materials to use. They make these choices according to their interests. Froebel insisted that children learn best when they are involved in practical activities. Froebel's philosophy is known widely for this important principle.

The kindergarten does not have a specific curriculum. Instead, it features games, creative play, songs, stories and crafts. All of these activities help to foster imagination and develop physical and motor skills.

Children can also practise their literacy and numeracy skills by engaging in conversation with the teacher and other children by speaking to the class, telling their news or doing role play exercises. They can practise their numeracy skills by weighing items in a baking exercise. Children also have the opportunity to learn about science.

The kindergarten framework consists of three principles:
- Games and songs
- Construction
- Gifts and occupations.

Games and Songs

The purpose of games and songs is to acquaint children with the life of animals and with humanity. Froebel incorporated his belief of socialisation as a method of teaching. The children and teacher gather in a circle to sing and play.

Children love singing and Froebel spent much time on the development of songs for all occasions. Songs were integrated into the kindergarten and were completed using plenty of movement. Froebel believed that songs would help children to develop their senses.

Many practitioners know plenty of songs but they forget that these songs can be included in the classroom. Some practitioners lack confidence in singing, especially in front of colleagues. However, it is important that songs are incorporated into kindergarten activities as much as possible. Children can become involved by practising with real musical instruments or by making their own instruments.

Construction

Construction pursues such activities as drawing, crafts, building blocks, music and movement.

Gifts and Occupations

One of Froebel's main priorities when developing his approach to education was to create specific materials to encourage children to engage in their environment. He had very individual ideas about how the materials should look and feel. He designed the materials himself and he called them 'gifts'. These gifts are exclusive to Froebelian education. They are mostly made of wood, some of which are still widely used today; others are in a different format.

The kindergarten gifts are manipulative materials and they are used to facilitate children's learning. They have a striking physical appearance and also a hidden symbolic meaning. They are given to children so that they can play with them and, in the process, learn. One gift is a set of six coloured balls. While the balls are fun to play with, they also help children to understand the concepts of shape, dimension and colour. Other gifts include wooden blocks and sticks. Gifts also help children recognise patterns commonly found in their surroundings. The aim of giving children these gifts is to explore the interests of children of various ages and stages.

Froebel believed that children should be encouraged to play with the gifts – again, we see how important play is. This helps them to learn concepts in mathematics, science and construction, for example. Children can experiment with the gifts in different ways and as they please. They can practise building and rebuilding the gifts. The gifts also represent 'the whole', especially the building gifts, as they begin as a whole and are then transformed into different formats to be finally replaced as a whole again. Similar to the Montessori approach, children are encouraged to put the gifts back in their correct location after use.

Froebel designed many of the gifts (mainly one through seven) before he died. The later gifts were designed by followers of his approach, taking into account his principles and what he deemed important.

Over time, Froebel's gifts became widely known and distributed throughout the world. They influenced the development of many young children down through the generations. The gifts are suitable for children aged 2–8. They are sequential: the first gift is the easiest to identify, and the gifts gradually increase in difficulty to develop more complex skills of perception. This is a prime example of the child working with materials that progress from concrete to abstract. Froebel's gifts lead children to discovery. They also promote the acquisition of language because children learn new words associated with each gift.

First Gift: Six Coloured Balls

The first gift is six coloured balls. They are made of soft yarn and can be compressed slightly. They are lightweight and easy to grasp or hold. The balls represent various colours of the rainbow: the three primary colours (red, yellow and blue) and also purple, green and orange. The balls help children to begin to appreciate colour, shape and texture. The children will differentiate between the various colours. The ball is also the first toy children play with and it represents the concept of being a 'whole'. Playing with the balls introduces children to the idea of movement and motion. In modern times, this gift remains popular for small children but has less of a role with preschool children.

Second Gift: Sphere, Cube and Cylinder

The second gift is a set of wooden objects: a sphere, a cube and a cylinder. All three solids have holes drilled in them. A string is provided so that the solid can be spun on it. The shapes can also be spun on a stick.

Children can put a shape onto the string, hold the two ends of the string between their thumb and forefinger and then use the other hand to spin the shape. This also winds the string. When the shape is released it spins, since the string unwinds. This allows children to observe other shapes being made.

This gift involves creating different patterns and designs by spinning the solids. Children will discover that by spinning one solid, they can see the shape of another, e.g. spinning a cylinder produces a sphere. Children can see that all objects are connected. This gift can help children to recognise different shapes in their environment.

Children can compare and differentiate between the shapes. Simple physics concepts can be discovered. Children can count the number of pieces or corners they have and can experiment with stacking one shape on top of the other. Children discover that the sphere and the cylinder will roll, but the cube will not. Children are also encouraged to be imaginative and to engage in imaginative play. Children may be introduced to spatial concepts such as on, under, front, back, in front of, behind, etc. In present times, this gift is less significant than in Froebel's original kindergarten.

The following gifts are the most popular and well-known gifts in modern times. Children can experiment building and rebuilding the block, as mentioned earlier. Children can use their imagination and can be creative.

Third Gift: Cube Divided into Eight Cubes
The third gift is eight cubes in the form of a single larger cube. The cubes come in a two-inch box and the box can be turned upside-down gently to remove the stack of cubes. Children are encouraged to take the stack apart and then attempt to put it back together. Froebel called this type of gift the building gift, where the emphasis is on the taking apart and the putting back together again. The gift highlights the parts in relation to the whole, this being the underlying concept. This gift shows children that parts can move through various forms and still return to the whole. Children can count the number of cubes and the number of faces, edges and corners that each cube has. Children also become familiar with the concept of symmetry.

Fourth Gift: Cube Divided into Eight Rectangles
The fourth gift is eight rectangular blocks which, when put together, form one large cube. This gift is similar to the third gift, with just a slight variation. The two-inch cube is again divided into eight pieces, but the pieces have a different proportion. As children take apart the cube, they will see how it can be used in different ways. Children are encouraged to compare this gift with the third gift. They can discuss the differences and similarities. As with the third gift, the focus is on dimension. However, this time there is a greater variety of shapes. Children make comparisons between these shapes and the shapes in their environment.

Fifth Gift: Cube Divided into 39 Pieces

This gift develops the idea of the cubes in the third gift. The fifth gift is presented as a larger cube with three blocks along each edge. It is expected that this large cube will break down into 27 cubes. The surprise of this gift is that three of the cubes are divided diagonally to form six triangular-faced blocks, and another three cubes are divided twice to form 12 smaller triangular blocks. Therefore, a three-inch cube actually divides into 39 blocks: 21 one-inch cubes, six triangle half cubes and 12 triangle quarter cubes.

With the fifth gift, children can experiment again with shapes. The new triangle pieces will introduce more possibilities for children to explore and will allow them to build more realistic buildings and structures. Children will be introduced to new words and names of shapes, e.g. angle, triangle and diagonal. Fractions and other mathematical concepts can be discovered, as can geometric shapes, sizes and differentiation.

Sixth Gift: Cube Divided into 36 Pieces

Like the fifth gift, the sixth gift is presented as a large cube. This time it consists of 18 rectangular blocks (as in the fourth gift), 12 square blocks (six rectangle blocks divided breadthwise), and six narrow columns (three rectangle blocks divided lengthwise). Like the fifth gift, it is best to use the sixth gift with children over the age of 5.

The sixth gift introduces new proportions to the three-inch cube. This is a return to concepts of size, as seen in the fourth gift. The new caps and the column bring a more constructive feel to this gift. Children are presented with the materials in a similar fashion to the third gift. Children can now use the new shapes and compare them to similar shapes in their environment. In this way, children gain extra experience in the concept of fractions. They are introduced to the notions of area and volume.

Seventh Gift: Two-dimensional Shapes

There are many variations on this gift. The shapes in this gift come from the many different shapes that can be found in the previous gifts: square, equilateral triangle, right-angled isosceles triangle, right-angled scalene triangle, obtuse isosceles triangle, circle, semi-circle, etc.

This gift is very significant in that there is a move from a solid surface to a flat surface. The gift allows children to experience objects in two-dimensional form. Children now move from concrete to abstract ideas. The previous gifts have seen the surface in connection with solids. Children now receive the embodied surface on its own, away from the solid. Children are therefore introduced to the idea of surface.

Shapes are introduced one at a time, until children are ready for the next shape. Children can examine these 'new shapes' and match them with the dimensional shapes that they have seen in previous gifts. It is in this way that children begin to see the connection between the solid form and its surfaces. These exercises require much more creativity on the children's behalf. Once children are familiar with the different shapes, they can begin to combine them to make new shapes, such as pentagon, hexagon, heptagon, octagon, trapezoid, trapezium, rhombus and rhomboid.

The seventh gift emphasis the different colours and the different forms of triangles. Children are introduced to geometry and fractions, symmetry, opposites and proportion.

Eighth Gift: Lines

This gift is divided into two sets: one set of straight lines and one set of curved lines (rings) of various lengths, and rings and half-rings of various diameters.

Children become aware of two-dimensional shapes after working with the seventh gift. The eighth gift now represents the edges or outlines of these objects. Once again, children move from concrete to abstract in their work.

Sticks

Children are invited to create things using the sticks. They will enjoy being creative and they are likely to complete some great shapes and patterns. Eventually, children can make bigger designs as a group.

This gift is ideal for demonstrating basic maths, addition, subtraction, multiplication and division. Children work with concrete objects to see the change in numbers. They might also find the sticks useful as a unit of measuring.

Rings

Before children begin working with the rings, they will examine the ring with the stick and they will note the differences. Through working with the rings, children are introduced to the curved line and the circle. They are likely to make some very attractive designs with the rings.

Children can examine their surroundings and make comparisons to the circles and curves around them. Eventually, children will work with both sticks and rings together. The rings allow children to discover diameter and circumference and the concept of the curve.

Ninth Gift: Points

The ninth gift involves small objects (e.g. buttons) in a variety of colours to represent the points. There are 32 each in eight colours: red, orange, yellow, green, blue, purple, white and black. This gift allows children to explore the use of the point in creating two-dimensional forms. Children learn how points form lines and define shapes. Children are now asked to be creative using only points. This gift is one of the higher levels of abstraction. Points have no dimension. Children begin with a small number of points, all the same colour, then progress to different colours.

Sorting and ordering objects is the foundation of basic mathematics. Once again, children can practise basic mathematics: addition, subtraction, multiplication and division. They can also explore the basic concepts of geometry.

Froebel's Categories of Gift Play

Froebel divided gift play into three categories:
- Forms of life
- Forms of knowledge
- Forms of beauty.

In forms of *life*, children use the gifts to create something they found in their life, e.g. a house. In forms of *knowledge*, children will explore the maths and science properties of the gifts, e.g. counting the sides of a cube. In forms of *beauty*, children use their own creativity to build designs from the material and play with the materials through music, art and movement.

Occupations

Froebel designed activities to accompany all of his gifts. He called these activities *occupations*. Every gift has complementary occupations; they give children learning experiences through play. Occupations allow freedom and they consist of things that children can shape and manipulate.

Examples of occupations include:
- Clay
- Cardboard work
- Wood carving
- Paper folding
- Painting
- Paper cutting and sticking
- Weaving
- Sewing
- Embroidery
- Interlacing
- Drawing
- Stringing beads and buttons.

Example of a Lesson with Froebel's Second Gift: Sphere, Cube and Cylinder

Materials

Froebel's second gift is a set of wooden objects: a sphere, a cube and a cylinder. All three solids have holes drilled in them. A string is provided so that each solid can be spun on it.

Presentation

■ Introduce the child to the gift and ask them if they know what might be inside the box. Shake the gift to add to the child's anticipation and interest.

■ Open the lid and show the child each object.

■ Invite the child to touch, feel and smell each object.

■ Ask the child to put one shape on the string.

■ Show the child how to hold the two ends of the string between their thumb and forefinger and use the other hand to spin the shape.

■ As the string unwinds and the shape spins, the child discovers that by spinning one solid they can see the shape of another, e.g. spinning a cylinder produces a sphere.

■ Discuss each action with the child and help them to see that all objects are connected.

Link with Froebel Categories of Play

This lesson links with Froebel's categories of play.

Forms of Life

■ Compare the objects to things from the child's life, e.g. a sphere can be compared to a football or an orange.

■ Show the child how to stack the shapes in different ways.

Forms of Knowledge

■ Introduce the child to the names of the shapes.

■ Ask the child to count the shapes.

■ Introduce the child to words such as 'surface', 'edge' and 'corner'.

■ Introduce the child to concepts such as 'on', 'under', 'front' and 'back'.

■ Basic physics concepts can be explored, e.g. the child can see which shapes roll (sphere and cylinder) and which stand (cube and cylinder).

Forms of Beauty
- Encourage the child to observe the different patterns and designs created by spinning the shapes.

Link with Aistear
This lesson links with the following themes, aims and learning goals of Aistear.

- Wellbeing

  Aim 2, Learning Goal 3: Children will discover, explore and refine gross- and fine-motor skills.

  Aim 3, Learning Goal 2: Children will express themselves through a variety of types of play.

- Identity and Belonging

  Aim 4, Learning Goal 4: Children will demonstrate dispositions like curiosity, persistence and responsibility.

- Communicating

  Aim 4, Learning Goal 6: Children will show confidence in trying out new things, taking risks and thinking creatively.

- Exploring and Thinking

  Aim 1, Learning Goal 1: Children will engage, explore and experiment in their environment and use new physical skills including skills to manipulate objects and materials.

  Aim 1, Learning Goal 6: Children will come to understand concepts such as matching, comparing, ordering, sorting, size, weight, height, length, capacity, and money in an enjoyable and meaningful way.

  Aim 4, Learning Goal 5: Children will develop higher-order thinking skills such as problem-solving, predicting, analysing, questioning and justifying.

Role of the Kindergarten Teacher

Froebel focused on the fact that women must be recognised in the education of children. He went on to promote women as teachers and founded training schools where he trained the first set of kindergarten teachers. There, teachers were informed that children should not be given information and facts alone. They should not be expected to learn by rote; instead, they should be very active in the classroom. Children in the kindergarten environment should be encouraged to express themselves and to be involved in the learning process. The kindergarten teacher will focus on the children's interests and plan lessons accordingly. These concepts were a dramatic departure from the norms of the nineteenth century.

Kindergarten teachers must be knowledgeable and qualified in the area of Froebel education and the developmental stages of children. They should be highly respected people with values that children will want to imitate. The teacher should be a sensitive, open and easily approachable person.

Teacher as Facilitator
One necessary role of the kindergarten teacher is to encourage children's self-expression through play, both individually and in group activities. The teacher must facilitate the children's use of Froebel's gifts and occupations. The teacher must stimulate learning through play.

Character building is a fundamental part of the learning process. The teacher must have high hopes that the children will have many good personal qualities, e.g. integrity, honesty and kindness. Children should have respect for themselves, for others and for their surroundings.

Teacher as Observer
Under the Froebel form of learning, the teacher carefully observes on a regular basis. These observations mean that the teacher can guide the children properly. However, teachers will not interfere with the activities in which children are involved. Effective and recorded observation of children is valuable to effective teaching and learning. As a result of completing observations, teachers can plan for the children according to their developmental needs.

The Importance of Family
Froebel emphasised the need for parents and educators to work in partnership in order to provide the best possible education for children. They must respect each other, help each other and offer support to each other. Parents can inform the practitioner about the child's personality, their likes and dislikes and their behaviour. This can facilitate the practitioner in ensuring that they provide the best ECEC experience for the child. In turn, the practitioner can observe the child and establish how the child learns, how they are progressing academically and how they are integrating socially.

The Steiner Waldorf Approach

Rudolf Steiner

Rudolf Joseph Lorenz Steiner was born in Austria on 27 February 1861 in the small town of Kraljevec, on the border between Austria and Hungary (now known as Croatia). He was the eldest son in a family of three children. His parents were Johann Steiner and Franziska Blie. Steiner had a rural upbringing that was typical of the time. The family often had to move from town to town in order for Steiner's father to find employment. His father was a railway telegrapher who often worked very long hours. His mother, a quiet lady, was the main caregiver.

As a child, Steiner found reading unusually easy and he was very prompt at grasping the concept of ideas. He was confident that there was a spiritual world. He had regular spiritual experiences and often found them difficult to comprehend. By the age of 15, Steiner was tutoring younger children as well as his peers. This helped to raise valuable funds for his own education. He had a particular interest in natural sciences and would often spend his pocket money buying second-hand books on philosophy.

In 1879, Steiner began his studies in natural history and chemistry at Vienna Technical

College. By this stage, he had decided to become a science teacher. During his spare time he continued to study any philosophy book available to him. He attended any philosophy lectures that were open to him at college. He was taking an increasing interest in the work of contemporary philosophers. While at college, he also taught himself the visual arts subjects, along with Latin and Greek. He also studied physics, chemistry, mechanics, botany, mathematics, literature and politics; and he passed exams in all of these disciplines. He regularly attended lectures on German literature, which introduced him to the works of Goethe (1749–1832). Goethe was a German poet, novelist and natural philosopher. Through reading Goethe, Steiner received the stimulus he needed to develop his own ideas further and to understand the spiritual experiences of his past. He also observed his college lecturers closely and he learned a lot about public speaking during this time.

In 1883, Steiner's scientific ability was acknowledged when he was invited by a publisher to edit Goethe's writings on natural science. This was a huge achievement for Steiner and it came at a significant time in his career. During this time, Steiner's own views on philosophy were maturing.

Throughout the 1880s, Steiner became a tutor to a family of four young boys. One of the boys was 10 years old when Steiner first started tutoring him. The boy was in very poor general health and was finding it difficult to master reading and writing. Through knowledge and observation, Steiner designed a programme of study for the boy. Within two years of working with Steiner, the boy's health improved dramatically and he had passed a secondary school entrance exam. The boy continued to flourish and he ended up becoming a medical doctor in his adulthood.

After receiving his doctorate in 1891, Steiner wrote his first book, *The Philosophy of Freedom*. The book was based on anthroposophy, the science of the spirit. In the book, Steiner explored the spiritual lives of humans. He began lecturing throughout Europe. He believed that the element of spirituality was missing from many subjects, including education, politics, agriculture, medicine and Christian religion. He wrote many journals and papers on this topic. Steiner devoted much of his life to anthroposophy. He also continued to write and lecture on the spirit of the human being, as well as art, drama, education, history, science and much more.

Steiner was invited by the director of the Waldorf-Astoria cigarette factory in Stuttgart, Germany to give lectures to the workers in the factory. It was from these lectures that Steiner was urged to develop his educational theory in greater detail so that it could enable him to open a school for the children of such factory workers. By now, World War I was over and people were looking for new beginnings. There was a feeling in Germany that a new method of education was required. On 7 September 1919, Steiner opened the first free Waldorf School in Stuttgart. The agenda was to devise a new curriculum and train and employ teachers to implement it effectively according to Steiner's guidelines. This school in Stuttgart is recognised as the most significant of all Steiner schools. It was a primary and secondary school with eight classrooms, catering for both male and female students. Students came from a range of socio-economic backgrounds, nationalities and religions, and there was huge variety in terms of the students' abilities and learning styles.

In 1924, aged just 63, Steiner became ill with stomach problems and had to stop lecturing. He died on 30 March 1925, before the completion of his autobiography. The notes from his lectures were published in numerous papers and books and were translated into several languages. Although Steiner was initially from a scientific background, he also used his knowledge of philosophy in his work. As a result, he became a popular and well-respected author and lecturer.

Core Concepts of the Steiner Waldorf Approach

This section provides detailed information on the core concepts of the Steiner Waldorf approach to ECEC, including:

- Education process
- Principles of education
- Environment
- Materials
- Curriculum
- The role of the teacher.

Steiner Waldorf Education Process

The Steiner Waldorf philosophy of education was launched in 1919 and is based on Steiner's beliefs, ideas and spiritual insights of human beings. His pedagogy is based on child development and the fact that children pass through various stages of development. The growing child and their characteristics were of huge importance to Steiner.

The education process is divided into three periods. Different stages of children's lives will be suited to different ways of teaching.

0–7 Years

Steiner believed that education begins at birth. The first seven years of children's lives are of greatest importance. It is at this stage that a lot of growth takes place and the children's inner needs come to the fore. Children conquer the skills of movement, speech, gesture and communication. Most of this is learned through imitation. One of Steiner's fundamental principles is the fact that children learn through imitation. The young child mimics everything they see, from physical movements to behaviour and attitudes.

Children absorb every aspect of their environment and they are open to external influences also. The focus at this point is on learning by doing. There are strong will forces at work during this period. Children learn naturally and successfully through doing. This stage lays the foundation for a healthy adulthood. This period is also where children can learn responsibility for the nurturing of a strong and healthy body. Children at this stage learn a great deal through their senses.

7–14 Years

At this stage, the focus is on the education of the heart, the imagination and social life. All lessons given by teachers of the Steiner Waldorf method should be presented as creatively and artistically as possible. Children become quieter and they have a readiness for more formal learning. They are open to a greater level of knowledge. They tend to have an active imagination and delicate feelings by this age. It is only at this particular stage that reading, writing and maths are introduced. It is important for children to have a daily routine. Children learn actively through the main lesson they are involved in.

14–18 Years

The focus at this point is on the education of thinking and the development of personal judgments. At this stage, children become young adults. They become increasingly clear and they can engage in rational thinking. Taught subjects can include science, singing, drama and art.

Steiner Waldorf Principles

Steiner focused his theory of education on three principles beginning with the letter R.

Rhythm

According to Steiner, children in general embrace regularity. This helps to strengthen their memories. In Steiner Waldorf schools, there is a day-to-day rhythm. A rhythm is a pattern or routine that helps children know what to expect. The purpose of this rhythm is to provide a balance of group and individual activities, and a balance of quiet and active times in the classroom.

There is often a weekly rhythm also, e.g. painting on Tuesdays, baking on Fridays. Daily and weekly rhythms can be part of a larger seasonal rhythm that may include the celebration of festivals or the changing of seasons. Working with rhythm provides a foundation for the understanding of time: what has gone before and what will follow.

A typical day might include the following activities:

- Arrival time: free play
- Ring time/Circle time: music, speech, drama
- Indoor creative play

- Home activities: cooking, sewing, tidying
- Artistic work: painting, crafts
- Outdoor play: fun outside in play area or garden
- Lunch
- Story time: a time where children come together to hear the kindergarten tell a good story.

Repetition

Through repetition comes experience, and it is through experience that children learn successfully. Repetition is very valuable: when children repeat an exercise it increases their familiarity and knowledge of it. For example, children thoroughly enjoy when familiar stories and poems are read to them, even though they may have heard them many times before. Repetition can help children to develop positive habits; when they practise something many times, this eventually brings perfection.

Reverence

Reverence is based on the concept that everything visible and invisible surrounding the children has an impact on them. Reverence for the tasks of life can be seen when children experience real work with real materials in a child-centred environment.

Steiner Waldorf Environment

The Steiner Waldorf approach is based on the concept that everything surrounding the child (both visible and invisible) impacts greatly on their development. Steiner therefore considered the 'whole child' and believed that children's learning is at its peak when they are provided with a peaceful and predictable environment that recognises their needs. Steiner established a unique and special classroom where this learning could take place. Children are educated together in mixed-age groups where there is no rivalry or competition.

A typical day in a Steiner Waldorf classroom will have different 'moods' associated with it. The creating of various moods to accompany different kinds of activities is done deliberately by the teacher in order to help children differentiate the kinds of behaviour that are appropriate for the particular situation. For example, a cultural event provides the opportunity to create a celebratory mood. Steiner emphasised the importance of young children experiencing wonder, awe and the feeling of gratitude for life. He believed in creating a mood of respect and love.

The environment (both inside and out) should be attractive and inviting. The teacher strives to create an environment that gives children time to play, encourages them to use their imagination and fosters a love of nature.

Indoor Environment

Steiner placed great emphasis on the aesthetic environment in order for children's learning to be successful. During early childhood, all of the child's senses are active. The teacher must be aware of this and must know not to over-stimulate the children. There should be calm, soft colours on the walls, with no displays of work or posters. The work that children produce is, of course, an important expression of their developing skills; however, these works are not displayed in the classroom. Steiner believed that young children love completing activities, but for them the process of completion is much more important than viewing the finished product on display. Children in the Steiner Waldorf classroom are not encouraged to dwell on their work after it is completed. The teacher takes note of the work and shows appreciation for it. They will then put it to one side and give it to parents at the end of the day or keep it in the child's portfolio until the end of the year.

There should be no excess noise, gadgets or television in the classroom. The use of technology is not compatible with the Steiner approach to ECEC. ICT is only introduced when children reach adolescence. Steiner believed that sitting still for long periods of time is not natural for young children. It takes away from play time and reduces concentration levels. Looking at a screen is a poor substitute for actual human contact; it does not allow the opportunity to interact socially. Steiner believed that children need real experiences, e.g. gathering the materials needed to make jam. Children need to see in real life the process of how things happen and how things are made, rather than watching this on television.

The environment is organised in an orderly fashion; it is simple yet attractive. There will be shelves of baskets containing scissors, crayons, toys and games. There will be a place for story books. A Steiner Waldorf classroom will not have any unnecessary clutter. The environment should be rich in poetry, painting, dance, drama, storytelling, singing and games.

Outdoor Environment

Every Steiner Waldorf school should have a safe outdoor play area for children. It should be spacious and equipped with trees, flowers, shrubs, hiding dens and sand pits. It is ideal to have a vegetable patch where both adults and children can work together and then watch the vegetables grow.

The outdoor area may also have an area for recycling waste from the classroom, e.g. juice cartons, yoghurt pots, etc. Perhaps there can be an area for making compost. Steiner was a lover of nature and the outdoors and proposed that every child have access to a garden. Children are encouraged to appreciate and value the natural world in order to help them to understand its pattern of the seasons. Being outdoors is always a good opportunity for children to mix socially; it also gives them a change of scenery from being inside. The children can go on nature walks and collect items for their nature table.

Materials and Toys

The materials in the Steiner Waldorf classroom are natural, multipurpose and are easily accessible to the children. Children have the opportunity to develop gross-motor and fine-motor skills, as well as hand–eye co-ordination. The materials often serve as preparation for reading and writing at a later age, e.g. a sewing exercise is a very useful preparation for reading print from left to right.

The toys are simply made of natural materials – many of wood – and are purposely undefined to allow for children's imaginations to take over, e.g. rag dolls with blank faces. The equipment in the Steiner Waldorf classroom includes:

- Simple manual tools
- Sewing materials
- Specially designed picture books
- Building blocks
- Woodwork table
- Art materials
- Materials for dressing up
- A home corner (equipped with cradles, prams, tables, chairs)
- Musical instruments
- A book corner.

Children are free to choose whatever activity they wish. They have freedom of choice. They might choose to work in groups or alone, or they might wish to work with the teacher. The children do not have to necessarily engage in intellectual activities. They are not given materials to help them with their reading, writing or number skills. These activities will come when the child reaches the age of 7.

In Steiner Waldorf schools, children are encouraged to share, work together, care for each other and respect the needs of others. Many items are made as gifts for family members.

Steiner Waldorf Curriculum

The purpose of the Steiner Waldorf curriculum is to provide children with a well-balanced experience of arts, science, religion and morality. Children can focus on the joy of learning rather than academic achievement. The Steiner Waldorf approach focuses on nurturing each child's unique capabilities by providing opportunities to play and engage in beneficial work activities. Steiner believed that it was the responsibility of the curriculum to facilitate the needs of children and to encourage free creativity. Steiner envisaged that his approach to education would enable young people to enter into the world knowing the purpose of their lives.

The academic subjects meet the developmental stages of the children. The core subjects are taught in thematic blocks and all lessons include a balance of artistic, practical and intellectual content. Whole class, mixed-ability teaching is the standard criteria of Steiner Waldorf education.

If children are presented with a creative curriculum that provides balanced experiences in a variety of subjects, they have the opportunity to develop into a strong, well-balanced adult. There are no textbooks in the pre-school years of the Steiner Waldorf approach; instead children simply enjoy their childhood and are allowed to play. For pre-school children, the academic side of the education process is not emphasised. There are no tests or competitions.

The Role of Play and Fantasy

Creative and imaginative play is greatly valued in Steiner Waldorf classrooms. Steiner highlighted the role of play in a child's development. It is another key element of early childhood education. Steiner was a believer that free play (especially imaginative play) enhanced the children's natural, healthy development. Play is considered to be just as important as work. The classroom does not have to be all about academia. It is in play that young children encounter their own learning situations. Play facilitates social skills and helps children to see things from other people's points of view. Play helps to strengthen the imagination of children and it is necessary in cognitive development. Through play, children develop a greater ability to concentrate.

Play in the Steiner Waldorf classroom is rarely adult led. It is more likely that the teachers will encourage the children to play among themselves, inventing new games and scenarios, playing pretend or dressing up. The teacher takes a passive role in the process of play. However, they will be active in doing other things in the classroom, e.g. observing the children at work, preparing new lessons, etc. The teacher will, of course, be available to intervene in play situations if this is required.

Children in the Steiner Waldorf classroom are equipped with well constructed toys to play with and share. The toys are deliberately simple and are made from natural materials. They are generally undefined, since this provides children with greater opportunities to use their imaginations. Creative play enables children to learn through investigation, exploration and discovery.

The children are given opportunity to engage in free play both inside and outside the Steiner Waldorf classroom. They have the opportunity to integrate socially and to use their imaginations to re-enact situations they have seen or experienced. Outdoor play is another important and valuable aspect of Steiner Waldorf education, and children are always encouraged to go outdoors. Toys are intentionally limited in the outdoor space. While the children will often have access to swings and sandpits, there are very few other toys. Instead, the children are encouraged to engage in natural play activities in a large, open space. Children in the Steiner Waldorf environment will always have access to a garden area, where they are encouraged to take an interest in nature.

Main Lesson

The classroom timetable in a Steiner Waldorf school is significantly different from that of a traditional school. The *main lesson* is a central feature of the Steiner Waldorf curriculum. Main lessons focus on cultural subjects within the curriculum, e.g. art, music, science or nature. The main lesson involves the thorough working of a chosen subject. For example, an aspect of science will be focused on in lesson blocks of approximately two hours per day over a number of weeks. Every day typically begins with the main lesson. The morning is seen as the ideal time for such lessons, since this is a time when children are more observant. Every lesson that is completed is connected to the next lesson. The teacher knows in advance what the lesson will be and they plan for it accordingly, making it as artistic as possible. After the main lesson, the activity in the classroom is changed. The overall result of the main lesson is a thorough understanding of important topics. This results in the children having access to a wide variety of knowledge and experience.

The main lesson can be approached in many ways: a group project or game, a story or poem or a painting exercise. The main lesson will continue until all of the children have made a connection to the lesson through various means. The main lesson is typically suited to 6 years plus.

Maths, Reading and Writing

Children in the Steiner Waldorf classroom are not presented with any kind of instructional materials to assist them to read and write. According to Steiner, children were not meant to read and write until after the age of 6. They can practise listening skills and speaking skills. They can tell stories and their individual pieces of news.

Mathematics and the use of mathematical language take place in concrete situations, e.g. at the cooking table, where the child is helping to prepare food. The child is introduced to such concepts as addition and subtraction, weight, measurement, quantity and shape. All concepts are grasped in a very practical way in accordance with everyday life.

Music

Music is an important form of expression. Children at various stages of their time in the Steiner Waldorf classroom learn about music. They regularly sing songs as a group during circle time. Music and songs help to create the calm atmosphere in the classroom. Eurhythmy (music or speech that is expressed through bodily movements) is also a valuable component in Steiner Waldorf education. Eurhythmy means that music or speech is expressed in bodily movement. Different movements correspond to different sounds or notes. Eurhythmy enables children to strengthen their muscles, co-ordination and listening skills. Eurhythmy is often taught by a specially trained eurhythmy teacher.

Arts and Crafts

Arts and crafts are a worthy element of the Steiner Waldorf curriculum. It is one way of engaging children in a topic that is current in the classroom. Learning through arts and crafts nurtures cognitive development and promotes many skills and abilities. Art work complements the intellectual work completed in the classroom. The training through art in Steiner Waldorf schools is not aimed at producing artists, but rather at educating children for the art of living a normal life. According to Steiner, it is important that children engage in group art activities and make practical objects, since this will help them to be creative in their daily lives and become social adults.

The art curriculum includes drama, drawing, painting, clay modelling and various handcrafts such as sewing, knitting, weaving and woodwork. Steiner highlighted the need for painting in the classroom, since painting is an example of self-expression. Painting allows children to express how they are feeling and it is also a great opportunity for them to use their imaginations. The three primary colours (red, yellow and blue) are given to the children first. They are later allowed to mix the colours and see the outcome of this.

History

Children are slowly introduced to the experience of time by studying how the day unfolds with daily, weekly and seasonal rhythms. Children can experience different festivals of the world and celebrate world events. They may study ancient or modern history.

Similar to the Montessori approach, the Steiner Waldorf approach values science education, allowing children to engage in the natural world, experiment, explore the outdoors and learn about plants and animals.

Storytelling

In Steiner Waldorf classrooms, there is a particular emphasis on the teacher actually telling a story themselves from memory rather than reading it straight from a book. Here, the teacher has direct eye contact with the children. The teacher has no distractions and no need to keep turning the pages of a book. The way the stories are told engages and expands the children's concentration span. The teacher must be very well prepared each day. Ideally, children are not shown any pictures while a story is read to them. This enables the children to imagine for themselves what the pictures look like. The aim is to allow children to use their imaginations and to make up their own images. This will help the development of true imaginative play.

Stories can focus on and emphasise celebrations and festivals. Through stories, children can learn all about the different cultures and ways of living. Traditional fairy tales and stories based on nature are used to teach the child right from wrong.

Steiner emphasised the importance of children's development of orality, especially in relation to cognitive skills. The children are always encouraged to speak in the classroom, to ask questions and to tell their news. It is also important for them to develop their listening skills. Children must be polite and listen to other people speaking. Children can also tell their own version of a story from a book by 'reading' the pictures. This gives children great opportunities to perfect their verbal skills. It encourages them to use their own words.

Puppet shows are common in Steiner Waldorf schools. These allow children to act out their own versions of stories, thus developing dramatic skills through the use of narration and dialogue.

Example of a Group Lesson: Making Bread

Materials
1 × large mixing bowl
1 × wooden spoon
1 × tea towel
1 × rolling pin
1 × large baking tray
1 × wire rack

Ingredients
500 g strong stone-ground flour, plus extra for dusting
½ teaspoon salt
1½ teaspoons fast-action yeast
2 tablespoons honey
3 tablespoons olive oil
300 ml warm water
Butter, for greasing
Seeds, oats or other toppings

Presentation
- Invite the children to sit around a large table where you will make the bread.
- Mix the flour, salt and yeast in a large bowl. Add the honey, oil and water and mix to form a dough. If the dough feels sticky, add a little flour; if the dough feels dry, add a little water.
- Invite the children to take turns in mixing the dough, until it becomes stiff. Turn the dough onto a floured surface.

- Show the children how bread is kneaded. A song or verse can be used to encourage the children.
- Return the kneaded dough to the mixing bowl, cover it with a damp tea towel and set it aside to prove. (It may take up to an hour for the yeast to rise and for the dough to double in size.)
- Once the dough has risen, it must be kneaded again before baking. Ask the children to demonstrate how this is done.
- Invite the children to take turns in rolling out the dough for baking.
- Place the rolled dough onto a greased baking tray.
- Invite the children to sprinkle a few seeds or oats on top of the dough.
- Bake at 200°C/400°F/Gas 6 for 25–30 minutes until the bread sounds hollow when tapped.
- While the bread is baking, the children can work together to clean the kitchen.
- Turn the dough onto a wire rack to cool. When the bread has cooled, the children can share it for lunch.
- It is important that the children do not focus too much on the quality of the finished product. Even if they have not achieved perfectly baked bread, they must be encouraged to see that they have created something together in a fun and engaging way.

Link with Steiner Waldorf principles
Rhythm
- Bake bread as a weekly activity to foster a sense of rhythm in the classroom.
- Show the children that there are stages and a sequence to everything we do.

Repetition
- Teach the children basic hygiene routines (washing hands, etc.) that they can repeat every day.
- Repetitive movement in kneading the dough will refine children's fine-motor skills.
- Encourage the children to recognise the scientific pattern at work in making bread.

Reverence
- Encourage all of the children to be involved in the process.
- Invite them to use their senses throughout the experience, e.g. touch the dough, smell the bread in the oven and taste the baked bread.
- Foster a sense of anticipation and excitement as the bread bakes in the oven.
- Show the children that baking requires great care, attention and concentration, e.g. measuring ingredients correctly.

Link with Aistear

■   Wellbeing

Aim 2, Learning Goal 1: Children will gain increasing control and co-ordination of body movements.

Aim 2, Learning Goal 3: Children will discover, explore and refine gross- and fine-motor skills.

■   Identity and Belonging

Aim 3, Learning Goal 3: Children will interact, work co-operatively and help others.

■   Communicating

Aim 3, Learning Goal 6: Children will develop counting skills and a growing understanding of the meaning and use of numbers and mathematical language in an enjoyable and meaningful way.

Aim 4, Learning Goal 3: Children will listen to and respond to a variety of types of music, sing songs and make music using instruments.

Aim 4, Learning Goal 6: Children will show confidence in trying out new things, taking risks and thinking creatively.

■   Exploring and Thinking

Aim 1, Learning Goal 1: Children will engage, explore and experiment in their environment and use new physical skills including skills to manipulate objects and materials.

Aim 1, Learning Goal 6: Children will come to understand concepts such as matching, comparing, ordering, sorting, size, weight, height, length, capacity and money in an enjoyable and meaningful way.

The Role of the Teacher in the Steiner Waldorf Environment

One of the greatest strengths of Steiner Waldorf education is the teacher's dedication and ability to cater for children's individual and cultural needs in the classroom. The first group of teachers encouraged by Steiner facilitated him in the development of his educational approach. Steiner believed that in order to become good educators, teachers must first focus on educating themselves. Teachers must maintain this throughout their lives. Steiner believed that it was only those teachers who were committed to doing this who could inspire the children in their care. Steiner Waldorf teachers should be equipped with an in-depth knowledge of child pedagogy and they must understand every stage of childhood. They must be trained to encourage independent activity and development through the child's self-initiated actions and play. The teacher must be confident in working with children individually and in groups. It is essential that the teacher has a calm and patient nature and is formally trained in Steiner Waldorf education.

The Steiner Waldorf teacher must be aware of the responsibilities they have, if they are to meet the developmental needs of the children in their care. Steiner had a number of guidelines to which teachers must adhere. They should focus on the whole child and all areas of their development: physical, intellectual, emotional and social. They must be dedicated to fostering a genuine love of learning within each child. They must treat all children equally and they must respect the backgrounds from which children come. The teacher's role as educator is not only based on creating a relevant curriculum; they must also be conscious of their own moral influence on the children. They must be very aware of their moods, gestures, motivation, body language and relationships with parents and work colleagues. Teachers must be professional at all times, since young children perceive and imitate everything that adults say and do. Children will observe how teachers handle materials, situations and relationships with colleagues and parents. Most important, the teacher must do their very best to educate the children and to be a role model for them. Everything surrounding the child (both visible and invisible) has a particular impact on the child.

Steiner believed that it is the responsibility of the teacher to maintain a suitable physical environment for the children in their care. The environment must be a warm, safe, homely atmosphere where each day is rhythmically repetitive. The teacher aims to provide an environment where the child feels comfortable and confident enough to be a regular contributor to the class.

The teacher has the responsibility to design a suitable curriculum for each child in their care. Each child has different strengths, capabilities and learning styles. Therefore, no child's curriculum will be completely identical to the curriculum of another child. The teacher will provide a suitable timetable for the day and will (to the best of their ability) vary the activities in which the children participate. The teacher engages in appropriate practical, domestic and artistic activities. These are activities that the children can easily imitate, e.g. gardening, celebration of festivals, arts and crafts, baking, storytelling and singing. The teacher is also a facilitator of imaginative free play and they nurture the children's power of imagination by telling carefully selected stories.

It is very important that there is close co-operation between teachers working together. If a teacher requires help or guidance with an element of the curriculum or a certain scenario, they will have the support of colleagues who help them to find a solution. The teacher works with colleagues to plan and record the lessons and to prepare appropriate stories, songs, verses and activities for the age, season or situation. Teachers regularly review their planning and the children's development. In Steiner Waldorf schools, especially when it comes to older children, it is quite common to have a class teacher as well as a number of specialist teachers that are more involved in certain areas, e.g. art. Specialist teachers take responsibility for certain lessons, while the class teacher takes responsibility for the majority of lessons, including the main lesson.

Observation of the whole child is regarded as an integral part of understanding child development, as is the design of child studies. The Steiner Waldorf teacher observes each child carefully on a regular basis and records what they see. These observations can of course be shared with parents.

Involvement with Parents

Another key concept of the Steiner Waldorf approach is the community aspect associated with it. There is an integrated approach, which involves teachers, parents and other family members. They all work together to ensure the successful education of children. It is important that there is a positive and smooth transition from home to school, and this relies on the teacher's good relationship with parents/guardians. The teacher's role often includes home visits and parent evenings. This provides parents with a clear understanding of the Steiner Waldorf approach and an explanation of what parents can do at home to support the work in the schools.

The HighScope Approach

David Weikart

The HighScope approach to ECEC was founded by David Weikart and his colleagues in the US during the 1960s. It remains a successful and well-known approach to education. The main objective of the HighScope approach is to improve the education of children by enabling them to participate in a programme of the highest quality.

The HighScope approach was originally developed for low-income families and children deemed at risk in Ypsilanti, Michigan in 1962. At that time, a high failure rate among students was highlighted there. Weikart became concerned about the inability of a local school system to produce literate adults. Weikart established a theory that this high failure rate was a result of children lacking the appropriate educational opportunities in school and a curriculum that was neither relevant nor of interest to children. Weikart also highlighted the fact that many children with poor grades early in their education often ended up with similar poor grades throughout their life. Weikart believed that this was also a result of an inadequate early childhood education. He refused to think that it was children who lacked knowledge or the ability to learn.

It was in response to the persistent failure of children from Ypsilanti to graduate from secondary school, and the fact that they were consistently scoring lower in tests than children of the same age from different areas that Weikart, who was an experienced teacher, studied in great detail the best practice and educational theories of the time. Weikart proposed to discover a new pre-school curriculum that would facilitate children of various intelligences to receive better academic awards in later years. Along with colleagues, Weikart initiated an experimental pre-school programme. Between 1962 and 1968, a pilot scheme was introduced for children aged 3–4. The name given to this scheme was the HighScope Perry Pre-school Project. It was a very beneficial study with many interesting conclusions. The study included 123 randomly chosen children; some of these children attended the project and some did not.

Upon evaluating this project, Weikart established some vital statistics. The children who engaged in the programme had greatly improved intellectually and socially. Participating children were more conscientious and they were graduating from secondary school and achieving higher scores in IQ tests. The study also showed that participating children were less likely to engage in antisocial behaviour or become dependent on social welfare. The children of Ypsilanti were finally receiving opportunities to become successful in education.

Taking these results into account (as well as the fact that reform of ECEC in the US was long overdue), Weikart and his colleagues proceeded to develop the HighScope Educational Research Foundation in 1970. The aim of the foundation was to continue with HighScope research and curriculum development. The educators proposed an intervention for children aged 3–4. This was aimed at focusing on pre-school children from poor areas and preparing them for success in school. It was also designed to promote active learning and to build on the fact that children are capable and determined individuals. Weikart perceived that children learn with greater success when they are learning about topics that are of interest to them (rather than simply learning for the sake of learning). Through active and meaningful experiences with people, materials, ideas and events, all children (regardless of age, race or gender) can learn without any difficulty. Participating in programmes such as HighScope would enable children to become independent, confident problem-solvers and decision-makers.

Core Concepts of the HighScope Approach

This section provides detailed information on the core concepts of the HighScope approach to ECEC, including:

- Principles
- Environment
- Curriculum
- Key development indicators (KDIs)
- The role of the teacher.

Principles of the HighScope Approach

The HighScope approach is based on three fundamental principles:
- Active participation
- Regular daily planning
- KDIs.

Active Participation

The HighScope programme is structured around the concept of active participation and learning through play. Children can become involved in choosing, organising and evaluating learning activities. The activities are completed under the teacher's careful guidance. Active participation occurs in a learning environment that has a rich variety of materials.

Regular Daily Planning

Daily planning is completed by the teacher in accordance with a developmentally based curriculum model and carefully completed child observations.

KDIs

Developmentally sequenced goals and materials for children are based on the HighScope 'key experiences'. The HighScope pre-school curriculum is built around 58 developmental milestones called KDIs. These are divided into eight curriculum content areas. (KDIs are discussed in more depth later in this chapter.)

HighScope Environment

The HighScope environment is an attractive one. It is bright and airy and it has a warm and welcoming atmosphere. Children feel confident to be themselves there and they are comfortable going there on a regular basis.

The classroom is organised with materials in order to facilitate independent learning. The classroom has ample space for the children to work individually or in groups. The room is equipped with child-sized furniture.

Both the indoor and outdoor environments are meticulously planned and organised by the teacher in a manner that will promote children's interests in the activities, active involvement with other children and opportunities to practise their problem-solving skills. A carefully planned outdoor area is important, as it gives children daily opportunities to observe and learn from the natural world. The children and the teacher will spend time outdoors most days, engaging in different types of play.

HighScope Curriculum

The purpose of the HighScope curriculum is to promote all areas of academic and social development. Weikart proposed providing children with a curriculum that focused on cognitive and intellectual development. There was no such curriculum like this before the HighScope approach and therefore there were high expectations for the programme to be a success. Having engaged in thorough research in local schools, Weikart and his colleagues decided on a new curriculum. Relevant theories on teaching and learning guided the development of the curriculum. The HighScope curriculum was established with children's happiness and development being the main priorities.

The design of the HighScope curriculum correspondences with John Dewey's philosophy of *progressive education* and also Jean Piaget's principle of *cognitive development*, which stated that children have a greater ability to learn when they are involved in practical exercises within their environment and given opportunities to learn through play. Weikart followed these principles. He saw these theories as the most accurate and relevant to his principles of active involvement and the use of real-life, purposeful materials. Piaget's theory was seen to be most compatible with the philosophical outlook of the HighScope programme.

Small-Group Time

Small-group time is a regular part of the HighScope kindergarten curriculum. A group of around five children and one teacher come together around a table at regular intervals and work with materials chosen by the teacher. During small-group time, children are given freedom and encouragement to work with the materials in a way that suits them; they are free to explore and to be creative. The teacher chooses the work carefully. The work may be based on the children's interests or developmental abilities. It can involve literacy or numeracy exercises. It can simply be something that is relevant to the children at this particular time, e.g. a birthday or season.

The teacher often begins small-group time by providing each child with a basket containing the materials required for the activity. The teacher briefly introduces the activity and then moves around the table, giving individual help and attention to each child. The teacher chats with each child and provides assistance as needed. When the children are engaged in the activity, the teacher listens and carefully observes. The teacher can imitate the children's play and help the children to expand their ideas and creativity. The teacher tells the children when the time is nearly over and everyone works together to clear away the materials.

Large-Group Time

Large-group time is the part of the day when the teacher and all of the children come together to participate in music and movement activities, storytelling and games. Large-group time may last 10–15 minutes. This is an enjoyable experience and everyone joins in. It gives the children a sense of common experience and it encourages them to be part of the group. The teacher may give roles to individual children so that everyone participates.

The teacher ensures that they have carefully planned for the day in advance of the group session. Large-group time involves activities that are of interest to the children, e.g. particular songs. Co-operative play is designed to be suitable for the children's ages and developmental levels. The children join in the group at a time that suits them; they are never pressurised to join. The teacher can introduce particular props to the group and they can observe and listen to any suggestions offered by the children. The teacher tells the children when the time is nearly over and everyone works together to clear away the materials.

A typical day might include the following activities:

- Circle time: music, speech, drama
- Plan–Do–Review (see below)
- Snack time
- Small-group time
- Large-group time
- Lunch
- Outdoor play.

The HighScope approach has a number of exclusive features that distinguish it from other approaches. These include:

- Organisation of the room
- Organisation of equipment
- Daily routine.

Organisation of the Room
The HighScope classroom is divided into a number of well-defined work areas, including a book corner, a home corner and an art area. All materials and equipment are natural and well manufactured. The children have the freedom to work on whatever they wish, without interruptions from the teacher or other children. The area can be altered from time to time in accordance with the children's interests.

Organisation of Equipment
All equipment and materials are readily available and easily accessible to the children at all times. Adult intervention is very rare and, as a result, the children can be independent. The materials are clearly labelled with pictures as well as words and are stored in their corresponding curriculum areas. The children can help to make the decision as to where and how materials should be stored.

Daily Routine

Children participate in outdoor activities and circle time on a daily basis. Children can plan different games to play outside. In the circle, the whole class gathers together to sing songs, talk about different topics and play games.

Throughout the day, the children will engage in group time. Sometimes this involves small groups, which are teacher led. The teacher will have gathered observations of the children and will have planned the group time accordingly. Group time can take into account the children's interests, the time of year and upcoming events in the community. Children can also engage in group time in larger groups, when the children themselves decide on the subject. Group time can be a good opportunity for sharing stories and news.

Children in the HighScope environment make choices, carry out their ideas and reflect on what they have learned throughout the day. These activities promote a genuine interest in learning and allow for independence.

The sequence of the day is based on a framework of:

- Plan
- Do
- Review.

Plan

In the HighScope classroom, children decide what they would like to do during the session. They plan their own activities. The teacher has a very passive role: they may offer encouragement, but it is the children who make all the necessary decisions.

Do

The *doing* stage involves children working with the materials they desire and on topics that are of interest to them. Children carry out the activity they have planned. They might work alone or with other children, creating and sharing ideas. The HighScope curriculum encourages children to work using their own initiative as much as possible. The activities can be either child or adult led. If the children have finished one task, they begin to plan another. The children take responsibility for cleaning up after themselves, sorting out materials and leaving them ready for the next child or group.

Review

The purpose of the review stage is for the children to reflect on the work they have just completed. This reflection may be in words, pictures or a short presentation. Children may like to share their reflections with the teacher and the other children. Quite often, the work that the children have completed will differ somewhat from the work they had originally planned. The children will work together to brainstorm and find answers. They will investigate what they have learned individually or as a group, what worked or didn't work and what improvements might be useful for similar activities in the future.

Key Developmental Indicators (KDIs)

For pre-school children, there are 58 KDIs in eight curriculum areas. Together, they form a framework that guides teachers in the planning process of beneficial learning experiences for the children in their care. KDIs are specifically organised to promote cognitive development.

KDIs are also known as *key experiences*. They are used to describe the development of the children and what they do when they are active in the HighScope learning process. KDIs are very useful for teachers: they act as a guide to help in the planning and evaluation processes. KDIs also allow the teacher to assess the children's progression on their observation record.

A full account of KDIs can be found at www.highscope.org. The pre-school KDIs are divided into eight categories:

- Approaches to learning
- Social and emotional development
- Physical development and health
- Language, literacy and communication
- Maths
- Creative arts
- Science and technology
- Social studies.

Approaches to Learning

Different children approach learning in very different ways. They learn different habits and preferences. The KDIs that relate to *approaches to learning* are:

Initiative: Children work using their own initiative to explore their immediate surroundings.

Planning: Children are in charge of the planning process. They create their own plans and act on them.

Engagement: Children will carry out activities in which they have a particular interest.

Problem-solving: Children have the opportunity to solve any conflicts or issues that arise in the environment in their own way and in their own time.

Use of resources: Children have access to relevant materials and are given the opportunity to gather these materials.

Reflection: Children are given the necessary time to reflect on the experiences they have completed. They can establish areas that were successful or areas that may require change for the future. Children can assess their performance of the activity.

Social and Emotional Development

The HighScope teacher works to the best of their ability to help children develop good relationships with adults and peers. The teacher does this by creating a nurturing environment to facilitate this social learning. The social skills that children develop will stay with them throughout their lives. The KDIs that relate to *social and emotional development* are:

Self-identity:	Children have a positive self-identity.
Sense of competence:	Children feel they are competent.
Emotions:	Children recognise, label and regulate their feelings.
Empathy:	Children demonstrate empathy towards others.
Community:	Children participate in the community of the classroom, e.g. sharing materials, waiting their turn and helping each other.
Building relationships:	Children build relationships with other children and adults, often through group work.
Co-operative play:	Children engage in co-operative play.
Moral development:	Children develop an internal sense of right and wrong.
Conflict resolution:	Children resolve social conflicts.

Physical Development and Health

Young children are generally active on a daily basis. The HighScope approach allows adults to introduce effective teaching strategies and learning activities to promote physical development. There is a growing awareness regarding the importance of physical education in early childhood. The KDIs that relate to *physical development and health* are:

Gross-motor skills:	Children demonstrate strength, flexibility, balance and timing in using their large muscles.
Fine-motor skills:	Children demonstrate dexterity and hand–eye co-ordination in using their small muscles.
Body awareness:	Children know about their bodies and how to navigate them in space.
Personal care:	Children carry out personal care routines on their own.
Healthy behaviour:	Children engage in healthy practices.

Language, Literacy and Communication

The HighScope curriculum enables children to become familiar with the alphabet and the letters and sounds that are associated with it. Children have the opportunity to play different games that involve language play and practice, e.g. making new words. The children will see the teacher write these letters and words and the children have unlimited access to books, word charts, etc.

The understanding of comprehension is important in the HighScope curriculum of language, i.e. an emphasis on children understanding what is being said to them. The teacher ensures that children regularly engage in conversation and use the appropriate vocabulary. The teacher questions the children and asks them to remember or to imagine. The KDIs that relate to *language, literacy and communication* are:

Comprehension:	Children understand language.
Speaking:	Children express themselves using language.
Vocabulary:	Children understand and use a variety of words and phrases.
Phonological awareness:	Children identify distinct sounds in spoken language.
Alphabetic knowledge:	Children identify letter names and their sounds.
Reading:	Children read for pleasure and information.
Concepts about print:	Children demonstrate knowledge about environmental print.
Book knowledge:	Children demonstrate knowledge about books.
Writing:	Children write for many different purposes.
ELL/Dual language acquisition:	If this is relevant to the child, they use English and their home language(s). This includes sign language.

Maths

The HighScope maths curriculum helps children to become increasingly aware of their surroundings and the various concepts in the area of maths. Children become aware of relationships associated in maths. They begin to notice objects that are the same and objects that are different. They can arrange objects according to similar patterns. They become aware of basic mathematical phrases. The KDIs that relate to *maths* are:

Number words and symbols:	Children recognise and use number words and symbols.
Counting:	Children count things.
Part–whole relationships:	Children combine and separate quantities of objects.
Shapes:	Children identify, name and describe shapes.
Spatial awareness:	Children recognise spatial relationships among people and objects.
Measuring:	Children measure to describe, compare and order things.
Unit:	Children understand and use the concept of unit.
Patterns:	Children identify, describe, copy, complete and create patterns.
Data analysis:	Children use information about quantity to draw conclusions, make decisions and solve problems.

Creative Arts

Creative arts are an important aspect of the HighScope programme. Creative arts promote skills in many areas of development, in particular cognitive, language and social skills. The KDIs that relate to *creative arts* are:

Art:	Through two-dimensional and three-dimensional art, children express and represent what they observe, think, imagine and feel.
Music:	Through music, children express and represent what they observe, think, imagine and feel.
Movement:	Through movement, children express and represent what they observe, think, imagine and feel.
Pretend play:	Through pretend play, children express and represent what they observe, think, imagine and feel.
Appreciating the arts:	Children appreciate the creative arts.

Art

In HighScope classrooms, children are encouraged to appreciate art. Children have access to a wide range of materials. They have the opportunity to be unique in their creations and to use their imaginations.

Music

Music is incorporated into the HighScope routine on a regular basis. Children can discover different sounds, dance to music, sing and be introduced to playing simple musical instruments. As with many of the subjects taught in the HighScope classroom, children have the opportunity to be creative.

Pretend Play

Children participate in pretend play on a daily basis in the HighScope classroom. Children can engage in role plays or different scenarios they may have read about or seen in real life. These experiences provide wonderful opportunities to practise language, learn new words and develop social skills. Children can be humorous and enjoy the fun element.

Science and Technology

Children can engage in purposeful science experience based on their surroundings. They can formulate questions and predict answers. They engage in practical problem-solving and in the development of observation skills. The KDIs that relate to *science and technology* are:

Observing:	Children observe the materials and processes in their environment.
Classifying:	Children classify materials, actions, people and events.
Experimenting:	Children experiment in order to test their ideas.
Predicting:	Children predict what they expect will happen.
Drawing conclusions:	Children draw conclusions based on their experiences and observations.
Communicating ideas:	Children communicate their ideas about the characteristics of things and how they work.
Natural and physical world:	Children gather knowledge about the natural and physical world.
Tools and technology:	Children explore and use tools and technology.

Social Studies

Through social studies, children can learn life skills in order to become valued members of society. Children can discuss expected behaviours and the various roles people take in society. They can reflect on different stereotypes and the reasons why they exist. Children discuss appropriate problem-solving techniques without becoming angry or upset. Children can practise making decisions in life, since they have the opportunity to make decisions in the class. Children are encouraged to work in groups (small and large) and to engage in discussion. The KDIs that relate to *social studies* are:

Diversity:	Children understand that people have diverse characteristics, interests and abilities.
Community roles:	Children recognise that people have different roles and functions in the community.
Decision-making:	Children participate in making classroom decisions.
Geography:	Children recognise and interpret features and locations in their environment.
History:	Children understand past, present and future.
Ecology:	Children understand the importance of taking care of their environment.

Example of Small-Group Time: Shapes in the Mystery Bag

Materials
Several different shapes (circle, square, triangle, etc.) made from a firm material
Several cloth bags
Crayons
Paper

Presentation
- Invite the children to sit around a circular table. (This is an adult-led activity.)
- Show the shapes to the children and encourage them to name the shapes.
- Encourage a group discussion, asking the children what they notice about the shapes.
- Explain to the children that you will play a game where they close their eyes, feel the shapes in the bag and try to remember the names of the shapes.
- Place one or all of the shapes in the bag and ask one child to close their eyes, reach into the bag, feel the shape and name it.
- Encourage the child to guess the shape without looking at it or removing it from the bag.
- When the child has made their guess, they can pull out the shape to see if they were correct.
- Now that the children understand the exercise, divide them into pairs so that they can try it for themselves.
- Give each pair a bag with several shapes in it. Encourage each child to do this exercise with their partner.
- As the children work through the exercise, help them in their exploration of the shapes. Observe how each child progresses with the exercise.
- When the children are familiar with identifying the shapes, invite them to draw the shapes using crayons and paper.
- When it is time for the exercise to finish, encourage the children to work together to clear away the materials. If possible, include a song that helps the children to do this.

Link with Aistear
- Wellbeing
  Aim 1, Learning Goal 3: Children will handle transitions and changes well.

Aim 2, Learning Goal 3: Children will discover, explore and refine gross- and fine-motor skills.

■ Identity and Belonging
Aim 3, Learning Goal 3: Children will interact, work co-operatively and help others.

■ Communicating
Aim 2, Learning Goal 1: Children will interact with other children and adults by listening, discussing and taking turns in conversation.

■ Exploring and Thinking
Aim 3, Learning Goal 5: Children will use letters, words, sentences, numbers, signs, pictures, colour and shapes to give and record information, to describe and to make sense of their own and others' experiences.

The Role of the Teacher in the HighScope Environment

As with every early childhood curriculum, the teacher plays a very valuable role. In the HighScope curriculum, the teacher is more commonly called 'the adult': they are more of a leader or facilitator than a teacher. For the sake of clarity, we will refer to them as 'the teacher' here.

The HighScope approach to education regards children as active learners who require support and challenges from the teacher. The teacher is aware of adult scaffolding and supports the children's plans and actions. The teacher helps the children to develop their own thinking and reasoning skills. The teacher encourages the children in many ways. Children are encouraged to be independent, solve problems for themselves, take interest in their environment and experiment with materials as they wish.

While the teacher takes a very passive role in the classroom, they have all the necessary traits and characteristics possessed by teachers. They are highly trained in the HighScope approach to education. They possess a broad knowledge of the subject of child development. They recognise the importance of observation in planning for children's needs. Therefore, they observe and listen carefully to everything that happens on a daily basis in the classroom. These observations are then recorded.

The teacher and children work in partnership. They work together as a team: there is no hierarchy. The teacher gives children control over events. Children implement the plan–do–review method. Throughout the day, the teacher will facilitate lessons with the children on topics the children themselves have chosen from a particular area. The teacher strives to provide the key developmental indicators (KDIs) within the classroom.

Assessment

HighScope teachers regularly take notes on children's daily activities. The teacher can then use these notes for future planning or correspondence with parents. The teacher will make an effort to explain the children's progress and development.

Involvement with Parents and the Community

Community involvement is a key concept of the HighScope approach. This is evident in the fact that the HighScope approach serves children from diverse backgrounds, with special needs and of different religions. Parents often volunteer: they attend regular parent–teacher meetings where they are able to discuss their children's progress, learning and overall development.

Staff and parents regularly communicate and parents often have valuable input. They can offer suggestions. They can discuss the children's recent experiences at home and in the classroom, along with any issues that may have arisen. Parents are encouraged to communicate with teachers on a daily basis. It is common for teachers to conduct home visits, where they can interact with parents in a relaxed and warm environment. The HighScope approach encourages parents to learn from their children, acknowledge the important work they do, take an interest and ask questions. This approach aims for good relationships between everyone involved.

Approaches to Early Childhood Education (5N1763): Assessment Guidelines

- **Assessment of module 5N1763: Approaches to Early Childhood Education**

  Note: This chapter provides suggested *guidelines for the assessment of module 5N1763, awarded by QQI. While students will find these guidelines helpful, they should follow closely the brief and instructions given by their own particular college in all instances.*

Marks are awarded under the following headings:

- Assignment: Exploration of the core concepts of a chosen educator (40%)
- Portfolio or collection of work: Exploration of the core concepts of four educators (60%)

Assignment

For this assignment, you are required to choose **one** educator: Maria Montessori, Friedrich Froebel, Rudolf Steiner or David Weikart (HighScope). You must present an assignment on the core concepts of their philosophy of education. Chapters 1–4 of this book will be useful to you in completing this assignment.

Marks are awarded under the following headings:

▨	Introduction	5 marks
▨	Development of topic	10 marks
▨	Application of theory to practice	10 marks
▨	Investigation of the role of the adult	5 marks
▨	Conclusion	5 marks
▨	References	5 marks
	Total	40 marks

Sample Brief

Approaches to Early Childhood Education (5N1763): Assignment Brief (40%)

For this assignment, you are required to explore the core concepts of one educator of your choice: Montessori, Froebel, Steiner or Weikhart (HighScope). Please present your assignment under the following headings:

1 **Introduction**
   ▪ Aim of assignment
   ▪ Objectives of assignment

2 **Development of topic**
   Outline the core concepts of your chosen educator.

3 **Application of theory to practice**
   Describe the significance of the educator's work to ECEC practices, i.e. how does their philosophy influence day-to-day practices in ECCE settings that follow their approach?

4 **Investigation of the role of the adult**
   Describe the typical role of the teacher in this environment.

5 **Conclusion/Recommendations**
   Summarise the most significant findings of your assignment, with recommendations for improvement.

6 **References**
   Correctly list all sources of information used in the assignment e.g. books, internet articles, etc.

Guidelines

Introduction

You must state your general aim, i.e. what it is you are hoping to achieve in your assignment. Your aim could be: 'To demonstrate an understanding of the core concepts of Maria Montessori's approach to ECEC'.

Break down the aim of your assignment into smaller parts or objectives. Examples of objectives could be to:

- Give a comprehensive account of the core concepts of the Montessori approach
- Describe how these concepts are applied in real-life Montessori settings
- Investigate the role of the adult in the Montessori environment
- Provide conclusions and recommendations on how the Montessori concepts can be applied
- Reference my work accurately and correctly.

The introduction is a good way for the reader to know what to expect during the assignment. It is also an opportunity for you to explain any new or unusual terms. For example, if Montessori is your chosen educator, you might explain the term 'developmental planes'.

It is important that you choose the core concepts of the educator. In Chapters 1–4 of this book, many concepts are discussed for each educator. For your assignment, it is up to you to discuss the most relevant concepts.

Development of Topic

Here you develop the points you mentioned in your introduction. Your introduction will serve as a good reminder for what to include in the development.

It is in this section that you explore the core concepts in detail. It is not enough to simply mention a concept: you are required to be comprehensive and to explain how a concept is applied in the setting. For example, if you mention an aspect of the Montessori curriculum, explain how this aspect is taught with specific lessons in the environment. Remember that you are asked to 'explore' the concepts, so listing the concepts is not enough.

It is a good idea to use a separate paragraph for each concept, so that the reader can easily understand.

Application of Theory to Practice

Here you explore how the core concepts of the educator relate to your experience of real-life settings. Examine any similarities and differences you have observed. This section of the assignment offers a great opportunity for you to include valuable information and opinions you have formed from your experience in ECEC settings.

You can illustrate a lesson plan that relates to one of the core concepts you have already discussed. Explain exactly how you would present a lesson to a child.

Investigation of the Role of the Adult

It is important that you focus on the role of the adult/teacher in your chosen environment. Often, the adult will have many different roles. Rather than listing all of the different roles, it is better if you choose those aspects that are most important (e.g. observation, assessment) and discuss them in some detail.

Conclusion/Recommendations

Recap on the points made in the development section of your assignment. Give your opinion or recommendation on a topic, e.g. explain how you believe a concept might be improved or could be implemented more.

References

Correctly list all sources of information used in the assignment, e.g. books, internet articles, etc.

Portfolio

For the portfolio, you are required to research all **four** educators: Maria Montessori, Friedrich Froebel, Rudolf Steiner and David Weikart. Unlike the assignment, you do not decide on the core concepts yourself. Here, you must examine all four educators under the headings provided.

Marks are awarded under the following headings:

▨	The importance of practical activities in the philosophy	5 marks
▨	The learning environment	10 marks
▨	Activities for individuals and groups	10 marks
▨	Implementation of a routine	5 marks
▨	Evaluation of a routine	5 marks
▨	Reflection on personal learning	5 marks
▨	Application of theory to practice	15 marks
▨	References	5 marks
▨	Appendices	5 marks
	Total	60 marks

Sample Brief

Approaches to Early Childhood Education (5N1763): Portfolio (60%)
For this portfolio, you are required to explore the core concepts of four educators: Montessori, Froebel, Steiner and Weikhart (HighScope). Please present your assignment under the following headings:

1 **The importance of practical activities in the philosophy**
   Explain the importance of practical activities in each philosophy.

2 **The learning environment**
   Describe the indoor and outdoor settings.

3 **Activities for individuals and groups**
   Give examples of individual and group activities and explain their importance to the children's development.

4 **Implementation of a routine**
   Plan and implement a routine according to a chosen philosophy.

5 **Evaluation of a routine**
   Evaluate your chosen routine.

6 **Reflection on personal learning**
   Reflect on your performance and assess how you might improve in the future.

7 **Application of theory to practice**
   Write how the educators' approaches are adapted into ECEC settings today.

8 **References**
   Correctly list all sources of information used.

9 **Appendices**
   Supply any additional information that is relevant to your work, e.g. lesson plan.

Guidelines

The Importance of Practical Activities in the Philosophy

Here you can explain the importance of practical activities in ECEC. Examine why all educators strive to engage children in practical activities. Describe how the practical approach benefits children in ways that rote learning does not. Provide an example of a practical activity promoted by each educator. Explain the purpose and benefits of this practical activity.

The Learning Environment

Here you can describe the typical classroom setting promoted by each of the educators. It is important to distinguish between the indoor and outdoor environments and to explain their place in the relevant theories. For example, Steiner placed a particular emphasis on children's need for access to the outdoors.

Activities for Individuals and Groups

You must identify different activities proposed for individuals and groups. Explain which theorists catered for different groups. Describe the opportunities offered by each type of activity. Give examples of typical individual and group activities. A typical group activity might be circle time.

Implementation of a Routine

Identify how different educators describe the implementation of routines. This is an opportunity to distinguish between adult-led and children-led routines, e.g. in the HighScope approach, children themselves engage in Plan–Do–Review. Describe different routines promoted by different educators. Focus on the different stages involved in the implementation of a routine.

Evaluation of a Routine

After completing an activity with a child it is important to evaluate it in order to understand how the routine went. You can assess the role of the adult and you can suggest any improvements for the future. Evaluations help to establish whether or not the activity was purposeful. Through evaluation, you will discover whether or not the activity had the appropriate and desired impact on the child.

   As part of your evaluation of an activity, ask yourself the following questions:

- What elements of planning were required for the activity?
- Did I discuss my activity with my supervisor or with other staff members?
- Was the activity appropriate to the children's development?
- How did the activity link with Aistear?
- How did I source materials for the activity?

- What resources did I use to devise the activity?
- Were my sources accurate?
- What were the steps involved in the activity?
- Did I give a clear description of the procedure?
- Was the activity a correct implementation of a core concept by a relevant educator?
- Was the activity a success?
- Did the children react in the way I expected?
- Did I stick to my plan or did I deviate from it?
- Were the children engaged by the activity?
- How did they interact?
- What strengths did I show in doing this activity? Was I confident, patient, etc?
- What weaknesses did I show in doing this activity? Was I unprepared, nervous, etc?
- Would I change anything if I were to do the activity again?

Reflection on Personal Learning

As part of your reflection on personal learning, ask yourself the following questions:

- How did I feel before the activity?
- How did I feel during the activity?
- How did I feel after the activity?
- Was I happy with my performance?
- Did I act professionally?
- What did I learn about myself in doing this activity?

Application of Theory to Practice

Here you explore how the core concepts of the educators relate to your experience of real-life settings. Examine any similarities and differences you have observed. This section of the portfolio offers a great opportunity for you to include valuable information and opinions you have formed from your experience in ECEC settings.

References

Correctly list all sources of information used in the assignment, e.g. books, internet articles, etc.

Appendices

Here you can supply any relevant information that is related to your portfolio, e.g. lesson plans, observation notes, etc.

Section 2

EARLY CHILDHOOD
EDUCATION AND PLAY

Introduction to Play

Characteristics of Play

Having studied both young animals and children at play, Burghardt (1984) identifies a number of characteristics of play:

- It is most common in the young.
- It has no obvious immediate function.
- It is a pleasurable activity.
- It can be quick, using bursts of energy.
- It is spontaneous and voluntary.
- It is relaxed, involving no fear or threat.
- Its sequence may vary.
- It relies on a stimulus to keep going, e.g. one child finds a pinecone on the ground and begins to play with it; another child joins in.
- It may involve developing a mastery of movements, e.g. climbing.

These characteristics highlight how useful and important play is as a tool for learning. Children do not have to be forced or coerced into playing. They do not need to be told to do it because it is good for them; they do not feel fearful or threatened by it. Most of all, children enjoy play. It makes sense, therefore, that ECEC should be based on learning through play – something children do naturally and spontaneously every day of their lives.

History of Play

Records of children's play date back to earliest times. Archaeological finds from ancient civilizations such as China, Peru and Egypt show drawings of play scenes. Artefacts such as dolls, tops and rattles, usually made from pottery or metal, have also been discovered. Throughout the centuries, anthropologists have studied play in many cultures. Even in the most 'primitive' ones, they have found evidence of storytelling, games and dancing (Mitchell 1937).

Ancient

Plato (c.424–c.347 BC)

The Greek philosopher Plato was a believer in the value of children's play. He urged the Greek state to promote children's games and he offered advice to mothers regarding the promoting play in the home. Plato divided children's development into four levels or stages.

- Infancy (0–3 years)   The child should be cared for and protected from fear or pain.

- Nursery (3–6 years)   Play and listening to fairytales should be the child's main occupation. Punishments should be infrequent and mild.

- Elementary (6–13 years) Girls and boys should be separated, but both should learn letters, mathematics, music, religion and morals. Boys should receive some military training.

- Middle (13–16 years)   Advanced mathematics, poetry and music can be taught. From age 16, boys should receive formal military and gymnastics training.

Plato believed that early experiences were very important because they have a lasting impact on final development. He believed that stories and fables told to young children should be carefully chosen in order to give children clear understanding of the concepts of good and evil. Plato believed that in order for adults to be good at something it is beneficial for them to have 'played' the skill during childhood, e.g. a good builder will have played at building things during childhood. Plato did not advocate children having a huge number of 'toys'. He proposed that children make their own toys from natural materials or that they be provided with 'tools' to mimic adult roles. Plato wrote a treatise called *The Republic* (*c*.360 BC) in which he proposed his views on public education. This work was highly valued by many later philosophers, including Jean-Jacques Rousseau.

Aristotle (384–322 BC)

Aristotle was another Greek philosopher. He worked with Plato and with Plato's teacher, Socrates. Aristotle valued play and physical exercise, especially during the early years. He believed that formal education should not begin too early, in case growth and physical development would be impeded. Aristotle placed great value on leisure time.

Quintilian (c.35– c.100 AD)

In Ancient Greece, public education was viewed as being in the overall interest of society. In contrast, education in Ancient Rome was very much seen as a private issue: the head of each family was the decision-maker with regards to their children's education. Quintilian was a Roman philosopher who was a firm believer in learning through play in the early years. He believed that children forced into formal learning at too young an age came to 'hate all learning'. He saw the value of observing children. He understood that children have different temperaments and rates of learning, and he believed that these differences should be accommodated. He stated that corporal punishment was degrading and that it simply was not required if educational instruction was good enough.

Medieval

The ideas of ancient philosophers such as Plato, Aristotle and Quintilian are actually quite modern. In many respects, they align with the teachings of educators such as Froebel and Steiner. However, during the Middle Ages (*c*.5th–15th centuries), beliefs about children and their development and play took a step backwards. During this time, children were expected to move from being dependent infants to 'mini adults' within the space of five or six years. In a sense, childhood ceased to exist. Children of the rich aristocracy practised archery, chess, hunting and school work from four or five years of age. Children of the poor worked as soon as they were physically able to do so. Childhood was not recognised again as a distinct period until the Reformation.

> In medieval society the idea of childhood did not exist…as soon as the child could live without the constant solicitude of his mother, his nanny or his cradle rocker, he belonged to adult society (Aries 1988).

It must be noted that there is some research that contradicts this view of childhood in the

Middle Ages. Orme (2001) and others have studied writings, records and archaeological finds from the time and they have found evidence of children having their own possessions and play activities.

Reformation and Renaissance

Martin Luther (1483–1546)

Martin Luther was an important figure during the Reformation. While he is best-known for his work in the reformation of the church, he also worked towards educational reform. In reflecting on changes in education in his society, he said:

> Our schools are no longer a hell and purgatory in which children are tortured over cases and tenses and in which, with much flogging, trembling, anguish and wretchedness, they learn nothing (Painter 1889: 67).

Luther was a careful observer of children, believing that the type of instruction offered to them should be adapted to their nature. He believed that children should be allowed to be active, run, jump and play. Luther believed that children should work hard at school and at home, learn a trade and be permitted to play.

John Amos Comenius (1592–1670)

John Amos Comenius was a Czech theologian who further developed child-centred education, beginning with the idea of the 'mother school'. This was a system of education to be used in the home by mothers of children aged 0–6. Comenius emphasised the importance of children learning through active, firsthand experience. These ideas are very much reflected in the later teachings of educators such as Rousseau, Pestalozzi, Montessori, Froebel and Piaget. Comenius likened children's development to that of a tree: if a tree is tended to carefully, it will reach maturity covered with fruit waiting to be plucked and used.

John Locke (1632–1704)

John Locke was a physician and philosopher. He was another important figure in childhood education and play. He believed that children should have playthings but should only be allowed to play with one thing at a time. He believed that this would teach children to be careful and respectful of their possessions and that if children were given too much they would become squanderers and wasters! He believed such children would never be happy with what they have and that they would always seek more and more. Locke was a firm believer in children making their own toys, with adults supervising and supporting their endeavours. Locke observed children at play and wrote about his findings.

Eighteenth and Nineteenth Centuries

Jean-Jacques Rousseau (1712–78)

Rousseau was one of the most influential philosophers of his time. In 1762, he wrote a hugely influential book entitled *Emile, or On Education*. It is a treatise on the education of the whole person for responsible citizenship. In it, he opposes many practices of the time, e.g. binding children in swaddling clothes and blankets to restrict their movement and make them sleep more.

Like Luther and Comenius, Rousseau believed that children develop in stages and that they should be facilitated in following what is naturally of interest to them at a particular time in their lives. In Rousseau's time, memory work was a significant feature of children's education. This rote learning was something in which Rousseau saw little value. Instead, he believed that children should be given opportunities to develop judgment and reasoning skills through hands-on experiences. He believed that children aged 0–5 should learn only through play and he rejected the idea that play was essentially doing nothing.

Rousseau advocated play for the development of a healthy body, which he saw as being essential for a healthy mind. He believed that children should be given opportunities to play at what were considered adult pursuits, e.g. football, archery, tennis and the playing of musical instruments. He warned that these play activities should not be turned into work by over-instruction or by making them too adult-led and competitive. Rousseau argued that for children play *is* work. He believed that the efforts of tutors to waste no time by filling children's heads with 'a pack of rubbish' were utterly futile (Frost 2010: 24). He argued that, through play and real-life experiences children obtain real understanding and skills such as observation, reasoning and judgment.

Johann Pestalozzi (1746–1827)

Johann Heinrich Pestalozzi was a Swiss teacher and educational reformer. A follower of Rousseau, he was a strong advocate of affording educational opportunities to the poor. In 1769 Pestalozzi bought a plot of 15 acres of land, intending to farm it. The land was poor and he didn't succeed. Pestalozzi then had an idea of opening a school on the farm, which he would call 'Neuhof' and where poor children would come and experience a mixture of 'education and industry'. Pestalozzi did not manage Neuhof well and this project failed, leaving him deeply in debt.

In 1799, Pestalozzi was given another opportunity to open a school. This opportunity came from the Swiss government and the school was opened in the town of Stans in central Switzerland. The French army had just invaded the town of Stans and, as a result, a large number of children were left orphaned there. Pestalozzi was put in charge of the orphanage. He was given no resources and initially ran it himself with a housekeeper. While the school at Stans was only open for a short time (the French army returned and took it over as a military base), Pestalozzi observed that the children made great progress during their time there. He again adopted the principle of mixing education and industry, combining work with learning and discovery. At this school, Pestalozzi opposed three particular educational practices common at the time: the exclusion of poor children from education, rote learning and cruel punishment.

In 1800 Pestalozzi went to teach in the town of Burgdorf, where he worked and then later founded a new school called the Educational Institute for the Children of the Middle Classes. This school was a financial success but Pestalozzi was disappointed because he was not succeeding in reaching and educating the poor. In 1801 he published a series of letters collectively called *How Gertrude Teaches Her Children*. This publication was widely read. In 1805 Pestalozzi opened the institution for which he is most famous, at Yverdon. While the school was not without its problems, it was visited by educators from all over the world and it had a lasting impact on educational practice. Pestalozzi originated the idea of *readiness*, i.e. a child must be cognitively ready to learn something and cannot be rushed into doing so. From his observations he saw that children have to experience objects and events in order to fully understand them, i.e. learning by doing. In *How Gertrude Teaches Her Children*, Pestalozzi stated that teachers (including parents) must kind and gentle in their approach at all times. He suggested that this could be done through language. Instead of saying 'Wash your hands', a teacher should say: 'Come here, child, and we will wash your little hands.'

While the word 'play' rarely appears in the work of Pestalozzi, he was an early advocate of *free play* as an educational method. Friedrich Froebel studied with Pestalozzi and this influenced his ideas of the centrality of play to ECEC.

Fredrich Froebel (1782–1852)

Fredrich Froebel was influenced by many of the educational philosophers that came before him. He is most famous for his concept of the *kindergarten*, meaning 'garden for children'. Froebel taught at Pestalozzi's school in Yverdon for two years. Although he felt that the goals of the school were noble, he equally felt that a lack of organisation at times impeded the fulfilment of these goals. In 1837 Froebel opened his first school in Blankenburg, Germany. Froebel likened the child to a young plant requiring tender care and nourishment in order to grow. Froebel's vehicle of instruction was play. He believed that all areas of development could be promoted through play: physical development through callisthenic exercises, social development through children playing and working things out together, sense development through exploring and manipulating playthings, and intellectual development through imitative or inventive use of the Froebel gifts and occupations. Froebel's gifts were to be manipulated and played with by the child in their own way and at their own pace. Froebel's occupations included activities such as paper cutting, weaving, threading, drawing and painting.

Froebel believed that play was a vital part of human life:

> Play is the purest, most spiritual activity of man at this stage, and, at the same time, typical of human life as a whole – of the inner hidden natural life in man and all things. It gives, therefore, joy, freedom, contentment, inner and outer rest, peace with the world. It holds the source of all that is good…play at this time [childhood] is of deep significance…the germinal leaves of all later life (Froebel 1887: 55).

Frobel believed in play with natural materials, e.g. pieces of wood used to make huts. He also believed in the value of gardening and other outdoor activities. He believed that every town should have a playground. However, his idea of a playground was very different from modern playgrounds with manufactured equipment. Froebel's version of a playground was very natural, e.g. an ordinary field with trees and flowers.

The Reality of Children's Play Throughout the Ages

Throughout history, regardless of whether or not the great thinkers, educators and governments valued play, children played with whatever materials were available to them. When European settlers landed in America, Australia and New Zealand for the first time, the Native American, Aboriginal and Māori children all played games that are still recognisable to us today. The first settlers to land in America observed Native American children involved in make-believe games mimicking adult pursuits of hunting, fishing, planting and harvesting. They played football, shinny (similar to hockey), quoits (rings), hoop and spear, bounce-on-the-rock, kick-the-stick, tossing games and chasing. These children had the finest of 'playgrounds' with acres of fields, meadows, streams and woodlands in which to build and defend forts, make bows and arrows, and play tag and hiding games. The European settlers, who wished to escape the cramped and dirty cities of their homelands, readily adopted these new ways and allowed their children much more freedom to play. They also maintained many games from their homelands, e.g. singing games, kites, blind man's buff, hopscotch, cards and dice games. Manufactured toys were limited (except for the children of the rich in Europe) and most were made from scraps of material, wood and metal, e.g. rag dolls. Play during this time (seventeenth and eighteenth centuries) was very gender focused.

Throughout history, children around the world have been forced to live in difficult circumstances because of political, economic and civil unrest. However, it is clear that children have an unwavering instinct and will to play. Even in times of child labour and abject poverty, children still play. This is evidenced in writings from American slave folklore, the Industrial Revolution in Europe, the Great Depression in America and the Great Famine in Ireland.

After the Industrial Revolution, children who lived in huge slum tenements in cities all over the world learned to play in the streets. In many cities, the authorities sought to curb this play, since children were involved in petty crime such as pickpocketing. A new game now emerged – avoidance. Children continued to play in the streets and, when adults or authority figures chased them, this in turn became a game of tag.

In response to deprivation in cities across the world, many governments began providing playgrounds for poor city children, e.g. London and New York. Some city councils were more aware of the importance of nature in children's lives and they realised that, while the urban playgrounds they created were of benefit, children also needed to experience the countryside. This lead to organised summer camps and the development of organisations such as the boy scouts in the early 1900s.

Jane Addams (1860–1935) was an American philosopher and activist who founded Hull House in Chicago in 1889. At its height, Hull House was visited each week by around two thousand people. Its facilities included a night school for adults, kindergarten classes, clubs for older children, a public kitchen, an art gallery, a coffeehouse, a gym, a girls' club, a bathhouse, a book bindery, a music school, a drama group, and a library, as well as labour-related divisions. Addams created a 'model playground' of over an acre, which was equipped with sand, building blocks, swings, a giant stride (like a huge maypole) and an outdoor games area. She was also an advocate of community events and festival celebrations.

Ireland in 1900 was just coming out of the Great Famine and was still predominately an agricultural based society. The majority of Irish children were living in rural areas, mixing work with play. Ireland had few large cities and it lagged behind other countries in terms of provision of outdoor recreational space for children, especially in poor inner city areas where children played mainly on the streets.

In the early twentieth century in America, the Playground Association of America worked towards providing all city-born children with good outdoor playground facilities. Hundreds of municipal playgrounds were opened in cities across the United States. This also happened in many other cities across the world. There was recognition of the fact that city children needed outdoor play opportunities. A significant criticism of the playground movement in America was the fact that playgrounds omitted nature: they had no grass, flowers or trees. Instead, they were equipped with manufactured play equipment bolted to the ground.

While manufactured toys have been around for centuries, they have largely been the preserve of children of the rich. Exquisitely made dolls, dolls houses, teddy bears, trains and train sets have existed for centuries. However, most children worldwide had little access to manufactured toys until the 1930s and 1940s; even then, children had one or two items each at most.

Many observers of children and their play patterns worry that as children receive more and more manufactured toys their natural curiosity and inventiveness has declined. Many toys nowadays require solitary indoor play. Video games are in abundance, where the game manufacturer essentially decides what the child does. Because of heightened awareness of health and safety issues, many children no longer play together on the streets or in nature. Most spend large amounts of time inside or in sterile playgrounds and parks. Many psychologists and educationists worry that this will impede children's coping and decision-making skills.

Decade	Most popular toys
1930s	Pogo stick, magic slate, Duncan yo-yo, Mickey Mouse doll, Monopoly, Sorry, View-Master, cap gun, trampoline, Snoopy Sniffer
1940s	Scrabble, Cootie, model airplane, Silly Putty, Slinky, bubbles, paper doll, Magic 8 Ball, Cluedo, Candy Land
1950s	Barbie, Play-Doh, Frisbee, Tonka trucks, Matchbox cars, Yahtzee, skateboards, hula hoops, Mr. Potato Head, Pez dispensers
1960s	Hot Wheels, LEGO, Action Man, Easy Bake Oven, Etch A Sketch, Superball, Game of Life, Sea- monkeys, Barrel of Monkeys, Operation, Scalextric, Twister, Spirograph
1970s	Atari 2600, Uno, Rubik's Cube, Simon, Dungeons and Dragons, Hungry Hungry Hippos, Connect Four, Star Wars action figures, Magna Doodle, NERF balls, space hopper, Clackers
1980s	Cabbage Patch Kids, Trivial Pursuit, My Little Pony, Koosh balls, Transformers, Pictionary, Teenage Mutant Ninja Turtles, Chia Pets, JENGA, All Terrain Armored Transport (Star Wars Walker)
1990s	Pogs, Tickle Me Elmo, Furby, Super Soaker, Beanie Babies, Game Boy, Buzz Lightyear, Power Rangers, Tamagotchi, Pokemon, K'nex construction kits, Pokemon trading cards
2000s	Wii, Playstation 3, Xbox 360, Sony PSP, Nintendo DS, iPods, Bratz dolls, ultra-lifelike dolls (Baby Annabell), animatronic toys (Robosapien and Roboraptor), hi-tech remote control toys (Flytech Dragonfly), Top Trumps, Geomag, child computers (Dora the Explorer laptop), electronic puzzle games (20Q), merchandise from the Harry Potter films

Styles and Types of Play

Play can be classified in two ways:

1   Overall style
- Structured play
- Free play.

2   Types of play
- Imaginative
- Construction
- Creative
- Physical.

Styles of Play

Structured Play

Structured play is planned, guided and led by adults. Structured play can be useful but there is a risk that if it is too adult-led children will lose interest. Offering the right amount of support is absolutely essential in providing for valuable structured play. Adults can provide support by demonstrating skills that the child can then try out for themselves, e.g. how to use a piece of equipment. Some theorists advocated a very structured approach. Montessori advocated that certain skills should be very clearly demonstrated by the adult, with the child carefully watching so that they could then copy exactly what the adult had done, e.g. spooning rice. She argued that children like to achieve perfection and are motivated by it. She was therefore a strong advocate of structured activity.

Another key ingredient of successful structured play is that the activity is at the correct level for the children. There is absolutely no point in presenting children with activities that are outside what Vygotsky called their *zone of proximal development*. If the activity is beyond what the child can do even with adult support, the adult ends up practically doing the activity for the child and this does not aid learning. Activities set for children should be challenging, but not beyond them. Practitioners should not feel that children have to produce 'presentable' pieces of work for parents; they should concentrate more on children's enjoyment in learning from what they do.

Free Play

Free play is not adult-led. Adults provide equipment, materials and resources for free play, but they do not direct it in any way. Advocates of free play believe that children learn much more from this style of play than from structured play, since they are more motivated by having created it themselves. In free play, children direct and figure things out for themselves and it is believed that children gain deeper understanding of what they are doing as a result of this. Free play can take place when children are on their own, in groups, in pairs or engaged in parallel play (i.e. where children play side-by-side but not with one another). In the past, much of children's play was free play. Children did not have many manufactured toys and they did not attend crèches and pre-schools with structured activities. Instead, they played with what happened to be available to them. It is a worry that nowadays so much of children's lives is structured and adult led. Some parents feel that they are in an ever-competitive environment, expecting their children to be making observable progress in pre-school. Practitioners should communicate to parents that process rather than product is of importance in the early years.

Types of Play

Imaginative play

Imaginative play includes pretend, symbolic and fantasy play. It is sometimes referred to as role play.

Pretend play

In this type of play, children practise and gain understanding of aspects of daily life. Children play school, shop, hospital, house, post office, restaurant, farm, etc. The role of the adult in pretend play is to provide an array of clothing and props for children to use. Clothing and props do not have to be 'perfect': children should be encouraged to improvise and make use of what is available to them. Small-world toys such as Playmobil can be used for pretend play.

Fantasy Play

Fantasy play is most common for children aged 3–8. During fantasy play children pretend to be something or someone that they cannot ever possibly be, e.g. Spiderman or Batman. This type of play should decrease as reasoning increases.

Symbolic Play

With this type of play children use objects in their play, but they pretend that the objects are something else. Symbolic play can be merged with imaginary play, e.g. pretending leaves are salad ingredients. Symbolic play becomes imaginary play (as describe above) when several objects are used together. For example, children can use mud, grass, leaves and berries as 'food'; they can sit on concrete blocks and makeshift tables eating food off slate 'plates', with sticks and pieces of stone as 'knives and forks'.

Providing for Imaginative Play

Parents and practitioners can provide dress-up clothes, including clothing from other cultures. Small-world toys and props can be used to recreate different scenes, e.g. house, shop, restaurant, post office, bank and school. (See Chapter 8 for more ideas.)

Construction Play

Construction play can either use manufactured or non-manufactured materials. Manufactured construction materials include products such as Aerofix models, LEGO, Scalextric, K'nex and Geomag. Children can also engage in productive construction play with non-manufactured materials such as boxes, egg cartons, kitchen roll, tins, glue, sticky tape, pieces of wood, nails, elastic bands, cloth and safety pins. The possibilities are endless. With construction play, some children (particularly older children) will have an 'end product' in mind; but this is not the most important part of the process for them. With this type of play, the adult can provide resources and ideas about what might be constructed. However, it is important not to try to direct this type of play or else children hand over to the adult.

Providing for Construction Play

Parents and practitioners can provide construction blocks, cardboard boxes, tape, paper plates, kitchen rolls and other 'junk' material that can be used for construction. (See Chapter 8 for more ideas.)

Creative Play

Creative play encompasses activities such as art, craft, drawing, painting, music and dance. The important thing about creative play is to provide plenty of materials and equipment to allow it happen. Creative play can allow children to express emotion and indicate upset or distress. Adults should not make judgments on children's creative work, since children become anxious and fearful about creating things that are acceptable to adults.

Providing for Creative Play

Children should have access to a wide range of creative materials, e.g. paint, brushes, sponges, play-dough, clay, collage materials, sand, crayons, markers, chalk, glitter, glue, etc. (See Chapter 8 for more ideas.)

Physical Play

Physical play can take place indoors or outdoors and it can involve equipment such as wheeled toys, climbing frames, balls, skipping ropes. During physical play, children run, jump, balance, climb and crawl. Physical play is vital for children's health: it not only keeps them fit but it also encourages them to eat and sleep well. Ball games, tag and tip-the-can all come under the category of physical play. It is this type of play that many children nowadays seem to miss, spending large amounts of time at home on computers or watching TV instead. In addition, in many pre-school and school yards children's physical play is curbed because of health and safety issues. They are told not to run and if the weather is cold or wet, they are often kept inside.

Providing for Physical Play

Physical play can be encouraged with large outdoor equipment, balls, hoops, wheeled toys, hop-scotch, skipping ropes, etc. (See Chapter 8 for more ideas.)

Hughes (1996) further categorises children's play into 15 play types. Some of these play types can be incorporated into the four main types described above.

Type of play	Description
Symbolic play	Using items to represent something else
Rough and tumble play	Playful fighting, wrestling and chasing
Socio-dramatic play	The enactment of real and potential experiences of an intense personal, social, domestic or interpersonal nature, e.g. playing house, going to the shops or even having an argument
Social play	Any social or interactive situation that contains an expectation on all parties that they will abide by the rules or protocols, i.e. games with rules, conversations, making something together
Creative play	Creating pictures or artefacts using a range of materials
Communication play	Using words, nuances or gestures, e.g. mime, jokes, play acting, singing, debate, poetry
Dramatic play	Dramatising events in which the child is not a direct participator, e.g. presentation of a TV show
Deep play	Play that allows the child to encounter risky experiences in order to develop survival skills and conquer fear, e.g. climbing a tree or walking along a high beam
Exploratory play	Exploring objects and what they can do, e.g. stacking bricks, mixing substances together to see what will happen
Fantasy play	Pretending to be someone unlikely or enacting far-fetched occurrences, e.g. racing driver or princess
Imaginative play	Play where the conventional rules that govern the physical world do not apply, e.g. children imagining they are dinosaurs
Locomotor play	Movement in any and every direction for its own sake, e.g. chase, tag, hide-and-seek, tree climbing
Mastery play	Controlling physical and affective ingredients of the environments, e.g. digging holes, changing the course of streams, constructing huts
Object play	Using objects for their intended or unintended purpose, e.g. sweeping brush
Role play	Play exploring ways of being, although not normally of an intense personal, social, domestic or interpersonal nature, e.g. dialling and talking on the telephone, driving a car

Stages of Play

As children get older, the ways in which they play change. These changes are often represented as stages of play. An age range for each stage is usually given, although (as with all areas of development) some children pass through stages sooner than others. A three-year-old child who has several older siblings may come into the pre-school setting already engaging in co-operative play. Likewise, a child who is the eldest or only child in their family many spend longer at the solitary and spectator stage. Adults should observe children's play and support them with transitions between play stages. This is particularly important when working with children who have special needs that may affect their social skills and ability to interact with other children, e.g. language delay.

Stage of play	Age range	Description
Solitary	0–2	Children play alone, interacting little with other children around them
Spectator	2–2½	Children play alone but watch what others are doing around them without joining in
Parallel	2½–3	Children play alongside others but not together
Associative	3–4	• Children begin to interact and play together but there is still a good deal of solitary play • Children begin to develop friendships and show preferences for playing with particular children • Play groups are usually mixed-gender
Co-operative	4+	• Children play together, discussing goals for their play • Play can be quite complex at this stage, with group members carrying out particular roles • As children reach primary school age they begin to play in single-gender groups and play can become stereotypical

Benefits of Play to Holistic Development

Aistear recognises the enormous body of research that shows that young children (particularly those aged 0–6) learn most effectively through play and that more directive methods do not work but actually curb children's natural desire to explore and discover. This section describes how play benefits all five areas of development: physical, intellectual, language, emotional and social (PILES). This links with Aistear's four themes: wellbeing, identity and belonging, communicating, and exploring and thinking.

Physical Development: Wellbeing

Physical play, particularly rough and tumble, deep and locomotor play, promotes gross-motor skills. Children develop balance and increase co-ordination through practising skills such as running, jumping, climbing, skipping, walking on tiptoe, hopping, pedalling, etc. Physical play also promotes health and wellbeing because it increases appetite and tires children so that they sleep well. Physical development also involves the development and refinement of fine-motor skills; creative and construction play are both particularly beneficial in this area. Play with small-world toys as part of imaginative play can also be useful, since children need to refine their motor-skills to make toy figures and animals stand up, etc.

Intellectual Development: Exploring and Thinking

Through play children can explore and think about a wide range of concepts in a non-threatening way. Play cannot be 'wrong' so children are much more likely to take risks with their learning when they are engaged in play. Children can begin to understand important mathematical concepts, such as number, matching, ordering, sorting, making and recognising pattern, adding and subtracting, and measuring (weight, length, time, volume, capacity, shape and space). Through construction play, children can practise reasoning and problem-solving skills. Some types of play (e.g. role play) allow children to explore aspects of their real life (e.g. a visit to the hospital or dentist). This helps them to understand these events and helps them to process concerns or worries.

Language Development: Communicating

Virtually all types of play involve communication. Children negotiate their roles, talk about what they are doing and talk about their plans for what will happen next. During socio-dramatic play children can learn new vocabulary (e.g. 'cash register' if playing shop). When playing games with rules, children have to explain rules to newcomers and verbally deal with situations when the game rules are broken. Adults can promote language development by suggesting new vocabulary while children are playing and labelling areas of the play environment.

Emotional Development: Identity and Belonging, and Communicating

Emotional development involves children learning to deal with their emotions (both negative and positive) in a healthy way. Emotional development also involves the promotion of a positive self-image and high self-esteem. Emotional development can be greatly enhanced through play. While at play children can try out new things in a non-threatening way. Play cannot be 'wrong' so children's efforts are always rewarding to them, thus boosting self-esteem and helping children to develop a positive self-image. Physical play, particularly rough and tumble, gives children a safe outlet for negative emotions, e.g. anger and frustration. Role play and pretend play can give children the opportunity to act out scenes from their lives that may perhaps be bothering them, thus giving the adult an insight into how the child is thinking and feeling.

Games that require co-operation between children and games with rules teach children to control their emotions and to deal well with situations that are not going their way, e.g. if the rest of the group don't want to follow a particular idea, the child may have to accept the group's decision even though they do not agree with it. Some games have a winner, which means that there will be losers also. Games such as these help children to cope with competition and deal with defeat. These games are particularly important nowadays, since many children come from small families. They do not have to deal with competition very often and sometimes they find it hard to handle when it does arise. They are used to parents 'letting them win' and can get upset when this does not happen.

Play environments should reflect the diverse nature of our society. Play opportunities should, insofar as possible, be available to all children in the setting. This is why it is very important that settings make provision for children with special needs, allowing them to fully participate in all play activities offered. Cultural diversity should also be reflected in the play environment, e.g. dress-up clothes and cooking utensils from different cultures. Gender is another important issue to consider. Both boys and girls should be encouraged to participate in all types of play. If one gender seems to be dominating a particular area of the setting, this should be discussed with the children and a workable solution found.

Social Development: Identity and Belonging, and Communicating

Social development basically involves the development of three related skills: (1) the ability to interact effectively with others, (2) learning and understanding the norms of the society in which the child lives and (3) moral development. Play can be a very effective way for children to learn and perfect these skills. Social play requires that children negotiate, take turns and follow rules. Creative play often requires children to share materials and equipment, thus teaching them to request things and wait for them if they are not immediately available. Accidents that happen during play (e.g. a child falling during physical play) require the other children to show empathy and to get help. Role play helps children to practise everyday skills: taking care of babies, making and serving meals, asking for food in a restaurant, asking for and paying for items in a shop, etc.

Play can be used to teach children who have difficulties in one or more areas of social development. For example, if a child in a setting has a tendency to pull toys from other children and not wait their turn, the teacher could organise a cutting and pasting activity where children have to share scissors and glue pots. The teacher can deliberately have fewer scissors and glue pots than are needed and they can then role play as part of the activity, showing the children how to ask nicely for things and to politely wait until it is their turn.

Theories of Play

Friedrich Froebel

Friedrich Froebel was born in Germany in 1782. His mother died when he was just nine months old. His father remarried twice, having a son with his third wife. Froebel went to live with a bachelor uncle and it is he who had most influence on Froebel's education, sending him to a primary school near where he lived. Froebel was an excellent student, displaying from very early on a love for mathematics, mapmaking, natural science and nature. At 15 years of age, Froebel became an apprentice forester where he cultivated his interest in plants and nature. However, he did not finish his apprenticeship, leaving to study maths and botany in the University of Jena in 1799. He later became a land surveyor and, for a time, he studied architecture.

Froebel's career as an educator began in 1805 when he took up a position in a school in Frankfurt. The then principal of the school, Dr Anton Gunner, saw great potential in Froebel as an educator. After two years, Froebel travelled to Yverdon in Switzerland where he spent two years observing and teaching under Johann Heinrich Pestalozzi at his Progressive model school. Froebel felt that he learned a great deal from Pestalozzi and agreed with many of his ideas. In 1826 Froebel published *The Education of Man*, in which he gave a detailed account of his philosophy of education.

Froebel returned to Germany in 1837 where he established the first *kindergarten*, a term he coined which means 'garden of the children'. The kindergarten was a new institution for the education of young children aged 3–7. Froebel's kindergarten provided a rich learning environment where children could explore and satisfy their curiosity and desire for learning. He was one of the first advocates of free play, a concept quite alien to most educators of the time. He developed a teaching school attached to this first kindergarten and from here he educated many teachers who went on to open kindergartens all over Germany and later worldwide. Froebel continued to teach and refine his ideas on early childhood education until his death in 1852.

Froebel was one of the first educators to see the value of free play as a learning tool. He called free play 'free self activity'. He was also a strong advocate of learning by doing, believing that children have to physically experience materials by touching, handling, feeling and smelling them. He was a firm advocate of social learning. He believed that children learn well in social groups, discussing ideas among each other. He was writing at a time where children, even young children, were expected to sit quietly and listen to a teacher's instruction; Froebel disagreed totally with this.

Froebel believed that children should have access to nature – grass, flowers, plants and trees. His kindergartens all had grassy outdoor spaces where children observed nature, planted and tended. Froebel was great believer in the value of songs and rhymes to teach concepts such as numbers, e.g. 'One, two, three, four, five/Once I caught a fish alive'.

Another significant feature of Froebel's approach to education is that of the Froebel gifts (see p.31). The gifts are made out of various materials (mainly wood) and each is used to facilitate children's learning of particular concepts. Concepts are not directly taught: the child is allowed to freely explore each gift, discovering for themselves what the gift is designed to teach.

Rudolph Steiner

Rudolf Steiner was born in 1861. After a very broad and extensive education in college in Vienna, Steiner went to work as a tutor to four young boys, one of whom was sickly and found it difficult to learn. Steiner developed an individual programme for the boy who began to make huge progress. (The boy actually qualified as a medical doctor in later years.) After receiving his doctorate in 1891, Steiner wrote his first book, *The Philosophy of Freedom*, which was based on anthroposophy, the science of the spirit. He began lecturing on his ideas throughout Europe. In 1919 Steiner was invited to lecture to workers at the Waldorf-Astoria cigarette factory in Stuttgart. Out of these lectures came a new school, the Waldorf School. In

1922 Steiner brought these ideas to Oxford at the invitation of Professor Millicent Mackenzie and this led to the founding of Waldorf schools in Britain. During Steiner's lifetime, schools based on his educational principles were also founded in Hamburg, Essen, The Hague and London. There are now more than a thousand Waldorf schools worldwide.

Steiner believed there to be three distinct stages: stage 1 (0–7 years), stage 2 (7–14 years) and stage 3 (14–18 years). Steiner believed that stage one is the most important. It is in this stage that children learn the skills of movement, speech, gesture and communication. One of Steiner's fundamental principles is the fact that children learn to a large degree through *imitation*. The young child mimics everything they see from physical movements to behaviour and attitudes. The child absorbs every aspect of their environment and is open to external influences. Steiner believed that children have a very strong will to learn at this stage and learn naturally through *doing*.

Steiner focused his theory of education on three principles beginning with the letter R: rhythm, repetition and reverence.

Steiner was a firm believer in peer tutoring and was an advocate of mixing children of different ages for all or part of the day. He was one of the first educators to introduce the idea of 'circle time' a time (usually at the beginning of the day) when children of all ages come together to talk and discuss their ideas.

Steiner's indoor play environment is quite different from many others. He did not believe in cluttering the environment with posters or displays of children's work. He believed that for children the process of completion is much more important than viewing the finished product on display.

Steiner believed the indoor environment should be organised in an orderly, simple yet attractive fashion. There should be shelves with baskets containing scissors, crayons, toys and games and a place for story books. The classroom should not have any unnecessary clutter as it is important that children can move around freely and are able to find what they want easily. A modern-day Steiner classroom for younger children would have no TV or computers, since Steiner strongly believed it was unnatural for young children to sit passively for long periods of time.

Like Froebel, Steiner believed that every school should have a safe outdoor play area for children. He believed it should be spacious and equipped with natural items such as trees, flowers, shrubs, hiding dens and sand pits.

Most of Steiner's play materials are quite plain and are made of natural materials. He believed such materials encouraged children to use their imagination.

Margaret McMillan

Margaret McMillan was born in New York in 1860 but returned with her mother and sister Rachel to Scotland after her father and younger sister died of scarlet fever. Margaret too had the illness, which left her deaf until she was 14 years old. In 1878 she went to study music for a year in Frankfurt, returning briefly to Scotland as a governess before travelling to Switzerland to train as a teacher. Later she became a member of the Froebel society, which was set up to train teachers using Froebelian methods.

One of Margaret McMillan's chief concerns was the ill health of poor children and their families. One of her main messages with regards to the education and care of young children was that children cannot grow and learn effectively if they are cold, hungry or ill. With the help of an American philanthropist, she opened a clinic for the poor. The clinic was first opened in Bow and was then moved to Deptford in southeast London. At the clinic, minor operations were carried out (e.g. adenoid removal). One unusual and very successful aspect of the clinic was the *night camp*. For nine months of the year children aged 6–14 slept outdoors in a church yard. Together with her sister Rachel, Margaret set up a large nursery school (which still exists). Emphasis was placed on good nutrition, baths and on playing outdoors. Every classroom had a veranda for use in wet weather. Margaret was a firm believer in the value of free play. She was elected president of the Nursery Schools Association in 1923.

Jean Piaget

Jean Piaget was born in Switzerland in 1896. Piaget initially studied philosophy, epistemology and zoology, obtaining his doctorate in 1918. After graduation he became interested in psychology, working with Alfred Binet on his famous intelligence tests. Piaget became interested in the wrong answers children gave to Binet's questions, believing that a lot could be learned about how children think from studying these answers. In 1921 Piaget returned to Switzerland, married and had three children. Piaget closely observed his own children's development, basing many of his theories of cognitive development on these observations.

Piaget believed that children's cognitive development occurred in four stages. At each stage, the ways in which children actually think about concepts will change. Some concepts may be beyond children if they have not yet reached that stage of development. Piaget's stages are:

- Sensorimotor (0–2 years)
- Preoperational (2–7 years)
- Concrete operational (7–11 years)
- Formal operational (12 years and upwards).

The important point about this aspect of his theory for children's play is that structured activities planned for children should match their stage of development. If children are engaged in self-guided free play this will not be an issue, since they will naturally play in accordance with their stage of development.

Piaget also proposed theories about how children deal with new information. He believed that children (and indeed adults) constantly take in or *assimilate* new information. Sometimes this new information 'disagrees' with what they already know. This causes a period of *disequilibrium* (imbalance). Human beings are motivated towards *equilibrium* (balance): we like to understand our environment. *Accommodation* is the term used by Piaget to describe the process whereby we reconcile new information with existing information in order to form new ideas. Usually, we are not aware of this process because the degree of disequilibrium is not great enough to stress us. Sometimes, however, if we find ourselves in an unfamiliar environment we become aware of this process.

Piaget proposed a theory of *object permanence*. This occurs at approximately 7–9 months, when babies first realise that objects exist even when they cannot see them. Piaget first noticed this with his daughter Jacqueline. At seven months, when Piaget hid a toy duck from her beneath the folds on her quilt, she did not seek to find it. This changed shortly after: she began seeking out objects of interest when they were hidden from view. Piaget proposed that this is why babies under seven months old do not generally make strange or cry when their principal carer leaves.

The term *egocentrism* was coined by Piaget. It was used to describe how children are very much bound by their own perspectives. Children generally see things from their point of view only.

Conservation is the idea that the properties of an object can remain the same even though its appearance may change, e.g. the same amount of orange juice poured into two different vessels will take on different appearances. Piaget believed that children under seven years of age could not grasp conservation.

Piaget did not write specifically on play but his theories can be incorporated into the play environment. Piaget saw the child as a 'lone scientist' and a discovery learner. He did not talk about free play as such, but it is not unreasonable to suggest that he would have favoured it. In relation to structured activities Piaget certainly advocated that it was important that children were not presented with activities that were too far beyond their stage of development, since this would throw them into disequilibrium. They would be unable to make sense of the activity and this would frustrate and stress them.

Lev Vygotsky

Lev Vygotsky was born in Russia in 1896. He was a psychologist and one of the principal advocates of social constructivist theory. He advocated the important role of language and social interactions in the development of thought. He believed that by talking with adults and their peers, children develop their thinking. When adults label and discuss concepts with children, this helps children to understand. (This idea is a departure from Piaget, who believed that the child generally made these discoveries on their own.) Vygotsky believed that children use language, even when they are alone, to help them solve practical problems (e.g. talking aloud when constructing something out of blocks).

The *zone of proximal development* (ZPD) was an important concept of Vygotsky. ZPD can be defined as the difference between what a child can do without help and what they can do with help. Teachers should set work that falls within the ZPD for children. If work is too easy, children will not progress their learning and they will become bored. If work is too difficult, children will become frustrated and disheartened.

Vygotsky also pioneered the concept of *scaffolding*. This occurs when work is set within a child's ZPD, and the teacher challenges and supports the child so that they can achieve the desired goal.

Vygotsky's theories are of great importance to the play environment. They emphasise the importance of planning activities that are inside the child's ZPD. His theory places emphasis on the importance of talking through challenges with the child. For example, if a child is constructing a rocket ship out of junk materials, the adult can scaffold the child's learning by asking probing questions such as: What materials do you think will work best? How do you plan to get it to stick together?

Vygotsky was an advocate of mixed groupings. He felt that by mixing different ages and abilities in a setting, the children could learn effectively from each other.

Sigmund Freud

Sigmund Freud is considered to be the father of psychoanalysis. He was born in 1856 in Moravia (now part of the Czech Republic). Much of his work has been more influential in the area of psychotherapy than education, although his research has application in the area of play therapy. Children can work through their anxieties and fears through play, thus promoting feelings of wellbeing and mental health.

One of the most important aspects of Freud's philosophy is the importance of the unconscious mind. Freud saw the mind as being divided into three parts: the conscious mind, the pre-conscious mind and the unconscious mind. He saw the unconscious mind as being an enormous storehouse containing all of a person's life experiences. He believed that the unconscious mind had a huge influence over an individual's thought processes and subsequent actions. Traumatic experiences, especially if they occur during childhood, are stored in the unconscious mind. They are at the root of many dysfunctional thought processes and behaviours in adulthood.

Freud believed that a person's moral personality was composed of three parts: id, ego and superego. The *id* is the self-gratifying part of the personality; it is driven by need and it is selfish. The *superego* (sometimes called the 'high priest') is the part of the personality that judges an action to be morally correct or not. The *ego* is the middle man: this part of the moral personality tries to balance the needs of the id with the moral demands of the superego. The superego is strongly influenced by environment, e.g. parents, teachers and community.

Freud stated that development occurred in five stages:

- Oral stage (0–2 years)
  The focus is on the mouth. Children put everything in their mouths. Id is very strong at this stage.
- Anal stage (2–3 years)
  The focus is on the anus, e.g. toilet training. Children begin to control the id for the first time.
- Phallic stage (3–6 years)
  The focus is on the genitals. Children play with their genitals. They are attracted to the parent of the opposite sex (Oedipus and Electra complex). The superego begins to affect the workings of the id and the ego.
- Latent stage (6–11 years)
  There is no physical focus at this stage. Children lose interest in the opposite sex and they usually play in single-gender groups. They continue to balance the id, ego and superego requirements.
- Genital stage (11 years and upwards)
  The focus is on the genitals. There is an increasing interest in sexual behaviour. Children develop relationships with both genders.

Freud believed that as a result of unpleasant experiences or thoughts individuals (including children) can suffer anxieties. Freud called this *angst*. Angst feels unpleasant, so individuals employ a number of defence mechanisms to help to avoid or alleviate it. Most of these defence mechanisms are unhealthy (e.g. denial: pretending a problem is not there) but one of them is seen as useful – sublimation. With sublimation, the individual channels negative angst into something harmless or indeed useful, e.g. going for a run. Children should be given opportunities to release anxieties, e.g. through physical play.

Play can be used in therapeutic ways by children. Play therapy is a relatively new field of study. Even without specialist play therapy, children can use play to release anger and frustration, e.g. kicking a ball, burying items in the sand tray, etc.

Anna Freud

Anna Freud was born in 1895, the sixth and last child of Sigmund Freud and Martha Bernays. Like her father, Anna was very interested in the area of psychoanalysis. She initially trained as a teacher, holding down a teaching position until she had to resign after contracting TB. With the outbreak of World War I, Anna travelled with her father and the rest of her family to London. Here, she founded the Hampstead War Nursery (renamed the Anna Freud Centre after her death). She also worked after the war in the Bulldogs Bank Home, an orphanage for child survivors of the concentration camps. This allowed Anna to work firsthand with children who had experienced very distressing childhoods, which points to a big difference between the work of Anna and that of her father: he worked mostly with troubled middle-aged women.

Anna was particularly interested in a number of different aspects of psychoanalysis. One of them was the importance of the ego in warding off displeasure and anxiety. She published a paper in 1936 called 'The Ego and the Mechanisms of Defence'. This built on her father's work and she identified additional defence mechanisms. Unlike her father, who believed that most defence mechanisms are unconscious, Anna believed that some of them are conscious and can be controlled by the individual, e.g. thought suppression (deciding not to think about something because it is unpleasant).

Another difference between Anna and her father was that she was much more interested in children from latency period onwards. While her father believed that our personalities are pretty much a reflection of our unconscious minds, Anna placed much greater importance on the value of the intellect. She believed that we can *think* about how we feel and we can make conscious efforts to change our feelings. Anna believed that daydreaming was a necessary part of childhood and that sometimes it is used as a substitute for unacceptable impulses.

Another area Anna was interested in was studying the effects of parental deprivation. During the course of her work, she met children who had experienced horrific childhoods. Many of them had witnessed their parents being killed or tortured in concentration camps. She found that many of these children coped remarkably well in terms of their emotions. She believed that the comfort and support these children gave to each other was the reason for this.

Like her father, Anna Freud saw the value of play in terms of its use in the alleviation of anxiety. In addition to this, Anna was a believer in children talking and thinking through what it is that is causing them anxiety. She spoke about the importance of adults taking time to observe and talk to children if they seem anxious or worried.

D.W. Winnicott

Donald Woods Winnicott was born in 1896. He was a very influential paediatrician and psychoanalyst. He was born into a well-known and prosperous family; his father, Sir John Frederick Winnicot, was knighted in 1924. However, D.W. Winnicott did not have an easy childhood. His mother, Elizabeth Martha Woods Winnicott, suffered severely with depression and he felt very protective and responsible for her. His memories of childhood involved 'trying to make my living by keeping my mother alive' (Minsky 1996: 134).

Winnicott trained as a doctor. After qualifying, he began working at Paddington Green Children's Hospital as a paediatrician and child psychoanalyst, a position he held for the next 40 years. Winnicott was a contemporary of Anna Freud. Like Anna Freud, Winnicott worked with young people displaced by war and children from dysfunctional families. It was through this work that he came up with the concept of the *good enough mother*. (Winnicott referred mainly to the mother in his research, reflecting the fact that most women did not work outside the home when he was forming his theories.) He realised very early on that there is no such thing as a perfect mother but that there are characteristics that a 'good enough mother' will have that are important to healthy psychological development. Likewise, by talking to and studying the lives of children experiencing psychological problems he was able to identify aspects of their lives that he believed lay behind their difficulties.

Winnicott believed that babies and children need to be frequently and attentively *held* by their mothers. Mothers are a baby's security blanket. Babies need frequent and affectionate handling. Later, this broadens to other people in the child's world – but initially, it is the mother who is the most important figure. The concept of holding does not just mean physically holding the child: it means anything the mother, family and wider society do to make the child feel secure and 'held'. Winnicott observed that this concept of holding was absent from the lives of many children he worked with, causing what he termed an *anti-social tendency*. He believed that if children do not feel secure at home, they will seek security elsewhere, e.g. within gangs.

> A child whose home fails to give a feeling of security looks outside his home for the four walls…looking to society instead of his own family or school to provide the stability he needs (Winnicott 1972: 228).

Winnicott believed that none of us are born with a clear sense of *self* and that it develops as we grow. In this way, Winnicott is very much an advocate of the nurture side of the nature/nurture debate. He did not believe that we are born with a certain type of personality. He believed that our personality grows over time and it is very much influenced by our environment.

Winnicott was very interested in the concept of the *premature development of the ego function*. Winnicott believed that when children have to grow up too fast (i.e. when their ego is forced to develop too quickly), their psychological development suffers and a *false self* is created. This could happen if, for example, the eldest child of dysfunctional parents has to care for younger siblings on a daily basis. Since his own mother had depression during his childhood, Winnicott was interested on the effects that this and similar family problems have on children. He believed that problems such as this caused a phenomenon he called *compliance*. The child tries to solve the problem by being a 'good baby'. In adulthood, their actions will always be motivated out of a desire to please others. This leaves the person open to abuse and being used by others.

On the other hand, children who experience 'good enough' parenting grow up trusting their world and are therefore free to be their *true self* most of the time. Winnicott believed that in reality we are all a mix of both our *true* and *false* selves but that, as long as the false self does not take over, we will be psychologically healthy. He realised that as part of life we sometimes have to 'people please'.

Winnicott is also very well known for his belief in what he called *transitional objects* or comfort objects, e.g. a teddy bear or blanket. He believed that these objects were very useful and important to help children to cope with transitions, e.g. separation from their mother when she has to return to work after maternity leave.

Unlike many other psychoanalysts, Winnicott saw play as being vital and central to healthy development. He believed that being a 'good enough mother' involved being a playful mother; playing games such as peek-a-boo is an essential part of parenting. Winnicott believed that play is vital throughout life, even in adulthood, since it is an essential way of relieving stress and anxiety. Children whose lives involve too much work and not enough play significantly lose out in this regard. Winnicott believed this to be a very serious matter for the psychological health of children.

Janet Moyles

Janet Moyles is a contemporary contributor to the theory of play in learning. She has written extensively on the subjects of play, teaching and learning. The concept for which she is best known is the *spiral of play* or *spiral of learning*. The spiral of play describes how children move in and out of different modes of play: directed play to free play, and back again. This movement increases the depth and breadth of their skills and knowledge.

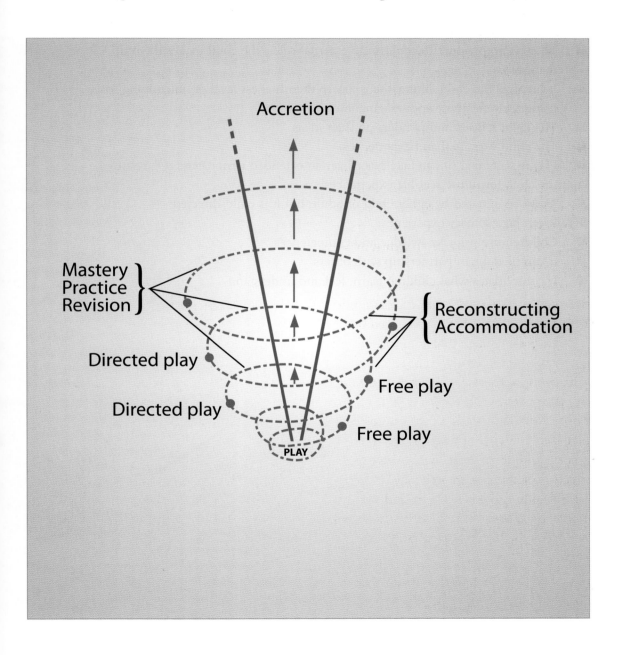

Tina Bruce

Tina Bruce is another contemporary contributor to the theory of play in learning. She has written extensively on the subject. She is best known for her concept of *Ludic* or *free flow* play. She has described what she believes to be the 12 most important characteristics of this type of play. It is important to understand these characteristics if the adult is to promote and encourage this type of play. The characteristics of free flow play are as follows.

- It is an active process with no necessity for an end product.
- The child is intrinsically motivated to engage in it.
- There is no pressure to conform to external rules: the child makes them up themselves.
- It involves the child 'lifting' their play to their highest level of functioning – using their creativity and imagination.
- The child reflects and ponders on their ideas.
- The child uses firsthand experiences.
- Play is sustained (it can take place over an extended period) and it prepares the child for future real-life experiences.
- It can be initiated by either child or adult, but it is child-directed.
- It can be a solitary experience.
- Children use prior knowledge and competences.
- It can be done in partnership with others.
- It consolidates what children learn, feel and understand.

Providing for Children's Play

Factors Influencing the Role of the Adult in Children's Play

The role of the adult in children's play is influenced by two principal factors:
- Age of the children
- Style of play: free play or structured play.

Age of the Children

As children get older they generally require less direct support with their play. Compare, for example, a non-mobile baby playing peek-a-boo with its mother and a child aged 4 playing with their peers at the water area in their pre-school. It can be generally stated that as children get older, adult involvement in play becomes less direct. The adult instead supports play through provision of play materials and by scaffolding and extending children's play through the use of questioning and suggestion.

Style of Play: Free Play or Structured Play

Whether children are engaged in free play or more structured play activities will make a significant difference to the adult's role. With free play, the adult's role is predominately about the provision of equipment, materials and resources. The adult may also help to support and extend children's free play by asking thought-provoking questions or making suggestions.

With structured play activities, the adult spends time planning age-appropriate activities for the children. The adult gathers resources and equipment and they will usually introduce and explain the activity. During the activity, they may model skills for the child, e.g. cutting out. While the child is engaged in the activity, the adult will recognise the child's efforts. As in free play, the adult will support and extend children's structured play activities by asking thought-provoking questions or making suggestions.

In summary, adults can support children in their play by:

- Providing varied, good-quality resources and equipment
- Being aware and identifying potential learning opportunities in all areas of the curriculum
- Modelling skills involved in play
- Interacting with the children, asking questions and making suggestions in order to support their learning
- Being familiar with key vocabulary, modelling and supporting children in their use of key words
- Working alongside children, modelling important skills and attitudes
- Reading with children from fiction/non-fiction books, giving them ideas for their play
- Acknowledging and displaying children's work (unless in a Steiner Waldorf environment)
- Observing children's learning and use of the materials
- Assessing children's development and progress to inform planning for future experiences.

The Role of the Adult in Children's Play

The adult's role can be summarised under two headings:

- Provision of appropriate equipment, materials and resources for play
- Supporting children's learning through scaffolding and extending their play.

Provision of Equipment, Materials and Resources

The equipment, materials and resources that adults provide will depend on the types of play in which children are engaged. Types of play will include:

- Imaginative: pretend, fantasy and symbolic
- Construction: small construction, large construction, junk play or modelling

- Creative: art, music, sand and water
- Physical.

(See Chapter 6 for definitions of these types of play.)

Imaginative Play
Pretend Play

Children imitate the people around them by recreating scenes from everyday life and acting out familiar roles. As imaginative play develops, children become able to incorporate narrative into their play. Their play becomes increasingly complex and the narratives children create include more characters and episodes. While children do not need extensive resources to become involved in rich and imaginative pretend play, resources do give them ideas and can help to develop and extend it.

Resources for pretend play could include some of the following.

Resources for pretend play	
Home corner	
Kitchen area	Sink, cooker, cupboards, table, chairs, fridge, microwave, dishwasher, rubber gloves, cups, saucers, cutlery, pots, spice rack, vacuum cleaner, pans, cooking/baking utensils, timer, clock, ice-cube tray, vases, tablecloth, towels, cloths, iron and ironing board, dusters, brush and dustpan, broom, kettle, aprons, toaster, containers, shopping basket, bags, lunch boxes, food (or play materials representing food), notice board, writing implements, recipe books, shopping list, first-aid kit, flowers, postcards *Note: It is important to recognise cultural diversity and include kitchen equipment such as woks and chopsticks.*
Living area	Sofa, chair, TV (perhaps one made from a cardboard box so that children can appear on TV), DVD player with DVDs, magazine rack, pictures, ornaments, flowers in vase, cushions, newspapers, cat, dog, telephone, plants, book, mirror, telephone and address book catalogues, family photos, puppets (for use with TV)
Bedroom area	Bed, cot, bed clothes, dolls (and clothing), hats, pieces of material, cloaks, clothes hangers, dressing table, mirror, jewellery and jewellery box, handbags, shoes, variety of scarves, hot water bottle
Restaurant/café	Signs for restaurant (opening times or chalk board for this to be written on), tables, chairs, table cloths, cups, plates, cutlery, glasses, straws, flowers, vases, cash register and money (coins and colour photocopies of notes), food (made from dough/foam, or commercially produced pretend food), order pads, pencils, napkins, placemats, menus, paper carrier bags, phone
Post office	Post box, post office uniform, signs, forms (tax, passport, TV licence), envelopes, paper, pens, cards, used stamps, labels, wrapping paper and sticky tape, parcels of various sizes, weights, scales, telephone, stamper and stamp pad, cash register and money, savings books, foreign currency, mailbag
Hospital	Various uniforms (doctor, nurse, ambulance driver), doctor's bag, rubber gloves, dolls, beds, bedclothes, bandages, cotton wool, plasters, medicine bottles, spoons, syringes, stethoscope, thermometer, old X-ray pictures, old plaster casts, crutches, scales, height measures, waiting area, telephone, note pad/prescription pad, clipboard, get well cards, reference books about the body, posters/charts, appointment book

Small-world toys can also promote pretend play: farm animals and equipment, toy cars and garages, fire engines and stations, police cars, dolls, miniature worlds (e.g. playmobil), pieces of construction toys (e.g. LEGO).

Fantasy Play

Fantasy play occurs when young children pretend to be something or someone that they cannot ever possibly be, e.g. Spiderman or Batman. This type of play is worthwhile, since it allows children to experience joy and feelings of power; it also helps them to burn off physical energy, increasing appetite and promoting sound sleep.

Resources for fantasy play could include some of the following.

Resources for fantasy play
Dress-up clothes and costumes of all types: police and fireman outfits, hats, football outfits, guitars, microphones, wigs, superhero outfits, witch and wizard outfits and props
Note: It is important to recognise cultural diversity by including saris, turbans, etc.

Symbolic play

With symbolic play, children use objects in their play but pretend the objects are something else. Many psychologists (particularly Steiner and Froebel) advocated the provision of natural materials for symbolic play.

Resources for symbolic play could include some of the following.

Resources for symbolic play
Stones, shells, twigs, pieces of wood, buttons, pieces of cloth, grass, leaves, pine cones, chestnuts, boxes, kitchen roll tubes, pasta shapes

Construction play

Construction play involves making or constructing items using either commercial or junk materials. Children's constructions may sometimes be planned in advance, the children may follow instructions or they may just evolve as they go along. Construction work is sometimes sub-divided into small construction work and large construction work.

Resources for construction play could include some of the following.

Resources for construction play	
Resources	Camera (for photographing work), train track and train, small-world people, farm animals, zoo animals, dinosaurs, cars, mark-making equipment, rulers, pens, pencils, labels (for children to name their own work), clipboards, plain paper, simple planning 'frames', measuring 'sticks', individual files in which children can photograph and file their own work
Commercial construction materials	
Small construction	Brio coloured blocks, Clic, Polydron, Constructo straws, waffle blocks, Flexi-Build, Interstar, Zoobs, K'nex, Magnetico, Lego, Rondino, Meccano, Cleversticks, Geo-links, wooden building bricks, Molto Blocks, Octoplay, Popoids, Kiblo, Star Builder, Sticklebricks, transformable shape blocks, Poly-M, Mobilo, wooden cubes, Georello, Zocketts *Note: There are also many themed environments available as small construction toys, e.g. Lego creator airport.*
Large construction	Soft blocks, hollow blocks, jigsaw bricks, large waffle blocks, large wooden blocks, Lego Soft, Lincabricks, Maxi-Bricks, NES Arnold Plasbrics, pre-school foam, unit blocks
Junk play materials	
Tools	Scissors, sticky tape, masking tape, paper clips, hole punch, Pritt Stick, PVA glue, velcro, elastic bands, pipe cleaners, Blu-tac, bag twists, clothes pegs, modelling tools
Paper	Newspaper, magazines, catalogues, wallpaper, card, crepe paper, sugar paper, newsprint, corrugated paper, tissue paper, foil, wrapping paper, poster paper, cellophane, paper plates, cards
Cardboard	Cereal boxes, egg cartons, juice cartons, shoe boxes, cheese boxes, toothpaste boxes, tissue boxes, kitchen rolls, smartie tubes, large cardboard boxes
Natural materials	Stones, pebbles, shells, leaves, twigs, feathers, chestnuts, pine cones, straw, wood shavings, sawdust
Assorted materials	Yoghurt cartons, lollipop sticks, polystyrene and plastic trays, wool, string, sequins, tin lids, plastic lids and caps (of all shapes and sizes), fabric scraps, foil pie dishes, buttons, ribbon, glitter, cork, pieces of carpet

Creative play

Creative play in this section includes art and craft, music, sand and water play. It is widely acknowledged that if children are given a broad variety of experiences in the area of creative play that important concepts and skills from across the curriculum are learned. However, if creative play is too adult-directed or is badly resourced it may offer the child very little.

Resources for creative play could include some of the following.

Resources for creative play	
Art/craft	Camera, card, clay, plasticine, playdough (with cutters and tools), collage materials, paper (including cartridge and sugar paper), fabric, glue, bubble wrap, cotton wool balls, string, rubber bands, mixing palettes, twigs, shells, leaves, flowers, pebbles, seeds, scissors (both right- and left-handed), pencils, crayons, charcoal, pastels, brushes, paint, water pots, aprons, old newspapers or plastic sheeting (to cover work surfaces)
Clay/dough	Chopping board (or suitable surface), cutting tools (scissors or dough tools), flour dredger, non-toxic powder paint or food colouring, rolling pins (plain and patterned), variety of containers (tins, egg boxes, paper bun cases) *Note: Change the smell of clay/dough by adding oils, spices and herbs. Change the texture by adding glitter, poppy seeds, rice, lentils, coconut, etc.*
Music	CDs and players, real and child-sized musical instruments (tambourines, maracas, guitars, keyboards, wind instruments, bodhráns, tin whistles, xylophones), boxes, rubber bands, sticks, bottles, spoons
Sand	Buckets, clean wet and dry sand, bulldozers, tractors, bun trays, kitchen roll tubes, clear plastic containers of various shapes and sizes, combs, feathers, cones, sticks, conkers, diggers, small-world toys, dumper trucks, egg cups, tins (e.g. custard), flour bags, brushes, lollipop sticks, funnels, jugs, moulds, pebbles, bags, bottles, flowers, rakes, sand tray, scoops, shells, aprons, sieves, dustpan and brush, spades/spoons, flags, cutters, sugar bags, take-away trays, trees (pieces of garden foliage), blocks, twigs, watering cans
Water	Aprons/play overalls, whisks, basins, cartons, bubble wrap, buckets, containers (with handles that fill up, with holes in the bottom, with holes in the side, with wide/narrow tops), corks, towels, dolls, fabric, rubber gloves, ferns, beakers, fishing nets, foil shapes and trays, boats, food colouring, funnels, glitter, sieves, slotted spoons, grapes, ice, jugs, ladles, large water tray (some have canals, bridges and water wheels), lengths of non-toxic plastic tubing, marbles, bubble bath, mermaids, yogurt pots, mop/bucket, non-slip floor, baby bath, cutlery, pebbles, penguins, pirates, plastic bags with holes, plastic bottles with holes pierced, cups, ducks, spiders, plasticine, play people, rocks, shampoo, shells, tea pots, soap, sponges, spoons, sprays, straws, washing up brush, watering cans

Physical play

Physical play can take place indoors or outdoors and can involve equipment such as wheeled toys, climbing frames, balls or skipping ropes (or no equipment at all). During physical play, children run, jump, balance, climb and crawl. Physical play is vital for children's health: it not only keeps them fit but it also encourages them to eat and sleep well.

Resources for physical play could include some of the following.

Resources for physical play
Balls, goal posts, wheeled toys (tricycles, prams, scooters push-pull toys), skipping ropes, chalk (for hop-scotch and other markings), large equipment (climbing frames, slides)
Note: It is important that there is enough space for children to engage in physical play such as tag, kick-the-can, etc.

Evaluating Play Materials, Toys and Equipment

When evaluating play materials, toys, equipment and play spaces there are a number of important factors that should be considered. One of the assignments for this module requires students to critique or evaluate a piece of equipment, a toy or a play space in an ECEC setting. This section, together with the guidelines offered in Chapter 14, will help with such an assignment.

Value in Relation to Children's Development

While all play materials, toys, equipment and play spaces offer some value in terms of the promotion of children's development, some are considerably better than others. Before purchase, thought should be put into what aspects of development will benefit from the item or play space. While some items and play spaces will be of particular benefit to a specific area of development (e.g. a football to physical development), a good resource will often benefit more than one area. Some theorists (particularly Steiner) believed that simpler items were better, since children begin to automatically invent uses for the item. Many modern electronic toys go directly against the teachings of play theorists such as Froebel and Steiner. Their complexity actually leaves little for the child to do (e.g. just press buttons). With many modern toys, all the complex work has been done by the manufacturer (e.g. the toy is programmed to make a 'moo' sound when the button with the cow on it is pressed). When assessing the value of a play item or space, it is useful to consider the five areas of development (PILES) along with the four Aistear themes that link with these areas: Wellbeing, Identity and Belonging, Communicating, and Exploring and Thinking.

Physical Development: **Wellbeing**
This includes health (including being a healthy weight) and physical growth, the development of gross- and fine-motor skills and the promotion of high levels of physical fitness.

Intellectual Development: **Exploring and Thinking**
This includes concentration levels, levels of motivation to learn new things, memory skills, problem-solving skills, creativity, use of imagination and understanding of new concepts (e.g. mathematical concepts).

Language: **Communicating**
This includes all aspects of language development: ability to listen to others, ability to take turns in a conversation, development of general and more specialised vocabulary (e.g. the language of mathematics), development of non-verbal communication skills, development of alternative forms of communication where necessary (e.g. sign language or use of Picture

Exchange Communication Systems – PECS), development of pre-reading and pre-writing skills and reading and writing skills.

Emotional: **Communicating, Identity and Belonging *and* Wellbeing**
This area of development is concerned with children learning how to deal with emotions such as anger and frustration in a healthy way. Another very important part of emotional development is the establishment of a positive self-image and high self-esteem.

Social: **Communicating, Identity and Belonging *and* Wellbeing**
This includes the development of all the skills required to interact effectively with others: perspective taking (the child is able to consider a situation from another's point of view); social information processing (the child accurately interprets what is going on in a given situation and acts appropriately); emotional regulation (the child is able to control their emotions, particularly anger and aggression); and understanding of the norms of society (the child understands how to say thank you, how to use a tissue when sneezing, etc.).
An important part of children's social development is their moral development. This involves the child learning how to think and act in morally demanding situations. Everyone the child comes into contact with will affect this aspect of the child's development, e.g. parents, family members, friends and ECEC practitioners.

> When assessing the value of play materials, toys, pieces of equipments or play spaces, it is useful to read through the areas of development as described above. Think about whether or not your choices promote any of the areas mentioned. You should explain how exactly you feel the item promotes the areas you include.

Assembly

Some play materials, toys, equipment and play spaces require assembly. There are several issues to consider.
- Are the children able to assist with assembly and would it be beneficial for them to get involved?
- If the item is too complicated for the children to be involved in assembling it, do you have the necessary skills to do it or do you need to get assistance?
- When assembled, is the item sturdy and well made?
- If the item is large and needs to be disassembled for storage purposes, is this easy to do?

Storage

In a busy ECEC setting it is important that play materials, toys and equipment are easily stored. Some manufacturers consider this factor and provide very well for it with sturdy storage boxes for their toys, e.g. K'nex and Duplo sets. Some manufacturers use lighter packaging, presenting their toys in lightweight cardboard boxes that are not very sturdy and are not realistically useful for product storage. In general, over the years packaging has become cheaper and less durable. Metal tins, wooden boxes and hard cardboard have been replaced with plastic bags and flimsy, throwaway boxes. As a result, settings need to buy durable storage boxes and shelving if they are to store their materials properly.

Safety

Providing safe play materials, toys, equipment and play spaces is most important. Toy manufacturers must adhere to strict guidelines when designing, constructing and packaging items and products for children. As consumers of these products, we must all take responsibility for safety. Only products that carry the correct safety symbols should be purchased. Even when this is done, adults should check toys and equipment carefully before giving them to young children (in case of loose or broken parts, sharp edges, etc.).

There are specific rules in Ireland and the EU to protect children from playing with unsafe play materials, toys and equipment. Specific rules also exist for ensuring the safety of children's products, e.g. baby prams, pushchairs, pacifiers (soothers), cots and clothing. Playthings and equipment such as swings, slides, pencils and pens are also regulated. Most of these rules are based on the standards that are developed by the European Committee for Standardisation (CEN). The National Standards Authority of Ireland (NSAI) develops standards governing safety, quality, design and performance of specific products for sale in Ireland.

Since 1990, legislation has been in place in Ireland which prohibits the placing of toys on the market unless they meet minimum safety requirements. This law is set down in S.I. No. 32 of the European Communities (Safety of Toys) Regulation 1990. In addition, EU rules state that any product offered for sale in the EU that conforms with certain specific health, safety and environmental protection standards must carry a CE mark. The CE mark is a declaration by the producer that the product conforms to all the applicable EU legislation.

CE mark

Another important factor to consider is the age of the child who will be playing with the product. Certain products that are safe for older children may not be safe for younger children, particularly children aged 0–2 years. Children in this age range naturally put items in their mouths in order to explore them. Products with small parts usually advise against purchase for children aged 0–3. These products carry a symbol to indicate this.

Not suitable for children aged 0–3.

What is a Toy?

A toy is defined in the law as a product intended for children under 14 years to play with. Playthings (e.g. sports equipment, metal darts, model steam engines or fashion jewellery) are not covered by the same legislation. These items should only be used by children old enough to understand the risks associated with them. Adults should supervise children using playthings, where appropriate.

Buying Safe Products for Children

Items should be:

▦ Strong and resilient (they should not break easily)
▦ Made of materials that do not burn easily
▦ Non-toxic.

Products that contain detachable or small parts should be marked as unsuitable for children aged 0–3. If there is a specific hazard associated with the toy this should be pointed out, e.g. fingers could become trapped by moving parts or hinges.

Safe Use of Children's Products

Toys with a CE mark indicate that they are safe to use for their *intended purpose* and for their *intended age group*, e.g. a toy suitable for a child aged 10 can be dangerous if used by a child aged 7.

Electrical Toys

Electrical toys should carry the CE mark to ensure compliance with EU safety standards. No electrical toy should be sold (or given out for free) if it exceeds 24 volts. All parts of the toy should be properly insulated to prevent a risk of contact with live wires. Safety instructions on electrical toys should be clear and precise; they should be easily understood and heeded by consumers.

Product Labelling

It is important to be familiar with the labelling that appears on toys. The following information should appear on the packaging or the product itself:

▦ CE mark
▦ Name, trade mark and address of the manufacturer, agent or importer within the EU
▦ Instructions for use
▦ Advice on the safe use of the toy (e.g. unsuitable for children aged 0–3).

The Irish technical standard mark can be placed on the toy along with the CE mark. This indicates that the toy complies with *all safety regulations*. The most common standard for toys in Ireland is called IS EN 71.

If you suspect that a toy is unsafe, you should contact the National Consumer Agency (NCA) so that they can investigate the matter. Similarly, if you or a child has been harmed by a toy, you should also contact the NCA for advice and information. NCA have published a booklet called 'A Guide to Toy Safety' (http://www.nca.ie/media/GuidetoToySafety1.pdf). It is well worth downloading this leaflet, since it will help you with your assignment on this module.

Durability

In today's economic climate it is important that toys, play materials (unless they are intentionally disposable) and equipment purchased by parents and ECEC settings are built to last. It is important that they are strong and sturdy and that they can withstand frequent washing and scrubbing. Buying the cheapest item is often a false economy, since the item may break easily. Some toys (e.g. LEGO, Geomag, wooden trains and tracks) are virtually indestructible.

Availability and Cost

During the Celtic Tiger years in Ireland, certain toys were in high demand and could be difficult to source. This resulted in inflation of the prices of these toys and it often made them very poor value for money. It is usually advisable to stay away from these 'must-have' toys, at least until the hype about them dies down. Practitioners in ECEC settings should shop around for best value. Internet shops are often good value, especially for specialist toys, e.g. Montessori equipment or Froebel gifts. These shops are usually able to keep their prices low, since they do not have the overhead costs of traditional toy shops.

Equality and Diversity

It is important that when buying play materials, equipment and toys for ECEC settings that the issues of equality and diversity are closely considered.

- Are children with physical disabilities represented in story books purchased?
- Do materials and toys reflect cultural diversity, e.g. dolls of varying ethnicity?
- Do dress-up clothes reflect cultural diversity, e.g. clothes from a variety of cultures?
- Do pretend play areas reflect cultural diversity, e.g. kitchen equipment from a variety of cultures?
- Do all children including those with disabilities have access to play equipment and play areas?

- Are adapted materials and equipment available when required, e.g. large-print books or left-handed scissors?
- Are all children encouraged to use toys and play spaces, e.g. do boys have equal access to the home corner?
- Does the play make a conscious effort to combat negative stereotypes?

Planning an Effective Play Environment

An effective play environment will be one where children are safe, fully involved, enjoying themselves and are learning. Different theoretical perspectives (see Chapters 1–4) have often very different opinions on what constitutes an effective play environment. The list below offers general suggestions on planning an effective play environment.

Indoor Space

- Children should have ready access to the outdoors.
- Indoor areas should be spacious and should be divided into specific areas, e.g. home corner, table top games area, art and craft area, sand and water area, construction play area, book corner.

- Low open shelving should be available so that children can access play materials, toys and equipment and return them to their proper place when finished.
- Theorists such as Steiner believed that surfaces should be painted in calming, neutral colours (e.g. pastels) and that loud or vibrant colours are unsettling for children after a time.
- All surfaces should be washable.
- Good-quality, sturdy pre-school furniture should be used.
- Children should have easy access to clean, purpose-built toilets and wash areas.
- There should be a separate area for children to eat.
- Floor coverings should be non-slip and easy to clean.
- The setting should be equipped with a good variety of well-chosen toys, play materials and equipment.
- Toys, play materials and equipment should be changed or rotated on a regular basis in order to keep children interested. (At the beginning of the year, retain some equipment so that it can be taken out at a later date.)

Outdoor Space

- Ideally, outdoor spaces should have a mixture of natural/grassy areas and artificial surfaces so that children can engage in different types of outdoor play.
- Soft surface play areas are expensive, but they are safe and very durable. Children can use this area of the outdoor space for playing with wheeled toys and for playing games such as tag. Large equipment (e.g. climbing frames) can be anchored down onto soft surfaces.
- Raised vegetable and flower beds are a good idea. If space does not permit, smaller containers can be used.
- If possible, an area of the outdoor space should be permitted to grow wild with long grass, flowers, weeds, etc. Paths can be made through the longer grass. Waterproof toy animals (e.g. rabbits and foxes) can be hidden in the grass.
- An area of well-mowed and maintained lawn is a good resource in warm weather: older children can play ball games and younger babies can crawl safely.
- There should be an area for children to shelter from the sun in hot weather, e.g. an awning.
- A large sand tray is very useful outside. (It should be covered when not in use to prevent cats or other animals using it as a litter tray.)
- Outside water trays should be raised on legs so that children can reach them but not fall into them. Children must be closely supervised when using the water tray.
- In good weather, a picnic area can be put in place so that children can eat outdoors. (This does not have to be a permanent fixture.)

9

Books and Storytelling

- **The importance of books and storytelling**
- **Storytelling techniques**
- **Books for children aged 0–6**
- **Promoting equality and diversity**

The Importance of Books and Storytelling

Books and storytelling are probably the most important resources in the ECEC setting. All areas of development benefit from books and storytelling.

Physical Development

Children develop fine-motor skills by handling books, turning pages and returning them to shelves. Often books and storytelling provide inspiration for physical play, e.g. children pretend they are characters from a story and this promotes movement. Storytelling can be used as a technique for imparting factual information, e.g. practitioners can tell a story about a boy who ate so many sweets that he ended up with no teeth! In this way, storytelling can be used to promote physical health and wellbeing.

Intellectual Development

Intellectual development includes: imagination, creativity, memory skills, concentration skills, concept formation and problem-solving skills. Storytelling and books promote all of these areas, so they are a cornerstone of ECEC. Children listen to stories and imagine what the characters look like and what they are feeling. As an extension activity to storytelling, children can be encouraged to create art and craft work related to the stories they have heard. Storytelling promotes memory skills: children usually listen very carefully to stories and remember large chunks of them. Words and phrases heard in stories can be remembered and used in different situations. When a story is told well, children will be enthralled. This promotes concentration: a vital skill for later learning.

Storytelling can introduce children to complex concepts and ideas that they don't often encounter in normal life, e.g. deception (*The Pied Piper of Hamelin* or *Chicken Licken*), environmental awareness (*The Lorax*), consumerism and the real message of Christmas (*The Grinch*), etc. Often books and stories present children with problems and dilemmas. Discussion of issues raised in books is very beneficial to problem-solving skills.

Language Development

Many aspects of language development are promoted through books and storytelling, e.g. the ability to listen to others and to ask questions. It is through books, storytelling, rhymes and poetry that children learn new vocabulary. One of the biggest indicators of literacy success in future years is the availability of books to children at home. Reading to young children on a regular basis allows them to develop pre-reading skills. These children are at a clear advantage when they enter the primary school environment; many of them have actually begun to read at this stage. The opposite is also true: children who are not read to do not develop pre-reading skills and are at a distinct disadvantage when they begin learning to read. The 2010 OECD/PISA report has shown that literacy levels among Irish children have fallen significantly over the last number of years, with 25 per cent of children who live in socially disadvantaged areas being unable to read to functional levels. We are now well behind countries such as New Zealand, Australia, Korea and Sweden, who have the highest results. One of the reasons for the introduction of the free pre-school year was to combat this problem. It is vital that ECEC settings take advantage of this and provide children with plenty of literacy opportunities.

Emotional Development

Emotional development is concerned with children learning how to deal with emotions such as anger and frustration in a healthy way. Another very important part of emotional development is the establishment of a positive self-image and high self-esteem. Books and storytelling can have a very important part to play in emotional development. A well-equipped, comfortable book corner can be used for children to relax and unwind away from the hustle and bustle of the rest of the room. Well-chosen books can be used to promote equality and diversity: children with disabilities and children from minority groups can feel represented and valued.

Social Development

Social development involves the ability to interact effectively with others, understanding of the norms of society and moral development.

Storytelling is a social activity. Children need to co-operate with each other so that they can all see. They develop an understanding of the idea that sometimes they must stay quiet and listen.

Social stories are very important for children who have difficulty in developing social skills, e.g. children on the autism spectrum. Many social skills are learned by children who simply copy what they see. Some children, however, require more explicit instructions and find social stories very beneficial. Social stories present children with day-to-day occurrences that may be challenging for them. Children then act out the social story and this gives them an opportunity to practise their social skills.

Here is an example of a social story, which can be used to teach children how to ask someone to play.

Asking Someone to Play

My name is _____ and I like to play with other kids. At break time, there are lots of kids from my class that I can play with. When I want to play with someone I need to do these things:

First I need to look at their face.
Next I need to say their name to get their attention.
Then I wait until that person looks back at me.
Then I say: 'Can I play with you?'
If the person says yes, then I get to play with this person.
If they say no, it is ok: I can find another person to ask.

It makes me feel happy that I know how to ask someone to play!

Many stories contain a moral. These stories can be useful for children for their own moral development. Children get to reason and think about how the characters in the story acted and they can apply this to their own lives. Some books directly tackle particular issues such as bullying or racism; these books can be used very effectively with children. *The Great Adventures of Larriot the Liger* by Megan Meyer is about a liger (tiger and lion hybrid) who is bullied by the other cubs. *Spaghetti in a Hot Dog Bun* by Maria Dismondy is a book about having the courage to be who you are.

Storytelling Techniques

Most of us remember someone from our childhood who was a naturally good storyteller. Good storytellers normally tell stories off the top of their heads, using voice, facial expression and gesture instead of books, pictures and props. True storytellers do make the distinction between storytelling and reading aloud, but for the purpose of this module storytelling will be taken to mean either.

For storytelling to be a success, children need to be seated in such a way that they can see properly. If there is no book involved, the children need to be able to see the storyteller's face so that they can read and enjoy their facial expressions and gestures. If the storyteller is reading from a book (particularly if there are pictures in it), the child needs to be close enough to the storyteller to see the book. Therefore, it is important that storytelling (particularly with younger children) is done in small rather than large groups.

When practitioners in settings tell stories, they sometimes arrange little chairs in a circle around the storyteller. Children are expected to sit on these chairs and not move while the story is being told. The practitioner holds up the book every now and then to show the children a picture. Sometimes practitioners wonder why children begin to lose interest when this setup is employed. Children should be allowed to sit or stand around the storyteller, particularly if they are reading from a book. This will ensure that they can see the book at all times. They should be allowed to point to parts of the picture and to ask questions. The storyteller can sit on the floor so that they are down low enough for children to stand behind them and see the book. If this does not happen, there is too big a gap (both physical and mental) between the book and the child.

It is very important for storytellers to observe their audience while they read or tell a story. This ensures that the storyteller can react to cues given by the audience. If children become agitated and lose interest, practitioners must finish the story quickly: there is no point in dragging it out and perhaps having to correct children who are fidgeting, etc. If children lose interest in a story, it is either not suitable for them or it was not told in an engaging way. It is true that some children have short attention spans, but if an entire group lose interest, practitioners need to evaluate what they are doing.

All children love well-told stories and they can be very interested in real-life stories, e.g. 'When I was little…' Practitioners should tell stories from their own lives from time to time. For example, if a group of pre-schoolers are getting ready to go to 'big school', practitioners can tell them a story about their own first day at school. It is not important that practitioners relay the facts here: it is more important that the story is positive and engaging. Props (e.g. an old schoolbag, book or lunch box) can add interest.

Even the most interesting story will not be engaging unless it is told in an interesting way. Practitioners should use different voices for different characters. It is important to overcome any shyness so that vibrant facial expressions and gestures can be used.

Props and other aids can be used to enhance storytelling.

- **Story sacks** usually take the form of a large cotton bag, filled with props related to the story. Commercial story sacks are available but they can be created by practitioners themselves.
- **Story boxes** are very similar to story sacks, except that the items appear in a box. Sometimes children are given the story box and they are challenged to make up a story about what is in the box.
- **Hot seating** is where people take on the role of characters from a story and other people ask them questions. The characters have to answer the questions in as much detail as possible. This technique is probably more useful with older children.
- **Story cards and boards** can be used to illustrate the story being told. They should be large enough to allow all children to see what is going on.
- **Puppets** (finger, shadow, string and hand puppets) can be used to illustrate a story. It can be fun for a puppet to actually 'tell' the story. Young children will actually look at the puppet while the story is being told and they will ask it questions, so practitioners do not need to worry about their ventriloquism skills.
- **Costumes**: Great interest is added if the storyteller dresses up for the occasion, e.g. dressing up as a witch to tell a Meg and Mog story.
- **Masks** can be made elaborately (papier-mâché and plaster cast) or simply (cardboard or paper plates). The storyteller can put the mask up to their face when speaking as a particular character.

■ Another terrific storytelling technique is **mixed language telling**. Children can be introduced to second and third languages through stories. The story is predominately told in the children's mother tongue, but key words are added in the second language. Children are able to figure out the meaning of the new words from the context of the story.

■ **Multi-voice telling** is where the storyteller 'gets help' from the children with the story. Children need to know the story well in order for this to happen. Stories that contain a refrain can be useful here, e.g. 'Run, run as fast as you can/You can't catch me, I'm the Gingerbread Man'.

■ **Sandwich storytelling** is where the storyteller asks questions during the story, e.g. Would you like the Cat in the Hat to visit your house?

Books for Children Aged 0–6
Attributes of a Well-Written Children's Book

There are millions of books published for children, but well-written children's books will have many common features.

■ Child or child surrogate (animal) is the hero/heroine.

■ Author uses engaging, lively language with distinctive dialogue.

■ Author is not condescending and is careful about using stereotypes.

■ Characters seem real, complex and dimensional and they show growth.

■ Author creates a completely believable and interesting world for the story's characters to inhabit.

■ Story possesses an economy of language and a coherent structure.

■ Story includes details that appeal to a child.

■ Story has clever twists and/or connections that make the reader say: 'A-ha!'

■ Story isn't overly predictable (although, for some picture books predictability can work).

■ Story makes a point without being overly didactic or preachy.

■ Illustrations (if applicable) expand in some way on the words of the story.

■ Story and illustrations are compelling and make the reader want to turn the page to see what happens.

■ Story has a clear climax/point of tension that is resolved in a satisfying way.

■ Author takes the reader on a journey and opens up new worlds and ideas to the reader.

■ Story moves and/or entertains, makes the reader laugh, cry and/or think. This satisfying feeling should linger with the reader after the book is over.

- On repeated readings the book offers fresh revelations or details that may not have been caught on the first reading.
- Story gives enjoyment to the child.
- Author is not afraid to be daring and take risks, e.g. willing to portray unlikeable characters or fantastical situations, willing to take on controversial subjects, etc.
- Author has a clear, fresh and interesting point of view on their subject.
- Be particularly careful about following any current trends; ideally the story should have some lasting value beyond mere trends.

(Adapted from Upstart Crow Literary Agency/Little, Brown Books)

Recommended Books for Children Aged 0–6

Below are lists of books that are particularly well-written and engaging for children. The books are divided into broad age ranges, although many older children will gain value from those books recommended for younger children and vice versa.

Children Aged 0–1

- *Faces (Baby's Very First Book)* by John Fordham
  This book and others like it acknowledge the fact that young babies have limited vision. High-contrast images, mirrors and crinkly pages consider the child's developing senses.
- *Farm (Baby's Very First Book)* by Jo Lodge
  This book is similar to *Faces* but it features farm animals.
- *Pets (Baby's Very First Book)* by Jo Lodge
  This book is similar to *Farms* but it features domestic animals.
- *Baby's Very First Touchy Feely Book* by Stella Baggott
  This book is part of the Usborne Touchy Feely range of books. It allows babies to feel different textures, e.g. lumpy crocodile.
- *That's Not My Puppy…* by Fiona Watt and Rachel Wells
  This book allows babies to explore different textures on the journey to finding their puppy. Others books in this series include *That's Not My Dinosaur…* and *That's Not My Monkey…*.
- *Hello, Spot!* by Eric Hill
  Each opening in this book shows the friendly puppy Spot meeting a different animal. Babies love getting to know the characters in this book.
- *Guess How Much I Love You* by Sam McBratney and Anita Jeram
  This books details the efforts of Little and Big Nutbrown Hare to express their love for each other.

Children Aged 1–3

- *The Very Hungry Caterpillar* by Eric Carle
  This book describes the life of a hungry caterpillar as he makes his journey from egg to butterfly.
- *Giraffes Can't Dance* by Giles Andreae and Guy Parker-Rees
  This book features Gerald the giraffe, who would love to join in with the other animals at the Jungle Dance.
- *Hairy Maclary* series by Lynley Dodd
  This series of books features a little dog called Hairy Maclary. In the stories, he meets various characters such as Slinky Malinki and Scarface Claw. All stories are told using brilliant, cumulative rhyming text and terrific pictures.
- *Mog the Forgetful Cat* by Judith Kerr
  This book features a cat called Mog, who has a problem with forgetfulness.
- *Owl Babies* by Martin Waddell and Patrick Benson
  This book features three baby owls (Sarah, Percy and Bill) who are very worried when their mother goes away and who are overjoyed when she returns.
- Dr. Seuss books
  These books are wonderfully engaging, e.g. *Hop on Pop*, *Dr. Seuss' ABC* and *One Fish, Two Fish, Red Fish, Blue Fish*. The books use rhyme and zany illustrations. The use of rhyme is brilliant: children learn how to read one word and, by changing just one letter in the word, they learn another word.
- *Brown Bear, Brown Bear, What Do You See?* by Bill Martin Jr and Eric Carle
  This book is a lovely introduction to learning about colours.
- *The Gruffalo* by Julia Donaldson
  This book tells about a little mouse's walk through the woods.
- *Busy Airport* by Rebecca Flynn
  This book is part of the Busy Books series. It features a busy airport.
- *The Rainbow Fish Bath Book* by Marcus Pfister
  This book teaches children about sharing. The 'bath book' features reflective holographic scales on the rainbow fish.
- *The Very Busy Spider* by Eric Carle
  This book is about the activities of a spider. The book is multi-sensory, so children can feel and see the pictures as they listen to the rhythmic text.
- Ladybird books
  The Ladybird series of books continues to be popular. The books are graded in terms of difficulty: levels 1–4. Levels 1 and 2 are suitable for children aged 0–3.
  Level 1 fairytales include *The Enormous Turnip*, *The Magic Porridge Pot*, *The Three Billy Goats Gruff*, *The Ugly Duckling*, *Goldilocks and the Three Bears* and *The Little Red Hen*.

Level 2 fairytales include *The Gingerbread Man*, *The Three Little Pigs*, *Town Mouse and Country Mouse*, *Little Red Riding Hood*, *Chicken Licken*, *Sly Fox and the Little Red Hen*.

Children Aged 3–6

- *Room on the Broom* by Julia Donaldson
  This book is about a witch and her cat, who share many adventures together.
- *The Tiger Who Came to Tea* by Judith Kerr
  This book is about a little girl called Sophie. She and her mother have tea with a tiger who comes to the door one day.
- *Peace At Last* by Jill Murphy
  This book features the Bear family – and Mr Bear's efforts to get a night's sleep.
- *The Owl Who Was Afraid Of The Dark* by Jill Thomlinson
  This book features Plop, a baby barn owl who overcomes his fear of the dark.
- Roald Dahl books
  Roald Dahl books continue to be very popular with children. Many of his books are more suited to children aged 6 and upwards. However, younger children may enjoy some of his books, including *Esio Trot*, *The Magic Finger*, *Danny – The Champion of the World*, *The Twits* and *James and the Giant Peach*.
- Ladybird books
  Levels 3 and 4 are suitable for children aged 3–6.
  Level 3 fairytales include *The Elves and the Shoemaker*, *Rapunzel*, *Thumbelina*, *Jack and the Beanstalk*, *Puss in Boots* and *Hansel and* Gretel. Level 4 fairytales include *The Pied Piper of Hamelin*, *Peter and the Wolf*, *Heidi*, *Snow White and the Seven Dwarfs* and *Dick Whittington and His Cat*.

Promoting Equality and Diversity

Books and stories provide a useful way of promoting equality and diversity in the ECEC setting. They can:

- Directly counteract social problems, such as racism and prejudice
- Counteract gender stereotyping
- Show people with disabilities in a positive, proactive light
- Educate majority populations about minorities (e.g. dress, language and customs)
- Reflect the diverse nature of our community.

Race

- *Bright Eyes, Brown Skin* by Cheryl Willis Hudson and Bernette Ford
  This book is about four children of mixed race who feel good about who they are and how they look. They enjoy the activities of a typical day at school and they are brimming with confidence and self-esteem.
- *Home* by Kate Petty
  This book looks at the homes of children from all around the world. There are photographs from countries in Africa, Asia, South America and Europe. Published in association with Oxfam, this book aims to draw parallels between children from many different cultures.
- *Play* by Kate Petty
  This book shows pictures of children from all around the world having fun playing alone or with their friends.
- *Hair* by Kate Petty
  This book features photographs of different hairstyles from all around the world.
- *Come Eat with Us* by Annie Kubler and Caroline Formby
  This book is a colourful flap book that shows different foods from all around the world.
- *All Kinds of People* by Emma Damon
  This book is a colourful flap book that considers similarities and differences between people all around the world.

Culture

There is a series of stories written by Jonny Zucker and illustrated by Jan Barger Cohen that explains and celebrates different traditions and festivals around the world.

- *Sweet Dates to Eat*: Ramadan and Eid
- *Apples and Honey*: Rosh Hashanah
- *Eight Candles to Light*: Chanukah
- *Four Special Questions*: Passover
- *Lanterns and Firecrackers*: Chinese New Year
- *It's Party Time*: Purim
- *Hope and New Life*: Easter
- *Lighting a Lamp*: Diwali

Disability

- *The Lost Puppy* by Kate Gaynor
  The main character in this book is a child with limited mobility. This book encourages children to look at their wheelchair as playing a positive rather than a negative role in their life.

- *Don't Call Me Special* by Pat Thomas
  This book introduces children to various disabilities in a way that is easily understood.
- *Hi, I'm Adam* by Adam Buehrens
  This book is written by a child with Tourette Syndrome, who explains the nature of his condition.
- *Ringo the Flamingo* by Neil Griffiths
  This book is about Ringo the Flamingo, who is not like any of the other flamingos in his flock because his legs don't work. The story shows how Ringo can contribute to the flock, despite his difference.
- *Why Can't Jimmy Sit Still?* by Sandra Tunis
  This book features a child called Jimmy, who has ADHD.

Note: While the books mentioned here portray disabilities/special needs in a positive light, it is important to equip the ECEC setting with books that do not deal specifically with disabilities/special needs, but instead show children with disabilities/special needs as regular children in regular stories.

Gender

There are many books on the market that deal with gender identity and gender stereotyping. However, many of them tackle the issue by depicting a reversal of gender stereotypes, e.g. a female builder or fire person. While this does no harm, it is important that gender equality is emphasised in ordinary, everyday ways – not just in terms of choice of profession. Books should show all genders involved in everyday tasks such as housework, laundry, gardening, etc.

Family Structure

- *The Family Book* by Todd Parr
  This book looks at different family structures.
- *Two Homes* by Claire Masurel
  This is a book about a young girl whose parents have recently divorced.
- *And Tango Makes Three* by Justin Richardson and Peter Parnell
  This is a book about two male penguins who come together to raise a young penguin chick called Tango.
- *Mommy, Mama and Me* by Lesléa Newman
  Rhythmic text and illustrations with universal appeal show a toddler spending the day with its two mothers.

10

Play and the Early Years Curriculum

- **Literacy through play**
- **Numeracy through play**
- **Science through play**
- **Social learning through play**
- **Music and movement through play**
- **ICT in play**
- **Equality and diversity in play**

Literacy Through Play

Pre-Reading Skills

The main purpose of literacy education in the early years is to give children a love of books and stories so that they have a desire to learn to read and to develop pre-reading skills. In many European countries children are not formally 'taught' to read until they are aged 6–7. In order for children to learn how to read, they have to understand the abstract concept that symbols on a page can have meaning. Since this is an abstract concept, it can be difficult for a young child to grasp. As with all other skills, some children make the link quicker than others and learn to read at a younger age. This is normal and children should be allowed develop at their own pace.

Fostering a Love of Books

The most important pre-reading skill that an ECEC setting can 'teach' is that *reading is fun*. If children love stories and books, they will be motivated to learn how to use them. In primary and secondary school, the common denominator between poor readers is that they do not like reading and have no interest in books. We must ask where this dislike begins and, more important, how settings can prevent this dislike developing in the first place.

It is true that when many children come into pre-school settings many of them have already been read to since they were babies. They can sit and pay attention as a story is being read, engaging readily with the story and asking plenty of questions. These children are already well on their way to reading: their parents and their home environment has ensured this. While it is important that ECEC settings continue the work of these children's parents, it is even more important that a love reading and books is created in the child who experiences little reading at home. Practitioners must observe these children and act accordingly. It is not good enough for a practitioner to simply say that a child has no interest in books. As with any other skill, it has to be developed. A child may not be able to sit still and listen to a story if they are with ten other children on little chairs in a circle, while the practitioner sits at the top of the circle reading from a regular-sized book and holding it up every now and then to show the pictures. However, this same child might be able to listen to a story if there are only three children present and they are sitting on bean bags right beside the practitioner and can see the pictures at all times.

ECEC settings need to invest in a good book corner. It needs to be comfortable: carpeted, suitable seating (e.g. beanbags), clean, tidy and well maintained. The area should be stocked with a wide range of different types of well-maintained books. Children's tastes in books vary, so a wide variety of types should be available for children to 'read' alone or with an adult. Types of books include picture books, textured 'feely' books, story books, pop-up books, factual books, big books, poetry and nursery rhyme books and joke books. Books can be accompanied by props, e.g. finger and hand puppets, story bags and story boxes.

Handling Books

Children must be shown how to handle books correctly, e.g. holding the book the right way up, turning pages singly and understanding reading conventions (i.e. that text is read from left to right). In order for children to learn how to handle books confidently, they need plenty of practice. They should be given time and opportunity to explore the book corner by themselves. If a story is being read to children who have not yet learned how to handle books, it is better if the story takes place on a one-to-one basis (or in a small group), since this gives the child the opportunity to turn the pages while the adult reads. In the English language, text is read from left to right. Children will learn this if adults run their finger along the text while reading. Children often then copy this when 'reading' books by themselves.

Rhymes and Songs

Books that include rhymes and songs are essential to the promotion of pre-reading skills. Rhyming patterns encourage children to pay attention to words, an essential pre-reading skill. When children become familiar with certain rhymes they begin to be able to predict what comes next. In this way, they are demonstrating that they have noticed word sounds and word order in sentences. Traditional nursery rhymes continue to be enjoyed by children. It is great if practitioners create props to go with them or if children are taught actions to accompany them. There are a wide range of books on the market using rhyme: old favourites (e.g. Dr. Seuss) and new ones (e.g. Hairy Maclary).

Predicting the Story

Children can be shown how to use cues on the page in order to predict the story line, e.g. illustrations. Children should be encouraged to tell the story themselves. When children are familiar with a story they enjoy telling the story and using the pictures as cues. This is why it is important to choose books that are well illustrated. Story boards and cartoon strips that have no print are also very useful for this purpose: children use the pictures to tell what is going on. While reading stories, it is good practice to ask children what they think is going to happen next and then ask them to turn the page to find out.

Words

One very important way of helping children grasp the idea that text is made up of words and that these words have meaning is by labelling children's artwork. If a child draws a picture, it is good to discuss the picture with the child and then in conjunction with them decide what they want to write on it, e.g. Daddy, our house, my dog Max. In this way, children create their own stories. This will promote a sense of achievement as well as reinforcing the idea that print has meaning.

Creating 'all about me' books is a very useful activity. Children bring in photos or draw pictures and the adult helps them to add captions. Hand and foot prints can be included.

Usually one of the first words a child recognises is their own name. Children's names can be printed clearly on coat hooks, work trays and lunch boxes. One nice idea is to print children's names on A4 card and then laminate them for use as lunchtime placemats. When children complete pieces of work they can be helped to print their name on it using the 'hand on hand' technique.

Items around the setting can also be labelled, e.g. cooker, fridge, table, window, door, etc. It is important that labels are clear and simple. If they are typed, ensure that a sans serif font is used.

Pre-Writing Skills

A number of aspects are particularly important with the development of pre-writing skills. ECEC settings should be aware of the following points.

- The development of writing, like the development of reading, should not be rushed.
- ECEC settings should concentrate on developing fine-motor skills in readiness for writing, rather than getting children to write letters at too young an age.
- Children who are asked to write letters and numbers before they are ready often develop poor writing habits (e.g. holding the pencil in an awkward way) and may begin to dislike writing as they feel they are not good at it.
- Writing should be done in a fun environment. It is much better that children begin writing as part of fun play activities (e.g. writing shopping lists while playing shop or taking an order in a play restaurant) than through the use of 'copy the letter' worksheets.

Fine-Motor Skills

There are many ways in which fine-motor skills can be developed in readiness for writing: threading buttons or beads, using peg boards, making jigsaw puzzles, etc. Some educationalists (e.g. Montessori) say that it is good practice for children to be shown directly how to hold a pencil: the children then practise just picking up and holding a pencil, not necessarily doing anything with it. Some settings use triangular pencils to help children with this. Once children can hold a pencil correctly, they then need to be given play opportunities to 'write', e.g. playing shop, bank, post office, restaurant, etc. This way children get plenty of practice 'writing' and their movements begin to become fluid and relaxed. These initial attempts at writing are called *emergent writing*. When writing is approached in this way, children hold writing equipment in the correct way and use writing in a context that makes sense to them. It is widely believed that this is better than getting children to trace around join the dot letters and other such worksheets. These worksheets put pressure on children to 'get it right' or 'be as neat as the person beside you', which can be off-putting. It is only after children are able to hold a pencil correctly and control it that these formal writing exercises can then be introduced.

Painting, drawing and colouring also give children opportunities to develop their grip and their fluidity. As children's drawing develops, their movements become more fluid and controlled. This is an essential pre-writing skill. When children begin to draw shapes that are starting to resemble letters, adults can extend this by showing them how letters are formed. One way of doing this is through the use of wet sand: the adult uses a stick in wet sand to show the child how the letter is formed, where it starts, what direction it takes, etc. The child copies the adult movements. Maria Montessori believed that this skill should be taught using sandpaper letters, i.e. the child uses their index finger to trace the letters as they are meant to be written.

Numeracy Through Play

Mathematics is an essential part of life. We use it while shopping, cooking, doing DIY jobs around the home, calculating how long a journey is going to take, etc. However, maths can be an unpopular subject. Many teachers and educational researchers believe that being competent at maths is all about getting a feel for it early on. This builds confidence and encourages the child to give maths a go. Unlike many other subjects, maths is quite black and white. Children can become easily discouraged by maths, quickly developing the idea that they are not good at it. This can have a seriously negative effect. It is vital that ECEC practitioners make a real effort to foster an interest in maths for the children in their care.

Jean Piaget believed that children under the age of 11 were predominantly concrete thinkers. This means that for children to understand maths they really need to experience it in a *concrete* way, rather than being taught it as a pencil and paper exercise. Many play experiences promote mathematical concepts and children should be given as many opportunities as possible. Mathematics concepts that can be promoted through play include:

- Counting
- Understanding the concept of number
- Ordering
- Matching
- Sorting
- Patterns
- Adding and subtracting
- Volume
- Capacity
- Measurement (e.g. time, weight and length)
- Predicting and estimating
- Recording (e.g. writing numbers)
- Shape and space.

Children should be introduced to a basic mathematics vocabulary in the ECEC setting. This should be done as part of normal care and educational routines and activities. Useful mathematics vocabulary includes:

▦ More than	▦ Add
▦ Less than	▦ Triangle
▦ The same as	▦ Square
▦ Biggest	▦ Circle
▦ Smallest	▦ In front of
▦ Widest	▦ Behind
▦ Longest	▦ Above
▦ Longer than	▦ Below
▦ Shortest	▦ Beside
▦ Shorter than	▦ Inside
▦ Match	▦ Outside
▦ Pattern	▦ On top of
▦ Take away	▦ Shared

Since children should be introduced to mathematics through play in ECEC settings, this section focuses on how different types of play assist in the development of pre-mathematical and mathematical knowledge and skills.

Pretend/Socio-dramatic Play

Pretend or socio-dramatic play can be useful for the development of many mathematical concepts. Children *count* when playing shop, playing restaurant or playing house. They use numbers on a telephone, cash register or calculator. They 'write' out a bill, share out resources or 'write' numbers on boards while playing school. *Matching* skills are developed when they set the table, match parts of costumes, match buttons with button holes on dress-up clothes, etc. *Sorting* skills are developed when children have to tidy up and place similar items together, e.g. dress-up clothes, kitchen equipment, pens and pencils. Clean up routines allow children to observe *pattern and order*. Through small-world play (using items such as toy animals, figurines and toy cars), children learn skills such as sorting, matching, pattern and order.

Creative Play

Creative play involves children exploring and using their bodies and materials to make and do things and to share their feelings, ideas and thoughts. Children can be creative by dancing, painting, playing with junk and recycled materials, working with play-dough and clay, and using their imaginations. While children are doing these things, they are also learning important mathematical concepts.

When children are taught (or teach each other) dance routines, they are learning about pattern and order. Painting and drawing allows children to learn about *volume*, space and shape, e.g. 'Have I enough paint?' Playing with junk and recycled materials helps children with problem solving, e.g. 'How am I going to make a rocket out of these materials?' Play-dough and clay allows children to explore shape (2D and 3D), space, length, adding and taking away, e.g. 'I have made a really long snake!'

Games with Rules

There are many games with rules that can allow children to experience mathematical concepts. Snakes and ladders, card games (e.g. snap), hopscotch and Ludo are all games that can teach children about *counting and order*.

Jigsaws are very useful for the development of mathematical concepts: children have to sort and order pieces in order to make them fit together. Children develop spatial awareness through their judging of whether or not pieces will fit together.

Construction

This type of play involves building something using natural and manufactured materials. Children can construct from junk materials or materials specifically created for construction play. Brands such as Gears, Duplo, Lego, Geomag, Meccano and K'nex can all be very educational. These products are often marketed at boys, so girls should be encouraged to use them also. Using construction toys or construction materials allows children to experience almost all early years mathematical concepts: counting, matching, ordering, sorting, making and recognising pattern, measuring, shape and space.

Providing beads and buttons for threading is also useful. Concepts such as number, sorting and matching can be encouraged with these activities. Children will also make different patterns while threading.

Water Play and Sand Play

Both water play and sand play can be very valuable in early mathematics. Play areas must be well equipped and they should be available for children during all free play sessions, not just every now and then.

Sand trays should have plenty of equipment: spoons, shovels, measuring jugs, funnels and small-world toys (e.g. diggers and animals). Water trays should have plenty of equipment, too: spoons, measuring jugs, funnels, sponges, objects that float and sink, etc. Through sand play and water play, children experience many mathematical concepts. They can learn a lot about volume and capacity in particular.

Outdoor Physical Play

Outdoor play includes: ball games; using push–pull toys and wheeled toys, e.g. tricycles; and larger pieces of equipment, e.g. climbing frames and slides. This type of play is very useful for the development of spatial awareness. Children may count for games such as hide-and-seek. They can draw markings on the ground for games such as hopscotch.

Special Equipment

Some settings will use specialist equipment for the teaching of mathematical concepts. These can include Montessori sandpaper letters, spindle boxes, golden bead series, number rods, binomial and trinomial cubes, numerals and counters, teen boards, fraction circles and skittles. Many of Froebel's gifts are concerned with the development of mathematical concepts.

Science Through Play

When people think about science they think about subjects like physics, chemistry and biology. While these are areas of science, in the pre-school years science is much more about creating scientific *skills* rather than specific subject knowledge.

Questioning and Prediction Skills

Children should be encouraged to ask questions about their environment and surroundings. Adults should also pose questions about the environment to children in their care.

Prediction is very much the basis of scientific thinking. When scientists are involved in research they often hypothesise (try to predict) what is likely to happen in their experiments. They then test out their predictions to see what the reality is. In ECEC settings, children can be encouraged to do this on a daily basis. Everyday questions can be posed:

- What do you think will happen if we put too much water on the plants?
- What do you think will happen if we don't wash our hands after going to the toilet?
- What do you think will happen if we don't put things back where we found them?

In addition to this everyday questioning, there are lots of really good experiments that can be done with pre-school children in order to encourage their prediction skills.

Floating and Sinking Experiments

Children try to predict from an interesting array of objects which ones will float and which will sink. Start with a few obvious ones so that children get the idea, e.g. stones, tennis balls, balloons, etc. Allow children to hold and feel the objects before asking them for their prediction.

When children gain confidence, move on to trickier objects, e.g. a needle, a pencil, an apple, an orange, a ruler, pasta shells, a piece of play-dough, etc.

Magnet Experiments

Children are given magnets and asked to predict whether they think they will stick to various surfaces in the classroom, e.g. table legs, fridge door, table tops, walls, doors, door handles, etc.

Balance Scale Experiments

Children use a balance scale and try to predict what way the scale will tip when certain selected objects are placed on it.

Observation Skills

Children should be encouraged to watch and observe the world around them. This encourages them to focus on details. Children can observe a spider web in the classroom or garden to see what the spider does. Children can observe worms or snails closely. They can discuss what happens with a painting when red and yellow paint are mixed together. Practitioners should always be on the lookout for interesting things for children to observe.

Experimentation Skills

Children should be encouraged to try things out to see what happens. For example, in the experiments described above, it is important that the children test out their predictions and then discover the reality. Experimentation skills need not be confined to formal 'experiments' like this: children can be encouraged to experiment in many informal everyday situations. Two children are *each* given a number of different implements to spoon a Rice Krispie bun mixture into bun cases (e.g. a fork, a teaspoon, a dessertspoon and a tablespoon). The adult simply gives the children the implements and lets them at it, providing assistance only if asked for. The children will usually work together to experiment with the implements until they find the best one (i.e. the teaspoon or dessertspoon). This not only fosters co-operation between the children, it gives them an understanding of volume.

Thinking Skills

Children should be encouraged to think about what they see. They should consider results and use them to form conclusions. Practitioners can encourage this through questioning.

- Why do you think that happened?
- Why do you think the dessertspoon worked best?
- Why do you think the pencil floated?

Social Learning Through Play

This area of the curriculum is mainly concerned with social and emotional development. An effective play curriculum helps children in many ways.

- Children develop positive self-esteem. Self-esteem is defined as a person's general evaluation of themselves, e.g. I am a capable person.
- Children grow in self-confidence. They trust their own abilities and they are not afraid to take risks and try out new things.
- Children develop an ability to deal with emotions in a positive way, e.g. talking about being angry, rather than acting on it.
- Children become more independent.
- Children develop a positive attitude towards learning.
- Children learn how to interact effectively with others, how to consider each other's perspectives and how to respect others.
- Children develop a better understanding of the social norms of the society in which they live
- Moral development.

Self-esteem

In order for children to develop positive self-esteem and self-image it is important that play opportunities offered are at the correct level for their age and stage of development. This way children will succeed, but not without having to make an effort. Praise and encouragement given to children when they put in an effort is best. Praising children when they have put in little effort devalues praise; children become confused and sometimes disillusioned with it. Children know how much effort they have put in themselves, so this should be closely observed by adults and acknowledged. Praise should be targeted: blanket praise (e.g. 'Good job!') is not as effective as targeted praise (e.g. 'I really like how kindly you spoke to Ashling when she fell; you made her feel much better.').

Self-confidence

Closely linked to the concept of self-esteem is self-confidence. Children should be given opportunities to experience success in order to develop self-confidence. Again this is why pitching play opportunities and activities at the correct level is vital. Children need to have a good chance of success without the activity being too easy. The educationalist Maria Montessori was a great believer in activities that had *control of error* built in. With such activities the materials themselves tell the child whether or not they have succeeded – the child does not need to rely on the adult to tell them. A jigsaw is an example of an activity with control of error built in: if the child has pieces left over then they know they have not completed the jigsaw correctly and will continue trying (maybe there and then or maybe at a later date).

Dealing with Emotions

Some play activities help with children's emotional development. Physical play allows them channel negative energy (e.g. anger) in a positive way. Through role play children can act out emotionally confusing or challenging situations in a safe environment. Some children use sand and/or water play to relax. During all play activities practitioners should encourage children to adopt a care perspective, i.e. to consider situations from more than one point of view. For example, if one child accidentally bumps into and hurts another child with their tricycle both children should be encouraged to see the incident from the other child's perspective.

Independence

Encouraging children towards independence is very important for their self-esteem, self-confidence and self-image. One downside of our extremely safety conscious society is that children's independence can be curtailed. Having said this, it is still possible to give children opportunities for independence and also be safety conscious. Children should be shown how to carry out certain tasks and then supervised while they do them, e.g. setting the table, pouring out water for lunch, washing up, sweeping the floor, tidying away after activities. Maria Montessori devoted a whole curriculum area to this, calling them *practical life* experiences. She believed that children enjoy doing things for themselves and should be allowed to do so.

Children should be actively involved in daily care routines. Toddlers should be encouraged to self-feed. Children should be encouraged to dress themselves. They can put on their own coats or boots to go outside. They can go to the toilet themselves and wash their own hands correctly. They can learn how to brush their teeth. Dressing skills can be encouraged with the use of a good dress-up box of costumes; clothing provided can include everything from elasticated waists and Velcro fastenings to buttons and zips. This way children can practise dressing independently in an unpressurised environment, i.e. they are not being hurried. Adults should give help if the children become frustrated – but they should not intervene too much. Another useful activity involves asking the children to dress each other. For example, children can help each other to put on their coats before going outside. It is much easier for children to fasten buttons and zips if they are in front of them, so this practice gives the child an opportunity to perfect the skill and to boost their confidence.

Children should be actively involved in educational routines also. Children should be involved in choosing activities, setting out equipment, tidying away equipment, filling paint pots, filling and emptying water jars for painting, covering work surfaces for messy play, wiping or sweeping up spills, choosing books for storytelling and tidying book shelves.

Another very important skill that must be developed by children in order to develop independence is the ability to follow instructions. Sometimes children lack the memory skills or the confidence to follow an instruction the first time it is given. Practitioners should be patient with children. Do not give more than one or two instructions at a time. Repeat the instruction if the child asks and provide encouragement as the child carries out the instruction, e.g. 'That is perfect! You have put the knife on the right and the fork on the left. Well done. Now do the same with the other knives and forks – good boy.' Generally, when young children ask for instructions to be repeated it is not that they have not been listening (or else they would not ask at all) but that they are not quite sure or confident enough to carry out the instruction. Practitioners should be careful to repeat instructions patiently without any impatience in their voice whatsoever. Sometimes visuals are useful for helping children to follow important instructions.

Positive Attitudes Towards Learning

The golden rule here is: success breeds success! If you ask someone what their favourite subject in school was they normally pick one they were good at. Attitudes towards learning and opinions about one's abilities develop quite early on (by about the age of 6). This is why it is important that children develop positive attitudes and beliefs about their own learning.

Marie Clay (1926–2007) was a renowned educator from New Zealand. She believed that children up until the age of 6 do not generally evaluate themselves against others. She believed that because of this it was vital to identify children struggling with learning (she focused particularly on pre-literacy skills) before they began to see themselves in a negative light and inferior to their peers. Based on this, it is very important that children aged 0–6 are given positive feedback about their abilities and achievements. By the time a child moves into first class they need to believe themselves to be capable learners. If this is not the case then children begin to expect to fail. Marie Clay developed a programme called *reading recovery*. This programme identifies children 'at risk' of literacy failure at the end of senior infants. When children are identified, they undergo an intensive reading recovery programme. The programme lasts 12–20 weeks and it usually involves 30-minute sessions, five days a week. Clay found that reading recovery had a 98 per cent success rate: those that did not succeed, she believed to have a specific learning difficulty (normally dyslexia). She believed that the main reason why reading recovery works is that it targets and helps children *before* they begin to see themselves as poor readers. In order to give children confidence in their own abilities, practitioners need to follow the two golden rules of ECCE: (1) offer interesting and varied play opportunities and activities that match children's stages of development, and (2) offer targeted praise and encouragement.

Social skills

Children can be encouraged to develop their social skills through play. All types of play are useful here. During imaginative play, children can practise different social situations, e.g. going to the doctor or buying food in a shop. These play experiences help children to practise and understand the norms of the society in which they live, e.g. you pay for what you take, you sometimes have to queue for services, etc.

During construction play, children learn to share materials and equipment. If children are involved in a joint project they may have to co-operate with each other and negotiate how something is to be done.

During creative play activities, children again may have to share materials and resources, e.g. borrow the red paint from the child beside them or share the glue pot. During creative play, children also learn how to comment on other children's work without offending.

During physical play, children often have to turn-take, e.g. on a slide. This encourages patience and encourages non-egocentric behaviour. Also, during physical play minor accidents can occur and these require children to empathise with other children and apologise if they are the cause of the accident. This is a very important part of social development.

Music and Movement Through Play
Music

From an early age, music plays an important part in many people's lives. Babies and young children are often surrounded by music, e.g. parents singing to them, listening to music while being driven around in the car or listening to music as part of children's TV programmes. The benefits of music to children are huge. In terms of physical development, dancing and moving to music promotes gross-motor skills and physical fitness. Listening to music and, more particularly, learning to play music is very beneficial to intellectual development. Children's language development can be promoted through singing favourite songs. Emotionally, singing and dancing to music releases tension and stress and gives a feeling of wellbeing. Socially, when children sing, dance or play musical instruments together they are learning important social skills. Music and dance are also part of our culture. It can be used to celebrate our own culture and also that of other nations. In this way, music and dance can be used as part of a setting's equality and diversity programme.

Children should be exposed to as wide a variety of music genres as possible. Some settings limit the children's music exposure to children's songs. While these are very useful and should be used, settings should consider other genres, e.g. rock, pop, classical, traditional Irish, world music, etc.

Settings usually make very good use of *singing* as an educational tool. Most traditional nursery rhymes can be put to music and enjoyed by children. Many are very beneficial for early reading and maths skills. Children are energised by singing and enjoy singing as part of a group. Singing songs familiar to a child can be soothing when they first enter a setting, so practitioners should find out beforehand what songs they know and like. They can be used as part of their settling-in plan.

Taped songs can be used, but live music is best. If practitioners can play guitar or another instrument, this is very useful. Practitioners do not have to be highly-skilled musicians, since most children's songs can be played using a few major chords.

Many settings make use of percussion instruments: tuned (e.g. xylophones) and un-tuned (e.g. drums, tambourines and maracas). Play with instruments can be both structured and unstructured and there are advantages and disadvantages with each approach. If instruments are left out all the time for children to play with, children have great access to them and can experiment with them at their own pace. However, this can have a wearing effect and can cause stress levels to rise for both the adults and the other children. If time with instruments is structured, this can stilt children's creativity: they feel they are performing and may become shy. Also, the amount of time they get with the instruments is reduced, since all the children are using them at the same time and one child may only get a short 'turn' at using them.

Children can make usable working instruments for themselves. Maracas can be made out of plastic bottles or tubs partially filled with rice. Xylophones can be made by filling glass jars with different amounts of water and tapping them with a spoon. Guitars can be made using an empty shoe box and some large elastic bands. Drums can be made out of cardboard boxes, saucepans, etc.

Movement

Young children love to dance and move to the rhythm of music. It is not only an enjoyable experience for them but it also helps to develop co-ordination and control over body movements. It is generally best if children are permitted to dance and move how they wish in ECEC settings. The enjoyment can be taken out of it if movement and dance is structured and taught. Movement and dance should not be performance-led at this age. Movement and dance can be used to introduce children to different cultural traditions. Children might like to watch short clips of dance from different cultures and then dance to music from that culture.

ICT in Play

ICT means information and communications technology. It includes the use of all types of technological devices: mobile phones, computers, the internet, digital cameras, DVD players, etc. Since the use of ICT sometimes involves communicating with the outside world (e.g. through websites), it is important that settings have clear policies in place for supervising children closely at all times.

Computers

Computers can be used effectively in the ECEC setting to help children gain confidence in using a mouse and keyboard. In addition, there is excellent software on the market today for use by even very young children. Software can often be purchased in bookshops or through educational suppliers (e.g. Prim-Ed). 'The Computer Classroom' is a software series that offers different packages for children of different age groups, beginning with pre-school and infant classes and going up to level 6 (children aged 10–12). 'Maths Made Easy' and 'Reading for Literacy' are other useful software programmes.

Digital cameras

Cameras can be used by children to photograph their work before it is dismantled or for introducing the topic of photography. Cameras can also be used by children to photograph special events. The children themselves should be shown how to use the camera and encouraged to do so, even if the resulting photographs are not perfect: the child is learning valuable skills.

Other ICT equipment

Children can be given phones to play with during pretend play. Children love to use 'walkie talkies' to communicate with each other, perhaps from inside to outside. There are many other electronic toys on the market, but overall play value should always be considered. Toys that are not versatile, repeating the same few functions time and time again are not generally worth the money.

Children can be given a treat every now and then and permitted to watch a DVD. They should be shown how to operate the equipment. Also children can be shown interesting internet clips, although it is vital that the adult watches the clip in its entirety before showing it to children.

Equality and Diversity in Play

There are a number of different reasons why it is important to consider the issues of equality and diversity in children's play. Children are growing up in a diverse society, so they must be not only aware of diversity but they must be positive in terms of their attitudes towards it. Children are aware of ethnic, racial and gender differences from a young age (3–4 years), so they need to see these differences as positive. They must be taught that everyone is equal. Children assimilate positive and negative, spoken and unspoken messages about difference from all aspects of their lives. ECEC settings need to be aware of this and they must help to counteract problems such as racism and sexism. Negative messages about a child's race, ethnic background, etc. can affect their self-image and self-esteem. Practitioners need to be acutely aware of this. They must positively promote the backgrounds and cultures of all children in the setting.

It is important for practitioners to examine their *own* attitudes to equality and diversity. In doing this, they will be able to challenge all incidents of bias, prejudice, discrimination, racism and sexism as they occur. Children must be helped if they are to 'unlearn' negative feelings towards difference. It is vital that the ECEC setting promotes positive attitudes towards equality and diversity. Practitioners can do many things to ensure this.

- Ensure that play experiences are accessible to all children, e.g. wheelchair users are involved in a music and movement exercise, perhaps by being pushed in time to the music.
- Encourage children to utilise all play areas and watch out for incidences of gender bias, e.g. girls taking over the home corner or boys taking over the construction area or dominating physical play. Challenge these incidences and explain that both boys and girls like to play in all areas.

- Provide a range of dress-up clothes that reflect the diverse nature of our society. Include turbans, saris, traditional African dress, etc. Parents may be able to help and offer advice with this.

- Encourage children not to be fixed in terms of their gender perceptions. Explain that men can be nurses and girls can work in the fire service, etc. The dress-up area can be used to encourage these ideas.

- Watch carefully for incidents of exclusion. Reflect on the reasons for the exclusion, record findings and work sensitively towards inclusion.

- Deal with incidents of racism as they arise. Reinforce the message later with suitable activities.

- Challenge children who make hurtful remarks. Give accurate information to the child. It is not enough to simply say: 'That's not nice.' An explanation must be given or the children are unlikely to learn from the experience.

- Support the child who has been hurt by the remarks. Encourage them to talk about how they feel.

- Teach children how to defend themselves. Teach them to politely but firmly say: 'That is not fair' or 'I don't like what you are doing/saying'.

- Puppets or dolls can be used as part of social stories to re-enact incidents. Children can then discuss what happened, how the people involved probably felt, what should be done, etc.

- Be considerate around particular days, e.g. Father's Day.

- Celebrate festivals from around the world. Parents may be a very valuable source of information here.

- Celebrate children's native languages, using their knowledge to teach the other children in the group.

- Find out and use correct terminology, e.g. black, deaf, Traveller or visually impaired. Encourage children to do the same.

- Ensure that you can pronounce and spell children's names correctly.

- The book corner is very important in terms of promoting equality and diversity (see Chapter 9). Ensure there are books providing everyday images of children from different cultures. Also consider how genders are portrayed.

- Play music and provide musical instruments from different cultures.

- Provide art materials that are suitable for demonstrating a variety of skin tones.

- Provide props for dramatic play: crutches, walking sticks, glasses with clear glass, etc.

Aistear

Aistear

A istear is the National **Curriculum** Framework for children aged 0–6 years in Ireland. Aistear was developed by the National Council for Curriculum and Assessment (NCCA) in partnership with the early childhood sector in Ireland and abroad. Aistear was published in 2008.

Aistear states its own purpose, which is to:

…provide information for adults to help them plan for and provide enjoyable and challenging learning experiences, so that all children can grow and develop as *competent and confident learners* within loving relationships with others. Aistear describes the types of learning (dispositions, values and attitudes, skills, knowledge, and understanding) that are important for children in their early years, and offers ideas and suggestions as to how this learning might be nurtured. The framework also provides guidelines on supporting children's learning through partnerships with parents, interactions, play, and assessment.

(NCCA 2009: 6).

Structure of Aistear

Aistear is presented in four documents or booklets. All four documents can be found at: www.ncca.biz/Aistear. In addition to this, NCCA have produced a series of audiovisual presentations on all aspects of Aistear. The presentations can be viewed and listened to on the same website. (Look under the 'Aistear Toolkit' section.)

The four Aistear documents are:

- **User Guide**
  This is a 24-page document that gives a broad outline of the purpose of Aistear, information on how it works alongside other developments in the sector (e.g. Síolta) and planning for the implementation of Aistear.

- **Key Messages from the Research Papers**
  This eight-page document gives a very general summary of the key pieces of research that informed the development of Aistear. A link exists within this document to the research papers in their full form.

- **Principles and Themes**
  This 59-page document details what should be included in an early childhood curriculum framework.

- **Guidelines for Good Practice**
  This 118-page document details how an environment can be created to facilitate children's learning and development. It describes how to create an environment that allows the principles and themes to be realised.

Principles and Themes of Aistear

This document details what should be included in an early childhood curriculum framework. Aistear identifies *12 principles* of early learning and development. These principles are presented in three groups:

Group 1: Children and their Lives in Early Childhood
- The child's uniqueness
- Equality and diversity
- Children as citizens

Group 2: Children's Connections with Others
- Relationships
- Parents, family and community
- The adult's role

Group 3: How Children Learn and Develop
- Holistic learning and development
- Active learning
- Play and hands-on experiences
- Relevant and meaningful experiences

- Communication and language
- The learning environment

Each principle is presented using a short statement. This is followed by an explanation of the principle from the child's perspective. This explanation highlights the adult's role in supporting children's early learning and development.

Below is an example of one of the principles presented in Aistear.

Example of a Principle

Equality and Diversity

Nurturing equality and diversity is important in early childhood. Promoting equality is about creating a fairer society in which everyone can participate equally with the opportunity to fulfil his/her potential. Diversity is about welcoming and valuing individual and group differences and understanding and celebrating difference as part of life.

- Support me to feel equal to everyone else and do not let me be excluded because of my ethnicity, culture, faith/no faith, home language, family background and type, special educational need, physical appearance, gender, or ability. Recognise, value and accept me and my family.
- You may have to treat me in a different way to other children, to ensure I feel equal. Thank you for respecting my cultural identity and that of my family. Remember too that I may need you to help me to integrate into life in Ireland.
- Help me to learn to value social and cultural difference and to recognise that I live in a diverse, multi-ethnic society. Help me to learn to recognise and challenge injustice and discrimination and to stand up for myself and others.
- Remember that learning is more meaningful, motivating and enjoyable for me when activities and experiences are based on my skills, strengths and interests and when they are linked to my home culture and language.
- Help me to be open to the ideas, stories and experiences of others, and to listen and learn from these.

(NCCA 2009: 8)

The 12 Aistear principles describe the characteristics of a quality early learning environment. Aistear then goes on to describe *what* children should learn: dispositions, attitudes and values, skills, knowledge and understanding.

Aistear's curriculum framework is organised under four *themes*:

- Wellbeing
- Identity and Belonging
- Communicating
- Exploring and Thinking.

Each theme begins with a short description of its importance for children as young learners. The theme is then organised into four *aims*, with each aim further divided into six *learning goals* (with some goals being more suitable for older children).

Aistear also provides some suggested ideas for the types of learning experiences that adults might provide for children while working towards learning goals. These ideas are known as *sample learning opportunities*. They are presented for three overlapping age groups:

- Babies (0–18 months)
- Toddlers (12 months–3 years)
- Young children (2½–6 years).

See Appendix 1 (p. 220) for a complete example of an Aistear theme, along with its four aims, six learning goals and sample learning opportunities.

Guidelines for Good Practice

The Guidelines for Good Practice document is divided into four main sections. Each section describes a different aspect of pedagogy. Pedagogy means the holistic development and education of children and young people.

The Guidelines for Good Practice are made up of:

- Section 1: Building partnerships between parents and practitioners
- Section 2: Learning and developing through interactions
- Section 3: Learning and developing through play
- Section 4: Supporting learning and development through assessment.

The guidelines then go on to demonstrate what good practice might look like in the four areas above. This is done through the use of a number of *learning experiences* or practical, everyday examples.

Section 1: Building Partnerships between Parents and Practitioners

This section of the Good Practice Guidelines outlines what partnership means and describes different ways in which parents and practitioners can work together to enhance children's learning and development. Aistear describes a partnership in this context as:

> Parents, families and practitioners *working together* to benefit children. Each *recognises, respects and values* what the other does and says. Partnership involves *responsibility* on both sides. (NCCA 2009: 7)

Partnership between parents and practitioners is of utmost importance and it benefits all concerned. Good partnerships are particularly important for children if they are experiencing periods of change or difficulty. Aistear recognises the need for practitioners to respect the confidentiality of information they receive, while at the same informing partners that confidentiality cannot be maintained where a child protection issue is believed to exist.

Partnership Benefits Everybody

When good partnerships exist, everybody benefits. *Children* feel more secure and confident moving from home to out-of-home settings. Learning opportunities are optimised and interest levels heightened when children see aspects of their home life (e.g. culture and language) incorporated into their out-of-home setting – and vice versa.

Parents feel that their opinions, knowledge, values (and perhaps language, culture and traditions) are understood, valued and respected by the setting. Information is shared both ways, encouraging parents to become more involved and perhaps more knowledgeable about their child's early educational experiences. Parents are more likely to feel comfortable visiting the setting and are more likely to get involved in events and activities organised in the setting.

Practitioners can learn from parents' skills and experiences. They can make learning more relevant and enjoyable for children and help children to develop a secure sense of identity. If parents are supportive of the setting, children will sense this and will also be more positive towards it. This makes the practitioner's work more rewarding and productive.

Creating and Maintaining Good Partnerships

Aistear's Good Practice Guidelines provide very practical guidance and suggestions as to how good partnerships can be created and maintained between practitioners and parents. The guidelines take the unusual but very effective step of providing examples of *learning experiences* in order to illustrate partnership in action. Aistear's Good Practice Guidelines focus on four ways for parents and practitioners to work together. They are:

- Supporting learning and development
- Sharing information
- Contributing
- Making decisions and advocating different approaches and courses of action.

Supporting Learning and Development

Practitioners should acknowledge that parents have provided children with most of their first learning experiences and should continue to be a big part of their children's learning experiences as they begin to spend time in out-of-home settings. Learning is most effective when information that parents have (about children's interests, skills, abilities and dispositions) is shared with practitioners. Likewise, practitioners should share information with parents about their children's learning. There are many ways in which this can be done effectively and Aistear offers a wide range of suggestions, some of which are listed below.

Practitioners can:

- Invite parents into the setting, i.e. an open door policy.
- Share information about the curriculum.
- Use a notice board to let parents know what activities children have done on a particular day.
- Send captioned photographs home regularly, showing parents their children's activities.
- Share information on children's interests both at home and in the setting and build on this information.
- Invite parents to share information about their culture and traditions and use this to support children's learning and development.
- Organise information sessions for parents, e.g. on Aistear.
- Publish a newsletter.
- Share resources with parents, e.g. books, CDs, small equipment.

Parents can:

- Ask the practitioner for suggested activities that can be done at home.
- Involve their children in everyday activities: cooking, shopping, cleaning, gardening, etc.
- Read with their children on a regular basis (perhaps join local library).
- Sing songs, tell stories and play games with their children.
- Talk to their children, encouraging them to ask questions.
- Limit the amount of time that children spend at passive activities, e.g. television.

Example of a Learning Experience

Supporting Learning and Development
Theme: Identity and Belonging
Aim 2
Learning Goal 2
Age group: Pre-school (full day care setting)

Precious is a Level 6 mature student on work placement once a week in the setting's pre-school room. Precious is originally from Ghana but has been living in Ireland for six years now. She is married with three children of her own. There is one little boy called Afram from Ghana in the setting. Each week, Precious brings something along from Ghana for the children to see, play with and learn. Today, Precious decides to dress up in traditional Ghanaian dress and prepare six identical smelling jars filled with three pairs of traditional Ghanaian spices for the children to smell. The children take turns in smelling the jars (each jar has a perforated lid) and then try to match the pairs of spices. Precious then tells the children the names of the spices and the types of dishes they are used in. Throughout the activity, Precious asks Afram for his contribution. In this way, she encourages Afram's sense of identity and belonging.

Sharing Information

Effective communication is a two-way thing. Information relevant to the promotion of a child's learning and development must be shared between practitioner and parents. For information to be communicated effectively, it needs to be in a form accessible to the receiver of the information. Practitioners should be mindful of parents with specific needs, e.g. literacy problems or language differences. Information should be treated in strictest confidence (unless, as stated earlier, a child protection issue is suspected). There are many ways in which information can be shared effectively. Aistear offers a wide range of suggestions, some of which are listed below.

Practitioners can:

- Develop an information booklet for parents. The booklet can detail all the relevant information about the centre: mission statement, aims and objectives, contact details, personnel, opening and closing times, fees and policies (e.g. behaviour management, healthy eating and first aid).
- Update and redistribute new information as required.

- Help parents to translate important information into their own home language. This may be useful to other parents whose language skills are not as good.
- Have regular, face-to-face meetings with parents. Settings need to be mindful of family circumstance (e.g. divorced couples) and also of issues such as language barriers.
- Share samples of children's work with parents.
- Use clear, open lines of communication with parents, e.g. text, email. Some settings use a communications copy for two-way communication.
- Share records with parents. Inform them about their children's successes and achievements. Discuss any issues of concern in person. Concentrate on finding solutions and planning ahead.
- Organise social events for parents so that they can meet each other, e.g. a summer barbecue.

Parents can:

- Get to know their child's practitioner and give feedback to them regarding how they feel their child is progressing in the setting.
- Let the setting know if anything occurs that could affect the child's mood or behaviour, e.g. introduction of a new family pet, death of a loved family pet.
- Share information about their language, culture and traditions.
- Parents of children with special needs are often the only link between the setting and other professionals working with the child. Parents need to keep settings informed and also help the setting respond effectively to the child's needs. Many parents of children with special needs have carried out a lot of research and are very knowledgeable about their child's particular need. This valuable information should be accessible so that it can be utilised fully by the setting.
- Evaluate the setting and give constructive feedback, if the setting provides for this, e.g. questionnaire.

Example of a Learning Experience

Sharing Information

Theme: Exploring and Thinking
Aim 4
Learning Goal 3
Age group: Pre-school (full- and part-time day care setting)

Little Scholars Nursery and Pre-school

Newsletter   **April 2014**

Our Day Out at the Fire Station

A big thank you to all the parents who came with us on our trip to the fire station last week: a fun time was had by all. The children sang all the way there and all the way back again! Since our return, we have been learning about fire safety in the home. The three things we have been talking about this week are: (1) fire prevention, (2) the importance of having a working fire alarm and (3) the importance of having an emergency escape plan in the home. We ask you to work with us on these extremely important issues.

We have lots of photos of the fire station trip, which are on display in the main hall. Please ask if you would like copy of any particular photo.

Rhyme of the Month

In recognition of our trip to the fire station, the children suggested that we include the words of Fireman Sam (short version!) in this month's newsletter. The children already know the words and actions, so they will be delighted to sing it with you.

Fireman Sam*
When he hears that fire-bell chime,
Fireman Sam is there on time.
Putting on his coat and hat
in less than seven seconds flat.

He is always on the scene.
Fireman Sam!
And his engine's bright and clean.
Fireman Sam!
You cannot ignore,
Sam is the hero next door.

Driving down the busy streets,
Greeting people that he meets.
Someone could be in a jam
So, hurry, hurry, Fireman Sam.
So move aside, make way.
Fireman Sam!

Themes for this Month
As you are aware, each week we choose a different theme on which to base our many activities. This month's themes are:
* Week 1: Community workers
* Week 2: Easter
* Week 3: Bugs
* Week 4: Egypt.

If you have any ideas or materials that might help us with our themes, please do not hesitate to speak with us.

*© Prism Art & Design Limited.

Look Who Has a Birthday in April!

- Katie O'Brien is **four** on 9 April
- Aleksy Burdalski is **four** on 13 April
- Ya Tan is **four** on 23 April
- Mark Gillespie is **five** on 26 April

We hope you all have a lovely birthday!

A Date for Your Diary

The six children going to school in September will be going on a fieldtrip to St Kevin's National School on 20 April. The infant teacher Mrs Jackson, whom many of you already know, has a number of activities planned. Come along if you can: you are more than welcome!

Contributing

Parents can make a very valuable contribution to their children's learning and development by sharing their time, experiences and talents with their children's out-of-home setting. Many parents possess knowledge and talents that do not already exist within the setting. For example, they may be able to play a musical instrument or share knowledge of their language and culture, if it is different from that of the setting. Grandparents who may now have additional time can also contribute to the setting. For example, they can talk about their own childhood and how things have changed since then, giving the pre-school children a better sense of time and place.

Sometimes settings (particularly infant classes in primary schools) have a formal Parents Association and parents can contribute through this. If settings are developing or amending policies or procedures, it is good to ask parents for their contribution, since they may be able to see the issue from a different perspective. When children's families can contribute to the setting, this can have a very positive effect on children's sense of identity and belonging. It strengthens the link between home and setting and it shows children that their home is supportive of the setting (and vice versa).

Parents themselves may benefit greatly from contributing. They can gain valuable information and they can also form new friendships and social networks. This can be particularly important to parents who are new in the locality. There are many ways in which contribution can be made effectively and Aistear offers a wide range of suggestions, some of which are listed below.

Practitioners can:

- Ask parents to share their knowledge and skills with the setting. Ensure that parents know that they are under no pressure to do so.
- Ensure that parents understand that their input is greatly valued and appreciated by the setting.

Parents can:

- Spend time in the setting. Share a learning activity with the children: play an instrument, coach a team, demonstrate a craft (e.g. knitting or origami), plant bulbs, make a book, accompany the children on a trip, tell a story using some words from your native language, if this is different from the language of the setting.
- Support play. Develop an outdoor play area. Help with a play activity: send in play props (e.g. dress-up clothes or empty shopping containers).
- Share information with the children and staff about who you are: Irish, Traveller, American, etc. Talk about what is important to you, e.g. family, festivals or interests.
- Talk to the children about your work. Organise a trip to your workplace or provide props from your work that can be added to the pretend play area.

- Help organise outings, sports days and other events.
- Fundraise for new equipment or facilities.

Example of a Learning Experience

Contributing
Theme: Wellbeing
Aim 2
Learning Goal 6
Age group: Infant class in primary school

Peter is a tillage farmer. He has two children at primary school: one in junior infants and one in senior infants. Peter was asked by the children's teacher, Ms O'Neill, to help and advise her to create two raised vegetable beds on the school grounds. Ms O'Neill felt that if the children were involved in growing their own vegetables, they would be more likely to eat them. Peter was happy to help out. Throughout the year, he came in for two hours every week to help the children plant, sow and tend the beds. Now they have a healthy crop of potatoes, carrots, turnips, broccoli, lettuce and scallions. The children love working outdoors and they love bringing home the fresh vegetables to show their parents. Many of the parents have told Ms O'Neill that their children are really enjoying this experience – and that they are eating more vegetables!

Making Decisions and Advocating Different Approaches and Courses of Action

Aistear acknowledges that parents know their own children better than anyone else. Therefore, it makes sense that parents be involved in decisions that are made regarding their children in out-of-home settings. There are many ways in which decisions can be made effectively. Aistear offers a wide range of suggestions, some of which are listed below.

Practitioners can:

- Consult with parents when policies are being developed or amended. This can be done in informal conversation or in formal ways (e.g. questionnaires).
- Ask parents to share any information that could contribute to better decision-making about the care of children in the setting.

Parents can:

- Act as advocates for their children, giving them a voice and seeking necessary services and facilities for them.

- Campaign and lobby for improvements, e.g. reduction in primary school class size.
- Provide valuable information for practitioners. This information may influence decisions made regarding children's care and education.

Example of a Learning Experience

Making decisions and advocating different approaches and courses of action
Theme: Wellbeing
Aim 1
Learning Goal 1 and 3
Age group: Babies in childminding and day care setting

Alison Burke is soon to return to work as a probation officer, having been on maternity leave, holiday leave and unpaid parental leave for the past year. Her new daughter Sarah is now 12 months old. Alison and her husband David would like to find a small, intimate day care setting or childminder for Sarah. They want Sarah to experience an environment as similar as possible to the home environment. The Burkes have come to live in a small, rural village and both commute to work in a large town 20km away. Both David and Alison feel that it would be best if Sarah could remain within her own community during the day, but they have not ruled out the possibility of bringing her with them to the large town (if there is nothing suitable locally).

The Burkes contact the HSE for a list of registered childminders and day care facilities in their local area and also in the large town. The Burkes find that there are three registered childminders in their local area, along with a large number of them in the town. The Burkes decide to check out the three local services first, making arrangements to visit each one. Before visiting each local service, the Burkes make out a list of key questions to ask. On visiting, they find that all three services are satisfactory. All three childminders are well qualified and have first aid. All three settings have a good range of toys and equipment, along with a safe outdoor play area. While the Burkes feel that all three services are of a high standard and tick all the essential boxes, they have a preference for Rose.

Rose provides a childminding service from her own home. She has a bungalow with access to a large, secure, well-equipped outdoor area to the rear. Rose minds two other children: one aged 2 and one aged 4. Rose has a very warm persona and she interacts very naturally with Sarah. Sarah seems to be happy in Rose's company. Rose gives Alison and David an information booklet about her service. She explains that she uses a 'communications copy' in which she records care routines and daily activities for each child. Rose regularly takes photos of the children while they are involved in their various activities and these photos are displayed in the setting.

Alison and David ask Rose for references from other parents. When they request references, the other parents have nothing but the height of praise for Rose and her setting. Alison and David meet Rose again. Together, they fill out a detailed application form. The form includes everything from contact details to Sarah's preferences, daily routines, medical history, allergies, vaccinations, likes and dislikes. In the weeks before Alison's return to work, Sarah goes to Rose three days a week, spending a few hours there each time. Things are going very well – and the future looks bright.

Section 2: Learning and Developing Through Interactions

Aistear recognises that relationships are at the very centre of early learning and development. Section 2 of the Good Practice Guidelines identifies a range of interaction strategies and methods that adults can use to enhance children's learning and development.

Effective interactions between adults and children need to be '*respectful, playful, enjoyable, enabling, and rewarding*' (NCCA 2009: 27). The Good Practice Guidelines offer detailed information on four interaction strategies. They are:

- Building relationships
- Facilitating
- Organising
- Directing.

Of the four interaction *strategies*, the first two (building relationships and facilitating) are very much child-led, while the last two (organising and directing) are more adult-led.

Building Relationships

This strategy is child-led. It highlights the fact that children learn by being with others, exploring with them and taking on risks and challenges with them. As part of this strategy, it is the responsibility of the adults to create an environment to allow this interaction to happen. The child directs and co-directs their own learning.

Facilitating

This is another child-led strategy. As part of this strategy, children learn through activities that they have initiated for themselves. In quality early childhood education and care, the child is encouraged to take or share the lead with adults.

Organising

This strategy is adult-led. In order for children to learn effectively, they must be in a well planned, well resourced environment. The environment must represent the identities and experiences of all children. The role of the adult is to plan and maintain this environment. In order for adults to maintain a quality environment, they must systematically reflect on their practice and ensure that the environment is of the highest quality.

Directing

This is another adult-led strategy. Children learn through activities that are well planned and guided by adults. Activities must be directed so that they build on the interests and experiences of the children. This strategy allows children to 'develop particular dispositions, values and attitudes, skills, knowledge, and understandings' (NCCA 2009: 28).

Aistear examines the four interaction strategies and then goes on to provide *sample methods* for each strategy. These sample methods are a very useful resource, since they explain how the adult can actually put the interaction strategies into place.

The following sample methods are suggested for *building relationships*.

Sample methods	The adult
Accepting and valuing children, their families and communities	• Welcomes all children, their families and communities • Finds out about each child's interests, background values and traditions • Provides props, toys, books and displays which represent all children in the setting • Helps children to learn about their communities
Engaging, discussing and communicating	• Joins with children in their play, activities and discussions • Shares jokes and funny stories, and has playful interactions with children as well as those that are serious • Helps children develop speaking and listening skills • Extends children's verbal responses where appropriate • Listens attentively and tries not to interrupt
Guiding children's behaviour	• Maintains a positive and safe learning environment • Works with children to draw up rules for the room and the playground or yard • Supports children in building resilience and in coping when things go wrong or when they are upset • Uses conflicts and awkward moments to discuss feelings • Works with children to solve problems and conflicts • Mediates when necessary in a firm and fair way to support children when they are feeling hurt
Naming and affirming actions and behaviours	• Names and describes what children are doing • Encourages children's efforts • Provides feedback (verbal and non-verbal)

The following sample methods are suggested for *facilitating*.

Sample methods	The adult
Negotiating learning and clarifying learning goals	• Encourages children to do things for themselves • Helps children to direct their own learning • Involves children in decisions about their own learning and gives them choices • Helps children to be clear about learning goals and encourages them to judge how well they have done something
Supporting participation and learning	• Acknowledges and nurtures children's ability to do things themselves through sharing control and empowering them • Assists children's initiatives, perseverance and decision-making • Encourages children to help and teach each other (peer mentoring) • Provides temporary assistance and support to children, through scaffolding, to move from one level of competence to another • Offers ideas, advice, suggestions and recommendations when asked or when appropriate
Thinking together to build meaning and understanding	• Plays, talks and works with children to make sense of experiences and learn from them • Follows children's leads • Helps, shows and explains when asked or when appropriate • Explores with children to find things out together rather than providing immediate answers

The following sample methods are suggested for *organising*.

Sample methods	The adult
Grouping children	• Decides why, when and how to bring children together in groups • Allocates time for children to negotiate group roles • Decides on which groups to work with at a given time • Provides individual, pair and small group experiences
Planning for and reflecting on children's learning	• Encourages children to plan activities • Plans, reviews, thinks and talks about children's experiences with them • Decides on the next steps in learning and provides tasks, activities and materials based on children's needs and interests
Scheduling and timetabling	• Organises learning experiences and monitors the ensuing interactions between children, between adults and children, and between children and the environment • Plans routines and transitions, involving children where possible
Structuring the learning environment	• Decides which equipment and materials will be available in the environment • Plans regularly and reviews the learning environment regularly, based on children's experiences and Aistear's aims and learning goals • Provides sufficient resources, time and space for all children to benefit from the experiences on offer.

The following sample methods are suggested for *directing*.

Sample methods	The adult
Assisting children's thinking	• Establishes an atmosphere that encourages talk and discussion • Listens carefully to understand what children are thinking and feeling • Builds on children's contributions, ideas and interests to extend conversations • Helps children to use their full range of thinking skills • Poses appropriate, challenging questions • Helps children to recognise their own progress and achievements and to build on these
Leading, labelling, describing and explaining learning	• Plans adult-initiated learning experiences • Explains to children what they will be doing and learning, and outlines how things work and what the 'rules' are • Reasons and clarifies actions and why things are being done the way they are • Tells, interprets, hypothesises, and thinks aloud
Modelling	• Teaches by example • Shows how to do things • Is mindful of the language, behaviours, values and attitudes portrayed as children imitate what they see and hear

Aistear suggests that all of the sample methods (shown in the tables on pp.163–5) can be combined and refined into six *interaction methods*. Aistear explores the six interaction methods in detail. Learning experiences are used to show the methods in action.

The six interaction methods are:
- Assisting children's thinking
- Modelling
- Naming and affirming children's actions and behaviours
- Negotiating learning and clarifying learning goals
- Structuring the learning environment
- Thinking together to build meaning and understanding.

See pp.26–51 of the Good Practice Guidelines for a full examination of Section 2: Learning and Developing Through Interactions.

Section 3: Learning and Developing Through Play

Aistear recognises the value of play in early learning and development. Section 3 of the Good Practice Guidelines deals with the subject of play and its role in the early childhood curriculum. Play is examined under various headings:
- What is play?
- Are there different types of play?
- Where do children play?

- What is my role as the adult in play?
- How do I prepare the play environment?
- How do I help children who find it difficult to play?
- How can I use play across Aistear's four themes?

Defining Play

Aistear describes play as 'ways of doing' and then goes on to further define it by describing ten of its characteristics. Play is defined as:

- **Active**
  Children use their bodies and minds in their play. They interact with the environment, with materials and with other people.
- **Adventurous and risky**
  Because of the pretend element of play, children are more comfortable taking risks and being more adventurous.
- **Communicative**
  Children share information and knowledge through their play. This can be done verbally or non verbally.
- **Enjoyable**
  Play is fun, exciting and humorous.
- **Involved**
  Play is deeply absorbing. Children become completely focused in their play, concentrating and thinking about what they are doing
- **Meaningful**
  Children play about what they have seen and heard, and what they know. Play helps them to build upon and extend their knowledge, understanding and skills in a way that is enjoyable and natural to them.
- **Sociable and interactive**
  Children can play alongside or with others. Sometimes they need to play alone.
- **Symbolic**
  Children imagine and pretend while playing. They try out skills, ideas, feelings and roles. They re-enact the past and rehearse the future, e.g. pretending to 'read' and 'write' before they can actually do so.
- **Therapeutic**
  Play can be very beneficial for children to express and work through emotions and experiences. This is the basis of the work of a play therapist.
- **Voluntary**
  Children choose to play. Their play is spontaneous.

Different Types of Play

There are many different types of play and children are often involved in more than one type at any one time. For example, children could pretend they are running a pizza restaurant (pretend play) while using play-dough to create pizzas (manipulative play). It is important that children experience a good variety of play types in order to support their learning and development across the four Aistear themes: Wellbeing, Identity and Belonging, Communicating, and Exploring and Thinking.

Aistear outlines five broad categories of play and gives a brief description of each:

Types of play	Description
Creative	**Creative play** involves children exploring and using their bodies and materials to make and do things and to share their feelings, ideas and thoughts. They enjoy being creative by dancing, painting, playing with junk and recycled materials, working with play-dough and clay, and using their imaginations.
Games with rules	Another type of play involves **games with rules**. Even babies and toddlers can partake in these, since peek-a-boo and turn-taking games have rules. In the beginning, children often play by their own rather flexible rules! In time, they also partake in more conventional games with 'external' rules. Language is an important part of games with rules as children explain, question and negotiate the rules. Rules are often an important part of pretend play where children negotiate rules about what can and can't be done.
Language	**Language play** involves children playing with sounds and words. It includes unrehearsed and spontaneous manipulation of these, often with rhythmic and repetitive elements. Children like playing with language – enjoying patterns, sounds and nonsense words. They also love jokes and funny stories.
Physical	**Physical play** involves children developing, practising and refining bodily movements and control. It includes whole body and limb movements, co-ordination and balance. These activities involve physical movements for their own sake and enjoyment. Children gain control over their gross-motor skills first, before refining their fine-motor skills. **Exploratory play** involves children using physical skills and their senses to find out what things feel like and what can be done with them. Children explore their own bodies and then they explore the things in their environment. **Manipulative play** involves practising and refining motor skills. This type of play enhances physical dexterity and hand–eye co-ordination. Over time, children need to experience a range of different levels of manipulation if they are to refine their motor skills. This type of play includes manipulating objects and materials. **Constructive play** involves building something using natural and manufactured materials. As children develop, this type of play can become more complex and intricate.
Pretend	**Pretend, dramatic, make-believe, role** and **fantasy play** involve children using their imaginations. Pretend play includes pretending with objects, actions and situations. As children grow, their imaginations and their play become increasingly complex. Children use their developing language to move from thinking in the concrete to thinking in the abstract. They make up stories and scenarios. Children act out real events and they also take part in fantasy play about things that are not real, such as fairies or superheroes. Children try out roles, occupations and experiences in their pretend play. **Early literary and numeracy** are clearly evident in this type of play, e.g. children make lists and menus and pay for cinema tickets. They also get the chance to play with different forms of ICT such as mobile phones, keyboards, cameras and calculators. **Small world play** involves children using small-scale representations of real things like animals, people, cars and train sets as play props. **Socio-dramatic play** involves children playing with other children and/or adults. It provides opportunities for children to make friends, to negotiate with others and to develop their communication skills. This play helps to extend language. The ability to write stories also has its roots in socio-dramatic play.

Play can also be defined by *who* is involved in the play.

- *Solitary play* means that the child plays alone. This is a dominant feature of younger children's play, especially children aged 0–2.
- *Spectator* or *onlooker play* is also a feature of younger children, although older children who are very shy or in an unfamiliar setting may also engage in this type of play. Here, the child watches others at play but does not engage directly in it. Children can get great enjoyment out of this type of play and they should not be pushed into joining in.
- *Parallel play* (also called *adjacent play* or *co-action*) involves the child playing separately from others but close to them, sometimes mimicking their action. This type of play is seen as a transitory stage: from solitary and onlooker types of play to a more socially mature associative and co-operative type of play.
- *Associative* or *partnership play* happens when children begin to play together, developing interactions through doing the same activities or playing with similar equipment, or through imitating.
- *Co-operative play* happens when children interact, take turns, share and make decisions about how and what to play. They collaborate, develop and negotiate ideas for their play. This type of play requires advanced levels of social maturity and organisational skills and is therefore more common in children aged 5–6.

Where Do Children Play?

Children will play anywhere, but it is important that children have good access to well-equipped indoor and outdoor play areas. It is important (within reason) that children can go outside if and when they wish to do so. It is ideal if indoor and outdoor play areas adjoin each other.

Given the unpredictability of Irish weather, some preparation is required for this to be possible. Children should have wellies, waterproof jackets and a change of clothes available in the setting. This will ensure that they can play outside in all types of weather. Aistear suggests that settings should actually embrace Irish weather and learn to work with it. This could mean having a rainy-day box 'that includes umbrellas, sieves, toy boats, toy ducks, containers for measuring rainfall, funnels, charts for recording the level of rainfall, containers for gathering water to recycle (to water flowers and plants indoors, for example), tin foil (for making hats), tapes to measure the size of puddles, and relevant picture books' (NCCA 2009: 55).

The Role of the Adult in Children's Play

Aistear states that, in order for adults to play an important role in children's play, adults must fully appreciate and understand the importance of play and its usefulness as a learning tool across all areas of the early years curriculum. Aistear examines the role of adults under the following headings:

- Planning and preparing the play environment
- Supporting play
- Reviewing play.

Planning and Preparing the Play Environment

It is the responsibility of the adult to provide an indoor and outdoor play environment that gives children a wide variety of rich play possibilities. The adult should plan and organise the children's environment based on assessment information and also the curriculum requirements of Aistear across its four themes. Aistear provides advice and practical guidance regarding how the children's play environment should be organised and resourced (see pp.56–8 of the Good Practice Guidelines).

In terms of organisation, Aistear recommends that the play space (both inside and outside) should be organised into smaller, child-sized play areas as opposed to one big space. For example, an inside space could be divided up into a pretend area, a library area, a construction area, etc. A large outdoor space could be divided up into a wheelie toy area, a climbing area, a natural materials area, etc. Children should have easy access to the outdoors and plenty of natural light available to them.

Children should also have a space within the environment that is their own personal space, e.g. a cubby hole. There should also be a space within the environment for children to be alone, if they so wish. Children's work should be displayed at the eye level of the children. Individual artworks should be named and dated. Materials and equipment should be stored in predictable locations that are easily accessible for the children. The environment should be kept tidy and the children can help to do this.

In terms of resourcing, the materials, equipment, displays and the physical environment itself should reflect the diversity of Irish society. Special resources should be provided for children with additional needs, as required. A wide variety of literacy and numeracy supportive resources should be provided. These can include books, writing tools and mathematical tools (e.g. rulers, weighing scales, calculators and height charts). There should be a wide variety and sufficient amount of open-ended resources that can be used by children as they wish: paint, play-dough, recycled materials, paper, etc. Environments should try to have as many 'real' objects as possible. Children can use these real objects for play, e.g. gardening tools, kitchen equipment and cleaning utensils.

Once an environment is planned and resourced in this way, the adult can now provide for play experiences that are safe, challenging, inclusive and enjoyable. The play can reflect children's individual strengths, interests, abilities and needs. The adult can now help the children to build on, challenge and extend their learning and development. This type of environment provides children with choices about what to do and when to do it.

Supporting Play

Aistear emphasises that the role of the adult in children's play is very much a facilitative (rather than directive) one. The adult uses their knowledge of play and their awareness of Aistear's themes to facilitate the children's play. The adult talks to children about their play and discusses their play choices. The adult is supportive without being interfering and they help children to extend or enrich their chosen play experiences. The adult must sometimes act as mediator when disputes arise and they must protect children from harm, if they are being rejected or bullied. The adult must help children who find it difficult to play.

Reviewing Play

Through various methods of observation and assessment, the adult gathers a wide variety of information about children's play. This information should be used for planning and extending children's future play experiences. It should also be used to make decisions about the play environment. For example, it might be observed that a particular play area is not being used by children and the play area can be altered to make it more appealing.

Children Who Find it Difficult to Play

Aistear recognises that, while all children can play, some may require extra support from the adult to benefit fully from play. Children who are impulsive or children who get into conflicts easily may find it difficult to play. Children who are withdrawn or isolated may also face challenges. There are likely to be children whose first language is different from the language of the setting. There may be children who have speech delays and children who have sensory or physical impairments. These children often need more specialised and focused support from the adult.

The role of the adult is to carefully observe what is going on and to plan accordingly. Depending on the nature of the difficulty, the adult can use many different strategies. The adult can change the physical or social environment. They can introduce a buddy system among the children. They can break down activities into smaller, more doable, parts. They can provide one-on-one support for some children and they can use special equipment or devices to help children with particular special needs.

Using Play to Develop the Themes of Aistear

The adult can plan the play environment so that children use different types of play to support their learning and development. Play can be used to incorporate Aistear's four themes: Wellbeing, Identity and Belonging, Communicating, and Exploring and Thinking.

The Good Practice Guidelines demonstrate how play can be used across Aistear's four themes. The guidelines present a total of 16 *learning experiences* to show how this can be done.

Four learning experiences are presented for each Aistear theme: one for babies, one for toddlers and two for young children. See pp.60–9 of the Good Practice Guidelines for these 16 learning experiences.

Below is an example of one learning experience that shows how play can be used to develop the themes of Aistear.

Example of a Learning Experience

Learning and Developing Through Play
Theme: Wellbeing
Aim 3
Learning Goal 3
Age group: Young children (sessional service – playgroup)

The children in the playgroup are outside on a frosty morning. Two boys, Fiachra and James, (both aged 4) discover a large spider's web. They call the playgroup assistant, Zola, over to have a look at it. They are fascinated by the different colours. Zola explains that it is the sun's reflection on the frost that is doing this. Zola is French and she tells them that the French word for a spider's web is *toile d'araignée*. The children laugh at each other's attempts to say the word! Zola asks the boys if they would like to take a photograph of the web and they race inside to get the camera, each trying to go faster than the other. Zola takes a photograph and uploads it to the computer. The boys study the photograph, trying to work out how the spider made the web.

The boys later tell Zola that they want to make a web, too. They assemble a range of materials, including glue, paper, markers, string, knitting wool and tinfoil. They spend a long time making their webs. Later, they proudly take photographs of the webs. *'Ils sont magnifique – quelles couleurs!'* says Zola. She explains to the children that this means: 'They are magnificent – what colours!'

After lunch, the boys run out to see the web but they have trouble finding it because the ice has melted. They are disappointed. During circle time, the group have a discussion about how ice and snow melt and how the ice melting made it difficult for Fiachra and James to find their web. The following day, another child brings in a DVD about a spider. All the children watch it. Over the following weeks, some children do projects on spiders while others investigate ice.

Reflection
How often do I encourage children to get involved in projects on things that are of interest to them?

(NCCA 2009: 61)

Section 4: Supporting Learning and Development through Assessment

The final section of the Aistear Guidelines for Good Practice is entitled *Supporting Learning and Development through Assessment*. This section describes what assessment is and shows how assessment can be carried out in early childhood settings. This section of the Aistear guidelines is covered in full in Chapter 14.

Other Approaches to the Early Years Curriculum

The subject of Section 2 of this book is ECEC and Play. The module entitled **Early Childhood Education and Play (5N1773)** includes the study of four approaches that are covered elsewhere in this book:

- **Montessori:**   Chapter 1
- **Froebel:**   Chapters 2 and 7
- **Steiner Waldorf:**   Chapters 3 and 7
- **HighScope:**   Chapter 4

In addition, Early Childhood Education and Play (5N1773) requires the study of two other approaches:

- **The Reggio Emilia approach**
- **Forest schools**

These two approaches are covered in this chapter.

Reggio Emilia Approach

Reggio Emilia is a city in northern Italy that has a unique approach to early childhood education. The approach was established by working parents directed by Loris Malaguzzi after World War II. Malaguzzi was inspired by John Dewey's progressive education theory and Jean Piaget's theory of cognitive development.

Every Reggio Emilia centre is staffed by six key professionals: an infant practitioner, a toddler practitioner, a pre-school practitioner, an *atelierista* (artist in residence), a *pedogogista* (educational philosopher) and a cook. These professional staff members are assisted by volunteers and helpers, usually parents and grandparents.

Principles

The Reggio Emilia approach centres on the belief that learning is enabled by human interaction and a suitable physical and cultural environment. In order for children to learn effectively, great care must be taken with the physical environment. Centres should be large, with plenty of indoor and outdoor space.

Light and beauty within the physical environment is considered to be vital: the centres have large windows that let in lots of light. Beauty is apparent in the setting and there are beautiful objects everywhere, e.g. vases of cut flowers, scented candles and mirrors. Classical music is often played in the background.

Each centre has a large communal space called the *piazza*. This is where children and adults of all age groups meet and interact. This interaction is seen as an essential part of children's development. Meals are also eaten together here.

Art is an essential part of the Reggio Emilia curriculum. Every centre has an *atelier* or art space where children can go to create pieces whenever they wish.

Role playing is seen as an important part of the curriculum and each centre has a dress-up area where clothing and props are provided. Each centre also has a reading area with soft seats and a large collection of books. Here, adults or older children read aloud for the younger children.

The Reggio Emilia approach sees parents as a fundamental part of children's learning. Practitioner reflection and documentation is also a key element to continued progress and improvement.

Materials

A wide variety of materials are made available to the children, e.g. buttons, stones, pieces of fabric, clay, paints, pens and glue. The materials are always naturally made and they are recycled many times in the classroom. Every centre has a 'projection box': a light box over which items of interest can be inspected closely.

Methodology

Mealtimes are set. However, outside of mealtimes children are free to pursue whatever it is that interests them at that particular time. Every day there is a morning assembly where ideas are discussed. This assembly time is considered to be vital: it gives children a democratic say in what goes on in the centre.

Teachers in Reggio Emilia schools work in harmonious partnership with children and their parents. Listening is seen as an essential skill for the Reggio Emilia practitioner. The calm, quiet physical environment facilitates this. Teachers must be skilled observers; they use these observations to plan for the needs of the children. Teachers use various methods to document children's work, opinions and ideas, e.g. journals and tape recorders.

Forest Schools

Forest schools promote a type of outdoor education in which children visit a particular forest or woodland each day to engage in personal and social learning, and technical skills. Children go to the forest or woodland in all weathers – except high winds. Protective clothing and shelters built in the forest ensure that this can happen. Children attending forest schools not only learn about natural sciences (botany, geography, biology and environmental science) but also skills such as teamwork and problem-solving. Forest schools are also believed to be very beneficial for children's physical health, self-esteem and self-image. Forest schools are also called *nature schools*.

The concept of the forest school was originally developed by H.L. Russell in Wisconsin, US in 1927. During the 1950s the idea was introduced to Sweden and later Denmark. In Denmark, forest schools became an embedded part of the curriculum for pre-school children aged 0–7. In Denmark it was observed that children attending Forest kindergartens were arriving at primary school with strong social skills, excellent group work skills, high self-esteem and confidence in their own capabilities. It was also found that they tended to have better physical health and lower stress levels. In the 1990s the idea of forest schools spread to the UK and there are now approximately 190 schools operating there. Forest schools are not prominent in Ireland at the present time.

Principles

In forest schools, basic needs are met first. Basic needs are defined in relation to Maslow's hierarchy of needs. Children are given tasty, nutritious food to eat. They are supplied with quality raingear and warm clothing and shelters are created in the forest to shelter the children from heavy rain.

There is an emphasis on safety. Fields and woodlands are fenced so that children cannot come to any harm and there are certain ground rules related to safety. Children go out in all weathers and seasons. They are given the freedom to explore the forest and they learn by doing. This freedom and choice reduces stress levels and problem behaviours.

Materials

Children use full-sized tools, e.g. shovels, saws and penknives. They are given lots of instruction so that they can use these tools safely. Camp fires and temporary shelters are created in the woods.

Methodology

Children are given the freedom to choose what they decide to do and explore in the forest. They may decide to pick blackberries or gather leaves. They may build a dam or stepping stones over a forest stream. They build dens and huts so that they can play at chasing. Adults offer knowledge when asked, e.g. the names of plants or berries. Adults take the time to explain what forest foods are safe or unsafe to eat. Adults demonstrate certain skills to the children, e.g. sawing timber for the campfire, cooking on a campfire or pitching a tent.

Assessment and Planning

Assessment

Aistear defines assessment as:

> ...the ongoing process of *collecting, documenting, reflecting on*, and *using* information to develop rich portraits of children as learners in order to support and enhance their future learning.

> (NCCA 2009: 72)

Broadly speaking, there are two types of assessment:

- Assessment **of** learning
- Assessment **for** learning.

It is important for practitioners to fully understand the difference between these two types of assessment and also to appreciate the purposes and uses of both.

Assessment *of* Learning

This is the type of assessment that has been traditionally used by our education system. Children are given various tests and assessments and the results are collected and reported. In pre-school settings, observations are carried out and findings are compared to norms for the child's age group. In primary schools, standardised tests are given. In Ireland, these include the Drumcondra Primary Reading Test (DPRT) and the MICRA-T (Mary Immaculate Reading Attainment Test). In secondary schools, end of year tests are used alongside major exams, such as the Junior Certificate and Leaving Certificate.

All of these tests are examples of assessment *of* learning. The purpose of this is to gather data about a child's progress and to use this data to inform others about the child's achievements. However, nowadays this form of assessment alone is seen as insufficient. It should not be the only form of assessment carried out with children in any setting or age group. Assessment of learning can also be called *summative assessment*, i.e. a summary or report of the child's progress to date is provided.

Assessment *for* Learning

Generally, with assessment *for* learning, assessment is part of the learning *process*. It is not something that happens at the end of learning, i.e. testing what has been learned. Assessment for learning can also be called *formative assessment* i.e., the intention is to form, shape or guide the next step in learning.

Assessment for learning (AFL) is always forward-looking. With AFL, the practitioner always shares the *learning intention* (learning goal) with the learner. The teacher then helps the child to unpack the learning intention, assisting them to understand exactly what it is they are being challenged to learn. As the child progresses through the learning experience, the adult gives the child feedback that is quite focused. This feedback gives the child a clear picture of what they are doing well and it also helps them plan for how they can further progress their learning.

What is Assessed?

Assessment enables the teacher to gain a lot of valuable information about children and their learning. They gain information about children's:

- Dispositions
- Skills
- Knowledge and understanding
- Developmental milestones.

Dispositions

Children's dispositions or personality characteristics have an impact on their learning. Children's dispositions will affect their concentration, perseverance, curiosity, willingness to try new things, positivity, resilience and tolerance.

Skills

Children's ability to learn will be affected by their skills in many different areas. These include the following skills.

- Physical skills, e.g. walking, climbing, cutting and writing
- Intellectual skills, e.g. memory, problem-solving and concept formation
- Language skills, e.g. listening, understanding, speaking, reading and writing
- Emotional skills, e.g. emotional regulation, emotional security, self-esteem and self-concept
- Social skills, e.g. interacting effectively with others, moral development and understanding social norms.

Knowledge and Understanding

Children's knowledge and understanding of the key aspects of the curriculum (e.g. Aistear or the primary school curriculum) will affect their learning.

Developmental Milestones

Children's development is uneven, e.g. a single child may have very advanced language skills but undeveloped physical skills. Children's development does not happen at the same rate for each child, either. Despite this, developmental milestones do exist and they are useful. These developmental milestones can help ECEC practitioners to notice early signs of potential difficulties. Practitioners can bring their concerns to parents and help them to contact other educational and health professionals.

Purpose of Assessment

Assessment is carried out for many reasons. In the ECEC setting, assessment can be carried out in order to:

- Understand where individual children are in terms of their physical, intellectual (cognitive), language, social and emotional development, so that activities are both developmentally appropriate and challenging for them

- Evaluate how well children are achieving the aims and goals of the early years curriculum
- Record children's learning, so that parents can reinforce and support this learning at home
- Inform parents about their children's developmental progress, which may help with the detection of early signs of developmental delay
- Observe children exhibiting problem behaviours, so that frequency, triggers and the response of staff can be investigated
- Allow children to reflect on their own learning and to discuss what motivates them and what they are interested in learning in the future
- Allow the teacher to reflect on their own teaching and to have the opportunity to try new activities, change routines, re-arrange the setting or use new resources
- Keep vital information on babies and young children, whose parents may need exact information (e.g. on fluid intake) if the child becomes ill and has to visit the doctor.

How Can Assessments Be Documented?

Samples of Work

Children should be encouraged to create a portfolio of their work. Portfolios can take the form of a scrapbook or folder in which pieces of work are kept. Photographs of larger pieces (e.g. construction pieces) can be taken and these can also be kept in the portfolio. Children should be involved in choosing which pieces go into their portfolio. Sometimes children like to bring home certain artworks and display them there. They should be allowed to do so, since a photograph or photocopy can be kept in their portfolio.

ICT

Once parental permission is given, photographs, video and audio recordings can be used to document children's learning and development. Practitioners can use video recordings in particular to observe groups of children while they are involved in activities. Sometimes, during the hustle and bustle of an activity, it can be difficult for practitioners to observe and evaluate learning. ICT helps practitioners with this reflective practice.

Daily Records

Practitioners (usually key workers) can make notes in a communications copy or other diary. The diary can be used to record lots of information regarding an individual child's care routines, e.g. what and how much they ate, when they slept and when they were changed. Notes regarding the child's daily activities can also be included in the diary, together with photographs of the child on particular days. The diary can be sent home to parents in the evening.

Checklists

The practitioner can use pre-prepared checklists in order to record particular aspects of children's learning and development. If the templates for checklists are planned carefully, the checklists can be very useful tools for recording all kinds of development, e.g. pre-writing skills.

Observation Notes

Practitioners observe the children in their setting all the time. Observations can be recorded quickly (in the form of brief notes) or in more detail. Various observation methods can be used and they will have corresponding reports. Time samples, event samples, narrative observations and pre-coded language observations can all be very useful.

How Can Assessments Be Stored?

Central Files

It is vital that central files containing certain types of information about children be kept in a secure location in the setting. It is advisable to have an office in the setting and a fireproof filing cabinet, which can be locked. The information in the central files can include such things as: parents' names and contact details, medical information and copies of reports from other professionals, e.g. physiotherapists. Usually, there is a separate file for each child and the files are alphabetically arranged in the cabinet. While it is important that this information is securely kept, it is also important that staff members have access to the information when required. In addition to hard copy (information printed on paper), settings may have information stored on computers. Computers should be password protected.

Learning Portfolios

Each child in the setting should have an individual learning portfolio into which selected samples of their work are stored. Portfolios can take the form of a folder, scrapbook or box. Again, children should be involved in decisions about what goes into their learning portfolio. This will encourage them to think about the quality of the work they are producing and the amount of effort they are putting into it. Photographs of larger pieces (e.g. construction pieces) can be taken and these can also be included.

Practitioner Files

In most settings, children have one key worker. Key workers should have a practitioner file for every child assigned to them. This may take the form of one big arch lever file with coloured dividers separating each child's information. Key workers can record all sorts of valuable information: observation notes, attendance records and records of conversations with parents or other staff members. The information in practitioner files may be transferred to the central file at the end of the year.

Methods of Assessment

Traditionally, assessment was seen as something that was very much adult-led. More recently, however, early years practitioners are beginning to value more child-led assessment methods. Nowadays, child-led assessment is used alongside traditional assessment methods.

Five assessment methods will be examined in this section:

- Self-assessment
- Conversation
- Observation
- Task setting
- Testing.

Two of these assessment methods are child-led: self-assessment and conversations. The remaining three assessment methods are adult-led: observation, task setting and testing.

Self-assessment

Self-assessment is a very important aspect of learning. When self-assessment goes well, children are able to think about what they have done, said or made. They can then reflect on what they would like to do differently or better next time.

In order for self-assessment to be worthwhile, children must have a clear idea of what it is they are trying to achieve. In this way, they have a yardstick with which to measure their work. Assessment can be measured in terms of learning goals.

Setting Learning Goals

Sometimes, adults can set learning goals for children. These learning goals can be defined by What I'm Looking For (WILF). For example, a teacher wants to do an art exercise with the children. Each child is given a sheet of paper showing the blank outline of a cake. The teacher wants the children to draw candles on top of the cake and colour them in so that the finished artwork looks like a birthday cake. In order to employ WILF, the teacher says: 'We are going to draw candles on top of the birthday cake. Then we are going to colour in it neatly.' The teacher then

pins a picture of a colourful birthday cake on the board, so that the children understand what they are supposed to do.

Sometimes, children can set their own goals. Adults have an important role in helping children clarify their own learning goals. This can be done by providing resources and prompting questions.

Resources can include:

- Books
- Magazines
- Internet access
- Photographs and examples of other children's work.

Questions can include:

- What do you think would happen if…?
- What do we need to…?
- Where do you want to start?
- What are you planning to do?
- What do you want to do?
- How do you think you should start?
- I wonder how we could…

Once children are clear on their learning goals, they will be able to start working through them and their learning will benefit greatly. Adults can help children to self-assess again. They can do this by asking questions that prompt the child to self-evaluate.

Questions can include:

- How did you make that?
- What did you use?
- How would it have turned out if…?
- Would you do anything differently next time?
- How did you think of that idea?
- What did you find easy about this work?
- What did you find difficult about this work?
- What part of this work did you enjoy?
- Are you happy with…?
- What did you learn from this?
- What would help you to do this better?

Conversation

Conversations between adult and child are very much a part of all assessment methods (with the exception of testing, where very little conversation takes place). Conversations are a useful part of assessment when the adult can employ various conversation strategies. These strategies give the adult a better of understanding of what children can do and understand.

Open Questions

These questions should be used most often, since they invite the child to think and elaborate on their answers. Examples of open questions include:

- Have you any ideas?
- Why do you think that happened?
- How did you do that?
- What were you thinking when?

Closed Questions

These questions are limited in terms of the response they require from children. These questions ask the child for short, factual answers. Closed questions should not be used all the time but they can be useful to get the conversation going. Examples of closed questions include:

- What colours did you use?
- Did you enjoy building the bricks?
- Which is your favourite picture?

Thinking Out Loud

Sometimes, if the adult 'thinks out loud' about a problem, this can prompt children to offer their opinions and suggestions. In this way, the adult can assess the children's understanding of particular concepts. For example, a teacher is transferring water from one vessel to another using a small spoon. The teacher says: 'This is going to take ages! I will have to think of a better way to do this.' This encourages the children to offer suggestions.

Expressing an Opinion

Children should be encouraged to offer an opinion and to justify it. For example, a teacher is reading a story during circle time. The teacher says: 'I think Paul was very selfish in this story. What do you think, Lara?' Similarly, during an art class, the teacher can say: 'What do you think we should use to stick this together, Amy?'

Listening to Children's Conversations

Adults should listen carefully to children's conversations while the children are at work together. Valuable information can be learned about children's knowledge and understanding. Notes on these conversations should be recorded.

Observation

Observation involves carefully watching and listening to children while they are involved in their daily activities and routines. Information gathered through observation is very important, since it gives practitioners information about what children know and can do already and what children *almost* know and can almost do. In other words, observation informs practitioners about the next steps for a child's learning.

There are a number of different observation methods that may be used, depending on what it is the practitioner wishes to find out. Observations may be planned or spontaneous. It is always better if observations are carried out by someone who knows the child very well, e.g. a key worker.

There are many different methods of observation:

- Narrative
- Pre-coded
- Checklist
- Time sample
- Event sample
- Movement charts
- Tables, pie charts and bar charts
- Photographs, audio and video recordings.

When practitioners are studying for their qualifications in college, they are asked to carry out a number of observations as part of certain modules (e.g. child development). These observations are often very detailed and take a huge amount of time to complete. This level of observation is not possible in the workplace: the practitioner would have little time to do anything else!

In the workplace, the emphasis is on *usefulness*. The aim of the practitioner is to record *accurate*, *useful* information about a child or group of children and their learning. The practitioner then uses this information to inform their work with the children. In this way, observation is a critical part of the learning process.

Narrative

With this observation method, the practitioner writes down in *storytelling format* what a child or a group of children are doing and saying during a given period of time. The practitioner usually takes quick notes while observing and then writes them up in more detail when they have time. If interesting issues or ideas come up during the narrative, the practitioner should take note of these and use them for planning future work with the child or children.

There are advantages to this technique. It gives a very rich and useful picture of children's thoughts, ideas, attitudes, problems, likes and dislikes. Information gained by listening and watching children carefully can be very useful for future planning.

There are disadvantages to this technique, also. It is quite time-consuming. A considerable amount of data is recorded over a short period of time. Narrative in its purest form requires the observer to observe and record only. This can be a problem in a busy workplace, where practitioners are required to multitask. Having said this, good narrative observations can be carried out while also interacting and working with children.

Pre-coded

Pre-coded observations are not really a separate observation technique, but rather a way of recording data more quickly while observing. Codes are used to indicate who is speaking to whom. What was actually said is recorded in longhand. The codes are decided by the observer and a key is given so that what is written makes sense to someone else reading the observation later on. For example, a practitioner named Ann wants to record an interaction she had with a pre-school child called Ellie Brady. The interaction can be recorded in a concise way, using pre-coded language:

A	$\longrightarrow$	EB	Bring the water over here, please.
EB	$\longrightarrow$	A	No, I can't. It will spill!
A	$\longrightarrow$	EB	Don't fill it up too much – then it won't spill.
EB	$\longrightarrow$	A	Ok…I'll just put a little bit in it.

Checklist

While checklists have been most commonly used for observing children's physical development and skills, they can be used much more widely than this. Checklists are a quick way of recording when a child has accomplished particular tasks. Items on checklists can be very varied. For example, a checklist for a child with autism could include items such as: 'Looks up reliably when name called' or 'Uses eye contact when reminded'.

There are advantages to checklists. They are quick to use, so they can be used for larger groups of children (e.g. a primary school class). They can be tailored to assess the learning goals being worked on at any given time, so they are very flexible.

There are disadvantages to checklists also. They do not provide detail about children's learning and development. Because they are created by the practitioner *before* observing the child, they can limit the focus to what is listed on the checklist. In this way, it is possible for the practitioner to miss important information about children's learning simply because it is not on the checklist. Having said this, checklists are useful and, as long as they are not the only method used, they are an important assessment tool.

Below is a sample checklist that could be used in a junior infant class in a primary school.

EARLY MATHS ACTIVITIES		
Student name:		
Strand unit	**Content**	**Achieved?**
Classifying	Can classify objects based on one attribute, e.g. colour	
	Can identify complement of a set, e.g. red/not red	
Matching	Can match equivalent and non-equivalent sets using one-to-one correspondence	
	Understands 'more than'	
	Understands 'less than'	
	Understands 'enough'	
	Understands 'as many as'	
Comparing	Can compare objects according to length, width, height, weight, quantity, thickness, size, etc.	
	Can compare without counting, e.g. 'more than', 'less than', 'the same as', etc.	
Ordering	Can order objects according to length and height	
	Can order sets without counting	

Time Sample

With time sample observations, the practitioner observes and records what a child or group of children are doing and saying at pre-determined time intervals. For example, a practitioner may decide to observe a child for 30 seconds every 15 minutes throughout the morning session of 9am–12.30pm. In this case, a total of 15 time samples would be recorded. Time sample observations give the practitioner a broad, general picture of how a child or group of children spends their time.

There are advantages to time samples. Because they are conducted over an extended period (e.g. every 15 minutes over an entire morning), they give a good general picture of the activities children are involved in and who their social groups are. Time samples are particularly useful for observing children's social interactions, e.g. if a practitioner has concerns that a particular child is not interacting well with their peer group.

There are disadvantages to time samples also. The main disadvantage of this method is that within a busy setting it may be difficult to remember to observe at the time intervals decided. Also, because only a snapshot is taken at each interval, valuable information may not be observed. However, practitioners can be flexible. They can decide to observe less frequently but for longer intervals, which could be helpful.

Below is an example of a time sample.

Time	Actions	Social group	Language
9.00	Circle time: RT and six other children sit on the ground for circle time. RT looks straight ahead.	RT, six other children and room leader	Not speaking
9.15	RT stands on her own behind the counter in the home corner. She is looking straight ahead into the room.	RT is on her own	Not speaking
9.30	RT stands behind the counter in the home corner. Another child (CF) is playing with the house phone and speaks to RT, who doesn't reply. RT smiles when CF presses buttons on the phone.	RT and CF	Not speaking

Event Sample

With event sample observations, the practitioner observes children over time at a particular event or activity (e.g. while at the sand tray). Event sample observations are also used to closely observe problem behaviour. This might be needed for a child who seems to be constantly getting into disagreements with other children. When used for this purpose, event samples give practitioners an *objective* view of what is actually going on. This is very important. Practitioners cannot rely on subjective data about children in their care; sometimes, what they believe to be correct can actually be very wrong.

There are advantages to event samples. Like time samples, event samples are usually conducted over an extended period of time, so the bigger picture can emerge. Issues that may be causing concern can be investigated in a systematic and objective way. For example, if the boys in the setting complain that the girls are always taking over the home corner and preventing the boys from playing there, this can be objectively investigated.

There are disadvantages to event samples also. In a busy setting, it can be difficult to record every time the targeted event occurs, especially when the observation runs over an extended period.

Below is a section of an event sample. The child being observed (TC) is viewed by staff as being constantly involved in disagreements with other children. The purpose of the observation is to objectively observe and document over the course of one day what is the

Time	P/UP	Antecedent	Description of behaviour	Consequence
9.12	UP	Group of four children playing at water tray area	TC fills small jug with water and begins to drink it. TC then spits out the water at CA. CA yells for room leader.	Room leader comes and asks both children what happened. Room leader explains to TC that spitting is not allowed and takes him away from area. TC has to stay by room leader's side for 10 minutes.
10.34	P	Group of six children sitting at the lunch table, having sandwiches and juice. CC pokes her finger into TC's sandwich	TC begins pounding CC's sandwich with his fist. CC pushes TC and TC falls backwards.	Room leader hears chair topple and tells TC to sit back up on his chair.
KEY				
P/UP: Provoked/unprovoked				
Antecedent: What happened directly before the behaviour being described				

nature of these disagreements. The observation should show whether or not the disagreements are provoked by the other children and also how staff respond to the disagreements.

Movement Charts

Movement charts (also called flowcharts) record a child's movements within the setting over a specified period of time. A floor plan of the setting is created and the information is recorded on this. Movement charts are generally used to monitor a child's use of equipment and resources. When complete, movement charts tell at a glance how a child spent their day. Sometimes a number of movement charts are carried out with different children in order to discover what toys and activities are most/least preferred by the class. This information can be used for planning the learning environment. For example, if a movement chart shows that the book corner is not being used at all, practitioners can think about ways of making it more attractive to the children.

There are advantages to movement charts. This method is quick and easy to use. Once an accurate floor plan is created, it can be photocopied and used to carry out observations with a number of different children. This method can very clearly show patterns of equipment usage, which provides good information for planning. This is a useful method for observing children's concentration levels.

There are disadvantages to movement charts. This method does not provide any detail about what children are actually doing at any given time. For example, a child may spend 20 minutes at the water tray but a movement chart will not reveal what the child actually did during this time. They may have engaged in a repetitive routine of pouring liquid from one vessel to another or they may have had a lively interaction with another child there. This type of observation does not pick up on the detail of what children are actually doing and saying. Also, if a child is very active and moves rapidly from one area to another, their movement chart can become very cluttered and confusing.

Sometimes it is useful for movement charts to be summarised into time segments. Rather than observing every movement of a particular child throughout the day, the movement of the child is summarised into main movements, i.e. the practitioner records the general movements of the child, giving the child's general location at different times of the day.

Below is a summarised version of a movement chart.

Location	Time
Home corner	9.30–10.15
Circle time	10.15–10.35
Computer area	10.35–11.00
Food area	11.00–11.15
Book corner	11.15–11.30
Art area	11.30–12.00
Home corner	12.00–12.23

Tables, Pie Charts and Bar Charts

Tables, pie charts and bar charts are not observation methods but ways of representing information. They can be used to display information about virtually anything. If they are created well, they can be a very clear and easy way to gain information.

Below is an example of a table that records children's fruit and vegetable intake over the course of a week. The children themselves record their fruit and vegetable intake. They place a picture or sticker on the table every time they eat a portion of a fruit or vegetable. Over the course of a week, the pattern of the children's fruit and vegetable intake will emerge.

Name	Monday	Tuesday	Wednesday	Thursday	Friday
Megan					
Mike					
Femi					
Shing					
Sam					

Photographs, Audio and Video Recordings

It is not advised that any video recording be carried out by students while doing observations. The reason for this is that the anonymity of the child cannot be preserved and parents of children will, quite rightly, object to this. However, practitioners may use both audio and video recordings if parents grant them permission to do so. Recordings can be very useful in determining children's learning and development. Practitioners can play these recordings several times and gain valuable insights that may not have been observed otherwise.

Audio tapes are a useful way of recording language, especially when children get older and begin to speak quickly. Audio tapes can be played back and useful notes can be taken. Photographs can be used for a whole host of reasons. Large pieces of children's work can be photographed for inclusion in their learning portfolios. Photographs can be taken of children engaged in various activities and these photographs can be displayed in common areas for parents to see. Children themselves can take photographs of things that interest them for inclusion with their project work.

Task Setting

Since children learn by doing, task setting is a useful way of assessing children's learning. Additionally, task setting is one of the principal tools of *assessment for learning*. Adults sometimes set tasks after a period of time or they may set a piece of work or a project for children after they have done work on a particular topic.

In order for task setting to be successful, children need to know exactly what it is they are being asked to do. They need to be 'let in on the marking scheme', so to speak, so that they have a clear idea of what is required for success. For example, the teacher sets up an obstacle course outside for the children. The teacher believes that the course will be useful for encouraging gross-motor skills and also social skills. The teacher takes the children outside to view the course. The teacher demonstrates how to complete each part of the course and the children copy these actions. The children then take turns completing the course on their own. The teacher then shows them how to time each other with a stopwatch.

Testing

In the early years curriculum, observation is the most common form of assessment used. Testing is not commonly used in the pre-school setting, but it may be used by health or other educational professionals in the pre-school when they are working with children suspected to have a special need. Commercially produced standardised tests are used by some professionals in order to test particular aspects of children's development, e.g. motor skills, social skills, language skills and behaviour. Results of tests are usually represented by comparing scores with those of other children the same age.

For most Irish children, the first time they are introduced to testing is in the second half of senior infants. This is when literacy and numeracy screening occurs. Screening instruments used in Irish schools include the Drumcondra Tests of Early Literacy (DTEL). These are screening and diagnostic tests suitable for use with pupils at the end of senior infants and the beginning of first class. The tests are used with children who are experiencing some difficulty in learning to read. The DTEL-Screening (DTEL-S) test and the DTEL-Diagnostic (DTEL-D) test draw on international best practice in early reading assessment in order to provide tests suitable for the Irish context. The tests complement a teacher's observations and assessments of a child's performance and increase understanding of particular difficulties. The tests provide information on young children's literacy difficulties so that instruction can be improved upon.

In addition to this, at the end of first class, all children complete a series of tests which may include: Drumcondra (both literacy and maths), Micra-T (literacy) or Sigma-T (maths) tests. Results are normally presented as a sten score, sten being an abbreviation for 'standard ten'. Sten scores are represented on a scale of 0–10. A score of 5 or 6 is average.

It is important to treat the results of these tests with caution, since certain factors can distort results, e.g. when English is not the child's first language. Having said this, testing does alert practitioners to children who may be experiencing difficulties and this is particularly important so that early intervention measures can be put in place.

Planning

All forms of assessment are carried out in order to help plan appropriately for children in ECEC settings. Assessments are also necessary to judge how well the plans of a practitioner are actually working. When practitioners plan effectively, they are well organised. As a result, this is very motivating and satisfying for them. Parents too appreciate an environment that is well planned and organised.

Plans can be long-term (usually yearly or monthly) or short-term (daily plans and individual session/activity plans). Some plans cater specifically for individual children. These are called individual learning plans (ILPs). Other plans cater more generally for groups of children.

The Planning Cycle

In order for planning to be successful, it must be carried out as part of a cycle. We do this all the time in our own lives, e.g. trying out a new dish for dinner. We *plan* for the dinner by researching recipes, asking friends for ideas, making a shopping list and buying what we need.

We *implement* the plan by following the recipe, cooking the dinner and serving it. We *evaluate* the plan by eating the dinner, deciding how good it was and thinking about what could be done differently next time. This information is then used to inform the next plan, and so on.

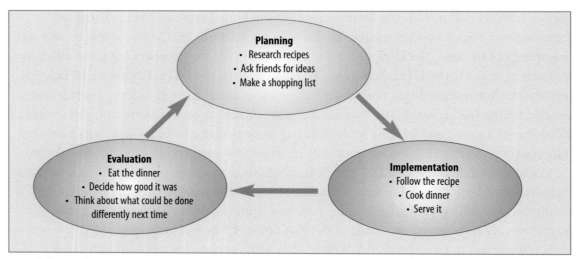

Good Practice When Planning

There are a number of principles of good practice that are important when planning. These include:

- Team approach
- Children's individual needs
- Children's opinions and preferences
- Diversity and equality
- Adaptability
- Health and safety
- Routines
- Parental involvement.

Team Approach

While individual practitioners (e.g. room leaders) will take responsibility for the writing, implementation and evaluation of their own plans, it is generally accepted that a team approach to parts of the planning process is very beneficial. Sharing of ideas and experience is very important, as is consistency within the setting. Different areas or rooms within the setting are not isolated entities, so daily routines need to be worked out (especially when facilities are shared).

Children's Individual Needs

In the Irish context, long-term curriculum plans and more detailed daily and session plans will use the Aistear curriculum framework to cater generally for children's developmental needs and interests. Where children have particular needs, ILPs will also be developed to ensure that these needs are being met. It is important that settings do not take a 'one size fits all' approach to planning.

Children's Opinions and Preferences

Children who are directly affected by the results of the planning process should be consulted with regards to their preferences, likes and dislikes. Watching and listening carefully to children while engaged in activities can also provide good information for planning.

Diversity and Equality

Experiences in the early years can and do affect children's perceptions and attitudes in later life. It is therefore very important that plans value and show respect for all members of society equally and that children are not excluded from taking part in any aspect of a plan, e.g. because of a physical disability. Practitioners must be aware of the *hidden curriculum*, i.e. messages that are being sent out to children unintentionally. An anti-bias curriculum respects diversity and equality and will reflect and value children's gender, family structure, culture, language, religion and traditions.

Adaptability

Plans are guides: they do not (and should not) have to be followed to the letter of the law. It is important that they are adaptable and can take account of unexpected or important events, e.g. Katie Taylor winning an Olympic gold medal for boxing could be used to talk about gender issues. This may not have been part of the long-term curriculum plan but the opportunity should be used nonetheless. A freezing cold day could be used to investigate what happens to water when it freezes, etc.

Health and Safety

While planning, practitioners need to consider very closely the health and safety of the children in their care at all times. All activities, setting procedures and routines should be checked for possible dangers. Changes must be made immediately if there are any concerns. For example, if children are going on a day trip to the fire station, a detailed plan for children's safety has to be put in place before embarking on the trip.

Routines

Children, like most adults, like to have a good degree of routine or predictability in their lives. Routines allow children to feel secure in the setting. Most settings (especially if certain facilities are shared) have daily routines or timetables that are followed by staff and children. Good routines will give children time to eat, rest, play outside, listen to a story, etc. Routines are not detailed. They are rather like your school or college timetable: they explain generally what happens at a particular time of day but they are not specific.

Parental Involvement

Planning can be greatly enhanced by parental involvement. Asking for parents' opinions and listening to what they have to say with regards to their children's needs does not give the impression that a setting does not know what it is doing. On the contrary, it gives the impression that a setting knows *exactly* what it is doing and that the staff are confident enough to ask for opinions and suggestions. Many parents have skills and knowledge that can be very beneficial to a setting, e.g. a landscape gardener may become involved in helping the children plant and tend a flowerbed.

Long-term Planning: Routines

Routines are general timetables that are used to give an overall picture of what happens on a day-to-day basis in a setting. Routines will cater for children's care and educational needs. Routines should be flexible and adaptable.

Settings will usually have very detailed care routines regarding specific tasks, e.g. nappy changing routines and feeding routines. These care routines exist to ensure that all staff members follow a set procedure and that they approach these tasks in an organised and safe manner. These routines help to ensure that mistakes are not made.

Detailed care routines will not be examined here. Instead, the focus will be on long-term routines in the ECEC setting.

Routines should:

- Provide structure and pattern to children's lives, giving them a sense of security
- Take account of the holistic development of the child, ensuring that all areas of development are considered in the routine
- Allow children some free, unstructured playtime
- Provide variety throughout the week, so that children do not become bored
- Give children quiet time or sleep time, depending on age requirements
- Meet children's hygiene and dietary needs
- Give children options and choices.

A number of factors must be considered when a routine is being planned.

Children's Needs

A good routine considers children's physical care needs and their educational and developmental needs. Before devising a routine, practitioners will ask questions, e.g.

- How much sleep do these particular children need?
- If children are not toilet-trained, how often should nappies be checked and changed?
- When should children have their meals and snacks?
- What play opportunities and activities are appropriate for children of this age?

Practical Considerations

Routines must consider practical factors, e.g. start and finish times of the setting. If facilities are shared, routines must take this into account. If the children are of mixed ages, this will influence the routine, e.g. quiet time for pre-school children when the babies are asleep.

Routine of the Home Setting

A routine in a home setting will often be quite detailed, since there may be a few children involved and both parents may be juggling work commitments. The routine of the setting may have to cater for school drop-offs and collections, nap times for the youngest children, meal times, homework time after school and outdoor activities.

Experience of the Practitioner

With experience, practitioners become very good at judging how long various parts of a routine are likely to take. It is advisable that if a practitioner is putting together a routine for the first time, they ask an experienced member of staff for their opinion. The inexperienced practitioner can sometimes create plans that have too much or too little in them.

Fixed Parameters of the Routine

The fixed parameters of the routine should be recorded on a skeleton framework. Fixed parameters are unchanging parts of the routine, e.g. start time, finish time, meal time and snack time. Once these requirements are met, the rest of the routine can be filled in.

Below is an example of a routine for the morning session of a pre-school.

9.00	9.30	10.15	10.30	11.15	11.45	12.15
Children arrive: free play	Choice of two structured activities	Snack time	Physical play (outside or in soft play cabin)	Choice of two structured activities	Free play	Story time

Long-term Planning: Curriculum

Following the introduction of Aistear in 2009 and the Free Pre-School Year Programme in 2010, most ECEC practitioners now produce long-term curriculum plans for their settings. This may mean some change, since many settings would only have created monthly or weekly plans before. Curriculum plans are usually developed to cover a full or half year and they are generally applied to children aged 3 and upwards. Other types of plans are created for children aged 0–3 years.

Yearly or half-yearly curriculum plans help practitioners to ensure that they have considered the learning aims and goals of Aistear in a comprehensive way. Curriculum plans show the big picture, rather than the detail of what is planned for a setting. In this way, curriculum plans are schematic. This is why curriculum plans may also be called *schemes of work* or *outline plans*.

One approach common in ECEC settings is 'theme of the week'. Activities undertaken during the week will link to this theme and also to the themes of Aistear and the aims and learning goals that go with these themes. In addition to this, children will also be involved in other activities during the week. These activities will also link up with the aims and learning goals of Aistear, e.g. free play activities. This is an important point: the aims and learning goals of Aistear are not just achieved through structured activities. Less structured activities are equally important.

When deciding on which activities to include in a curriculum plan, the following points should be considered:

- Children's preferences, e.g. what types of activities do the children enjoy most?
- Daily routine: activities must be planned so that they fit in with the children's daily routine, e.g. story time could take place towards the end of the day when children are ready to curl up on beanbags and listen to a story.
- Suitability: activities must be developmentally appropriate for children so that children are challenged and stimulated.
- Link to Aistear: activities should link closely with the themes, aims and learning goals of Aistear.
- Equality and diversity: activities should promote a positive world view, e.g. important festivals from other cultures can be celebrated.
- Health and safety, e.g. cookery activities must take into account any food intolerances or allergies.
- Resources: activities must be planned so that they can make use of the available resources.

Below is a section of a curriculum plan for a pre-school.

October		
Week number	**Theme of the week**	**Activities**
Week 1	Autumn	• Forest walk • Irish native trees • Story: *The Gruffalo* • Leaf gathering and leaf collage • Art activities with autumnal colours

Week 2	Wild animals found in Ireland	• Study of animals: fox, rabbit, hare, badger, deer and hedgehogs
		  • animal home
		  • animal young
		  • animal stories
		  • dangers animals face
		  • hibernation
		• Cookery: chocolate and shredded wheat hedgehogs

Week 3	Fruit	• Why we should eat fruit • Types of fruit: pictures, samples and names • Trying new fruits • Cookery and cutting fruit: fruit salad • Collage: fruit basket
Week 4	Halloween	• Traditions • Circle time: What happens in your house at Halloween? • Story: 'The Witch Who Was Frightened of Halloween' • Making bats and spiders • Decorating the room for Halloween • Making pumpkins

Curriculum Planning for Children Aged 0–3

Generally speaking, curriculum plans are not suitable tools for practitioners working with babies and children aged 0–3. Instead, practitioners should see the child's day in terms of *learning experiences*. Learning experiences fit around the daily care routine of the baby or toddler. When a baby sitting on the floor reaches for a toy, they are learning about spatial awareness. When a toddler slaps the water in the water tray, they are experiencing water. When they pick up sand and allow it to run through their fingers, they are experiencing sand.

Short-term Planning

While long-term curriculum plans tend to be broad and general, short-term plans tend to be much more specific and detailed. Short-term plans are called different things in different settings, e.g. activity plans, detailed plans or session plans. In this section, we will use the term 'activity plan'.

Activity Plans

Detailed activity plans ensure that activities run smoothly. They are particularly useful for students and for practitioners trying out new activities for the first time, since they prompt the adult to think carefully about issues vital to the success of the activity.

It is useful to ask the following questions:

- What is the aim and learning goal of the activity?
- How does this link to Aistear?
- What equipment and resources do I need for this activity?
- How long will the activity take?
- Is the activity suitable for all children in the group?
- If not, how can it be adapted to suit everyone?
- Are there any health and safety issues that must be considered?

In some settings, plans will have a very specific format. Montessori settings will make use of the *work cycle* and the *three-period lesson* (see Chapter 1). In other settings, the format will be far less prescriptive.

Below is a sample activity plan. This sample shows one way of presenting an activity plan; different settings may use different layouts.

Activity Plan

Theme of the Week:	*Wild Animals Found in Ireland*
Activity:	*Chocolate and Shredded Wheat Hedgehogs*
Time:	*9.30–10.15*
Number of children:	*8*
Age of children:	*3–4 years*
Practitioner:	*Áine (plus student)*

Themes, aims and learning goals

Theme	Aims	Learning goals
Wellbeing	**Aim 2:** Children will be as healthy and fit as they can be	Children will: • Discover, explore and refine gross- and fine-motor skills • Understand that no food is bad, but some should only be eaten occasionally (e.g. chocolate) • Show good judgment when taking risks (e.g. carrying glass bowl)
Communicating	**Aim 1:** Children will use non-verbal communication skills	Children will: • Understand non-verbal rules (e.g. taking turns in waiting for the microwave) • Listen to and receive information • Use language for asking questions and requesting

Theme	Aims	Learning goals
Exploring and thinking	**Aim 1:** Children will learn about and make sense of the world around them **Aim 4:** Children will explore ways to represent ideas, feelings, thoughts, objects and actions through symbols **Aim 4:** Children will have positive attitudes towards learning; and develop dispositions such as curiosity, playfulness, perseverance, confidence, resourcefulness and risk-taking	Children will: • Use new physical skills to manipulate objects and materials (e.g. breaking up chocolate/Shredded Wheat, mixing, placing/dotting eyeballs) • Develop a sense of time (e.g. two minutes in the microwave, waiting for the chocolate to harden) • Become familiar with and associate symbols (pictures, numbers, letters and words) with the things they represent (e.g. gathering equipment and ingredients shown on poster) • Demonstrate growing confidence in being able to do things for themselves

Equipment

- 8 × small aprons
- Poster of the equipment needed for this activity
- 4 × large tinfoil plates
- 4 × large glass bowls
- 8 × tea towels
- Microwave oven
- 4 × dessertspoons
- Fridge
- Sink

Materials

- 8 × Shredded Wheat bales (2 bales per team)
- 400g cooking chocolate (100g per team)
- A golfball-sized piece of white, ready-roll icing, quartered (¼ per team)
- 4 × icing pens (preferably black)
- Washing up liquid

Health and Safety Issues

- Check the children's allergy information (dairy and wheat).
- Ensure the children carry glass bowls safely and understand the risks.

Method

1   Place the relevant equipment and materials on a table that the children can reach.

2   Arrange the children into four teams (two children per team).

3   Explain the activity to the children. Encourage the children to discuss issues around the activity, e.g. How often should chocolate be eaten?

4   Ask the children to put on their aprons.

5   Show the children a poster of the equipment needed for this activity. (The poster will show a tin foil plate, a bowl, a spoon, squares of chocolate, etc.) Ask the children to collect the relevant equipment from the table.

6   When the children have all the materials to hand, ask them to crush the Shredded Wheat onto a tinfoil plate, using their hands.

7   Ask the children to break the chocolate into small pieces in the glass bowl.

8   Invite the children to come up to the microwave to melt the chocolate. Explain that chocolate takes 2 minutes to melt in this microwave but this might be different from their microwaves at home. Show the first team how to set the microwave for 2 minutes. Each team takes their turn in setting the time and melting their chocolate. Once their chocolate is melted, they return to their table, being careful to use tea towels to safely hold the glass bowls.

9   Ask the children to add the crushed Shredded Wheat to the melted chocolate. Assist them in using the dessertspoons to stir the mixture.

10 Demonstrate how the children should pile their mixture onto the tinfoil plates. The mixture must be divided into four, so that four hedgehogs are created by each team.

11 Show the children how to make eyeballs for their hedgehogs by rolling up small pieces of icing. Assist the children in attaching the eyeballs to the hedgehogs. Guide the children in using the icing pens to draw eyes on the hedgehogs.

12 Invite the children to place the plates of hedgehogs in the fridge to set.

13 While the hedgehogs are setting, invite the children to carefully bring their equipment to the sink so that it can be washed.

14 Demonstrate the washing up for the children and allow them to take turns in washing, drying and putting away the equipment.

15 Once the hedgehogs are set, they are ready for the children to bring home.

Extension Activities

Extension activities are follow-on activities. They must relate to an activity that the children have just carried out. A suitable extension activity for the Chocolate and Shredded Wheat Hedgehogs, would be reading a story about hedgehogs. *Hodge the Hedgehog* by Amy Sparks is a story about a hedgehog who does not like to share. This story would be an interesting extension activity for the children.

Evaluation

After an activity, it is useful to complete a short evaluation. The evaluation will focus on issues such as: organisation, timing, learning goals, etc. It can be useful if a brief evaluation is written on the bottom of an activity plan. This means that the practitioner will be aware of any pitfalls when they go to repeat the activity at a later date.

Individual Learning Plans (ILPs)

Individual learning plans (ILPs) are used to tailor the broader, overall curriculum (e.g. Aistear) to the individual child and their specific needs. As with other areas of planning, there is no standard way of presenting ILPs. Many different versions are used in many different settings. The examples presented in this chapter are meant as a guide only.

ILPs are important because they:

- Help the practitioner to focus on the specific needs of the child
- Ensure that children's unique interests and strengths are considered
- Inform overall curriculum and individual session planning
- Help the practitioner to monitor the child's individual progress
- Ensure that equipment and activities are appropriate for the child
- Help the practitioner to review, evaluate and improve their performance.

ILPs are particularly useful in helping staff to work effectively with children with additional needs in one or more developmental areas. ILPs for children with special needs are referred to as Individual Education Plans (IEPs) by the Department of Education and Skills (DES).

How to Create and Use and ILP

The best person to create an ILP for a specific child is the practitioner who knows the child best and who works with them most. This person is often referred to as the child's key worker. The starting point for creating an ILP for a child is to find out what their interests and developmental needs are. This is done in two ways: observing the child closely in the setting over a period of time and consulting with others who know the child well (e.g. parents or colleagues in the setting).

Often, ILPs will have a relatively tight area of focus (e.g. a child's language development) and the plan will set specific goals and targets in this area only. The child's other areas of development may not require the special attention of an ILP, since they may be sufficiently catered for by the general curriculum and session plans. However, some children have more complex special needs and their ILP may target more than one area of development. If there are other agencies working with the child (e.g. a speech therapist), they may have specific recommendations for the setting and these recommendations can be incorporated into the ILP.

Sometimes, ILPs are created for children with specific strengths in a particular area (e.g. a child who has already begun to read at pre-school). The ILP could include extension activities for this child so that they remain stimulated in the environment.

It is important to note that ILPs are not created only for children with long-term additional needs. They can be created over short periods of time. For example, if a child is going through a difficult time at home and this is causing behavioural problems in the setting, a short-term ILP can be put in place.

The following procedure can be followed in devising an ILP:

- Identify the child's need
- Set clear aims and goals
- Create the ILP.

Identify the Child's Needs

Most ILPs are initiated by an adult who notices that a child may have a particular additional need. This may be realised as a result of planned assessments, health checks or formal observations carried out in the early years setting. Sometimes, ILPs are initiated because a parent or carer expresses a general concern about an area of the child's development. Further assessments and observations will then be carried out in order to ascertain the exact nature of the child's additional need. For example, if a child in the setting seems to be very aggressive towards other children, event sample observations can be carried out to establish the facts: how often the child behaves aggressively, what happens before the aggressive behaviour, how adults in the setting deal with it, etc. Once the objective information has been collected, the ILP can be devised.

Set Clear Aims and Goals

Once a child's specific needs have been identified, the next step is to set a small number of clear aims and goals for the child. In this way, all staff working with the child will have a clear understanding of what the priorities are. If a child has complex needs, it is best to concentrate on one area at a time, rather than trying to tackle everything at once.

Create the ILP

Once the aim and goals of the ILP have been decided, the next step is to think about and record the strategies that will be used by the setting to work towards their achievements. Everyone who works with the child must be aware of these strategies so that the effect of them can be maximised.

Below is a sample ILP. It has been developed for Jake, who is a fraternal twin. Jake's speech is very limited. He makes one- to two-word utterances and his pronunciation is very unclear. His twin, Liam, has much more advanced speech and Liam tends to answer for Jake a lot of the time.

Individual Learning Plan (ILP)

Name:	Jake
Age:	3½ years
Date of plan:	3 October 2013
Date of review:	4 October 2013
Key worker:	Joan
Aim of plan:	To encourage Jake's spoken language

Goal	Strategies	Comments
Encourage Jake to speak for himself	• Put Jake and Liam into different groups for activities • When Liam begins answering for Jake, gently say: 'We will let Jake talk, Liam, good boy.'	
Give Jake more opportunities to use language	• Use one-to-one story time to encourage Jake to speak about the pictures in the story, etc. • Make better use of *expanding* and *labelling* techniques in interactions with Jake throughout the day	

ILPs are only effective if they are integrated into the overall plans for the setting. If they are not, they become unsustainable, since practitioners must also cater for the needs of the other children in the setting. Because of this, they cannot focus solely on an ILP for one child. In the example above, staff will employ the strategies indicated in the plan. They will do this throughout the day, while Jake is taking part in the activities planned for all children in the setting. The only additional activity just for him is the one-to-one story time.

ILPs must be regularly evaluated and reviewed. It may be that the chosen strategies do not working, e.g. Jake may not wish to do one-to-one story time while everyone else is doing something different. Equally, if the chosen strategies work very well, the child may no longer need an ILP for this area of development.

It is important that parents are involved in ILPs. They should be consulted at *all* stages of the planning process. If appropriate, they can implement the strategies in the home setting, too. For example, in the case of Jake, his parents could make a conscious effort to encourage Jake to speak for himself and they could also begin to use expanding and labelling strategies at home. Once parents are aware of the reasons behind an ILP for their child, they will usually greet it with enthusiasm.

Early Childhood Education and Play (5N1773): Assessment Guidelines

CHAPTER OUTLINE

- **Assessment of module 5N1773: Early Childhood Education and Play**

Note: This chapter provides suggested guidelines for the assessment of module 5N1773, awarded by QQI. While students will find these guidelines helpful, they should follow closely the brief and instructions given by their own particular college in all instances.

Marks are awarded under the following headings:

- Assignment 1: Critique of a toy, piece of equipment or play space   (30%)
- Assignment 2: Play activity   (30%)
- Skills demonstration: Storytelling activity   (40%)

Assignment 1

For this assignment, you are required to choose a piece of play equipment, a toy or a place space in the ECEC setting. You are required to thoroughly examine and evaluate it and present an assignment describing: the criteria you used for assessment, the process of assessment and a description of your findings.

Marks are awarded under the following headings:

▨	Logical rationale	5 marks
▨	Comprehensive list of criteria for assessing the item	5 marks
▨	Detailed assessment of the item	10 marks
▨	Detailed assessment of the role of the adult	5 marks
▨	Considered recommendations for changes/alternative uses for the item	5 marks
	Total	30 marks

Sample Brief

Early Childhood Education and Play (5N1773): Assignment Brief (30%)
Assignment 1: Critique of a toy, piece of equipment or place space
For this assignment you are required to select and assess a toy, piece of equipment or play area. Please present your assignment under the following headings:

1   Title page
2   Table of contents
3   Introduction: aim, objectives and rationale
4   Description of toy, piece of equipment or play area
5   List of criteria under which the toy, piece of equipment or play area will be assessed
6   Written account of findings
7   Evaluation
8   The role of the adult
9   Conclusion
10 Recommendations
11 References
12 Appendices

Guidelines
Title Page
The title page will normally show your name and PPS number. It will give details of the module title and the title of your assignment, e.g. Early Childhood Education and Play (5N1773): Assignment 1 – Critique of a toy, piece of equipment or place space.

Table of Contents

Provide a list of contents with page numbers. This will be done at the very end, when you know exactly what is in your assignment and on which page each section appears.

Introduction: Aim, Objectives and Rationale

You must state your general aim, i.e. what it is you are hoping to achieve in your assignment. Your aim could be: 'To choose a toy and critique it using a number of important criteria'.

Break down the aim of your assignment into smaller parts or objectives. Examples of objectives could be to:

- Compile a comprehensive checklist of assessment criteria with which to critique my chosen toy
- Use the checklist to assess my chosen toy
- Write up and evaluate my findings
- Outline and evaluate the role of the adult in relation to the toy.

You must provide a rationale for this particular assignment. Explain your reasons for choosing the particular toy. For example: 'I chose to critique Lego for this assignment because it is a toy that has been on the market for many years. Most settings have this piece of play equipment, so I thought it would be useful to assess and observe children using it in order to discover why this toy has continued to be popular since it first became available in the 1940s.'

Description of Toy, Piece of Equipment or Play Area

Give a detailed description of your chosen toy, piece of equipment or play area. The inclusion of visuals (e.g. scanned pictures) can aid this description.

List of Criteria under which Toy, Piece of Equipment or Play Area will be Assessed

You might decide to present this part of your assignment as a list of questions displayed in a table.

Criteria	Result of assessment
Does the toy carry international safety symbols?	
Can the toy be stored easily?	
Does the toy promote physical development? How?	

Written Account of Findings

Here you explain in detail the findings of your assessment. It is good to organise your findings under headings, as shown below.

- Safety
- Play value: Does it promote physical, intellectual, language, emotional and social development? How?
- Ease of storage
- Value for money
- Durability.

Evaluation

Here you consider the results of your assessment and outline whether or not it was a good toy, piece of equipment or place space. Talk about its positive and negative aspects.

The Role of the Adult

Describe how the adult can support children's learning and play in using this toy, piece of equipment or play space.

Conclusion

Summarise the main points of your assignment. Restate what you set out to do at the beginning of your assignment. Give an account of how you carried out your research and then briefly restate your findings.

Recommendations

Consider how the chosen toy, piece of equipment or play space could be improved upon or used more effectively.

References

Correctly list all sources of information used in the assignment e.g. books, internet articles, etc.

Appendices

Supply any additional information that is relevant to your work.

Assignment 2

For this assignment, you are required to submit a lesson plan of a play activity for a group of children aged 0–6. The plan must be devised in consultation with an adult in a supervisory role.

Marks are awarded under the following headings:

Logical rationale	5 marks
Comprehensive planning	5 marks

▪	Effective implementation	5 marks
▪	Detailed evaluation of learning outcomes from the activity for the children	10 marks
▪	Considered reflection on the personal role of the candidate in the activity	
	uses for the item	5 marks
	Total	30 marks

Sample Brief

Early Childhood Education and Play (5N1773): Assignment Brief (30%)
Assignment 2: Play activity
For this assignment, you are required to submit a lesson plan of a play activity for a group of children aged 0–6. Please present your assignment under the following headings:

1   **Title page**
2   **Table of contents**
3   **Introduction: aim, objectives and rationale**
4   **Record of consultation with an adult in a supervisory role**
5   **Details of anticipated developmental benefits of the activity**
6   **Explanation of how your chosen activity fits with the themes, aims and learning goals of Aistear**
7   **Details of resources, materials and/or equipment required to carry out the activity**
8   **Details of planning and implementation of the activity**
9   **Evaluation of the activity in terms of (1) success of planning and implementation and (2) developmental value of the activity**
10   **Evaluation of your role in making the activity a success**
11   **Description of ways in which the activity could be extended at a future date**
12   **Conclusion**
13   **Recommendations**
14   **References**
15   **Appendices**

Guidelines
Title Page
The title page will normally show your name and PPS number. It will give details of the module title and the title of your assignment, e.g. Early Childhood Education and Play (5N1773): Assignment 2 – Play activity.

Table of Contents

Provide a list of contents with page numbers. This will be done at the very end, when you know exactly what is in your assignment and on which page each section appears.

Introduction: Aim, Objectives and Rationale

You must state your general aim, i.e. what it is you are hoping to achieve in your assignment. Your aim could be: 'To choose, plan, implement and evaluate a developmentally appropriate and enjoyable play activity for a group of children in my work placement'.

Break down the aim of your assignment into smaller parts or objectives. Examples of objectives could be to:

- Research a range of play activity and then consult with my work place supervisor as to their suitability
- In consultation with my work place supervisor, choose one suitable play activity for me to plan, carry out and evaluate
- Research and outline the anticipated developmental benefits of the activity to the children in my care
- Show how my activity fits in with the themes, aim and learning goals of Aistear.

You must provide a rationale for this particular assignment. Explain your reasons for choosing the particular activity.

Record of Consultation with an Adult in a Supervisory Role

Describe how you consulted with your work placement supervisor before carrying out the activity. This could take the form of minutes of a meeting between you and the supervisor. You should prepare for the meeting by having a number of potential ideas to show them. In the minutes, you could describe how you showed your supervisor the brief and explained the nature of the assignment to them. You should minute the details of the discussion that followed and any results or decisions that followed the discussion. When you have the minutes typed or written up properly, you could ask your supervisor to sign them as proof of consultation.

Details of Anticipated Developmental Benefits of the Activity

Detail how you feel the activity should benefit children developmentally. Most students start with physical development (fine- and gross-motor skills), then move on to intellectual, language, emotional and social (PILES). It is good to have a paragraph on each. Begin each paragraph with a brief definition of the area of development you are focusing on and then describe how you feel the activity could benefit that particular area.

Example:

'Social development involves the development of three main skills – (1) development of the ability to interact effectively with others, (2) development of an understanding of social norms and (3) moral development. My play activity where children played a game of snakes and ladders promoted all three of these areas. Children had to co-operate with each other, they had to take turns (a social norm) and they had to play the game by the rules (moral development).'

Explanation of How Your Chosen Activity Fits with the Themes, Aims and Learning Goals of Aistear

For completion of this part of your assignment, read the section of this book that deals with Aistear's themes (see Chapter 11). You can also download a copy of the Aistear booklet 'Principles and Themes' online (http://www.ncca.biz/Aistear/).

It is important that you consider all four Aistear themes: Wellbeing, Identity and Belonging, Communicating, and Exploring and Thinking. You must look at the aims and learning goals for each theme and explain how your chosen activity could be used to promote them.

Example:

'The children as part of their play activity have made play-dough and are currently using pastry cutters and other implements to shape it as they wish. This activity promotes a number of Aistear's themes, aims and learning goals. Under the theme of Wellbeing, Aim 2 (children will be as fit and healthy as they can be), this activity promotes a number of learning goals. By making the play-dough, mixing it and kneading it, the children are increasing control over their body movements and co-ordination (Aim 2, Learning Goal 1). The activity also helps them to discover, explore and refine gross- and fine-motor skills (Aim 2, Learning Goal 3). Cleaning up after the activity promotes Aim 2, Learning Goal 6 (hygiene awareness).'

Details of Resources, Materials and/or Equipment Required to Carry Out the Activity

List all the resources, materials and/or equipment required to carry out the activity. This is an essential part of the planning process and is necessary for the activity to run smoothly.

Details of Planning and Implementation of the Activity

Here you can make a numbered list of what you need to do before the activity (planning) and during the activity (implementation).

Evaluation of the Activity in terms of (1) Success of Planning and Implementation and (2) Developmental Value of the Activity

Critically evaluate the success of your activity. Under (1) Planning and Implementation you should consider questions such as these.

- ▨ Did I try out the activity beforehand myself?
- ▨ Did I have all equipment and materials ready?
- ▨ Did I have enough equipment and materials for all children involved?
- ▨ Did I allow enough time for the activity?
- ▨ Did the children have a clear sense of what to do?

Under (2) Developmental Value of the Activity, you should return to sections 4 and 5 of your assignment. Review your consultation with your supervisor and your list of anticipated developmental benefits of the activity. Once you have reviewed this material, describe how you feel the activity actually benefited the children. Give a reason for each point made.

Example:
'I felt the children gained practice using their gross-motor skills when they were required to mix the water into the flour using small wooden spoons. I noticed that some of the children were able to hold the spoon correctly and mix effectively, whereas others had to be shown how to hold the spoon and mix while holding the bowl so that it did not slip away from them. By the time all the dough was mixed, most of the children had achieved this skill. I allowed them to get as much practice as they wanted before moving on to shape the dough.'

Evaluation of Your Role in Making the Activity a Success
The adult's role in children's play can be summarised under two headings:
- ▨ Provision of appropriate equipment, materials and resources for play
- ▨ Supporting children's learning through scaffolding and extending their play.

You should evaluate in this section how well you fulfilled these two roles before *and* during this activity. You should include some theory here, e.g. Vygotsky (see Chapter 7).

Description of Ways in Which the Activity Could Be Extended at a Future Date
Describe how this activity could be extended at a future date. For example, if you carried out a paper cutting and pasting activity with the children, you could extend this another day by bringing other things to cut and paste (e.g. fabric, wool) as part of a collage activity.

Conclusion
Summarise the main points of your assignment. Restate what you set out to do at the beginning of your assignment. Give an account of how you carried out your activity and then briefly restate your findings.

Recommendations

Consider how the activity could be improved upon in the future.

▪ Was it suitable for the age group you were working with?

▪ Could be it be better planned?

▪ Is there anything about your performance that could be improved upon?
   You should also detail here how you feel this activity could be built upon in future
   activities in the setting.

References

Correctly list all sources of information used in the assignment e.g. books, internet articles, etc.

Appendices

Supply any additional information that is relevant to your work.

Skills Demonstration

For this assignment, you are required to perform an oral presentation, reading a story to a group of children aged 0–6. You are required to voice record your presentation for assessment purposes. You are also required to submit a written assignment on the storytelling.

   Marks are awarded under the following headings:

▪ Logical rationale	5 marks
▪ Effective performance, including:	20 marks
– Ability to hold audience's attention	
– Effective interaction with audience	
– Successful use of voice	
– Appropriate use of aids/resources	
▪ Comprehensive evaluation, including:	15 marks
– The techniques and aids/resources used	
– The potential value of the story/activity for a group of children (0–6)	
– The candidate's personal role in the performance	
Total	40 marks

Sample Brief

Early Childhood Education and Play (5N1773): Skills Demonstration (40%)

For this assignment, you are required to perform an oral presentation, reading a story to a group of children aged 0–6. You are required to voice record your presentation for assessment purposes. You are also required to submit a written assignment on the storytelling. Please present your assignment under the following headings:

1 Title page
2 Table of contents
3 Introduction: aim, objectives and rationale
4 Record of consultation with an adult in a supervisory role
5 Details of anticipated developmental benefits of the presentation

6 Explanation of how your chosen presentation fits with the themes, aims and learning goals of Aistear
7 Details of resources, materials and/or equipment required to carry out the presentation
8 Details of planning and implementation of the presentation
9 Details of storytelling techniques you intend to use to enhance the storytelling presentation
10 Evaluation of the presentation in terms of (1) success of planning, implementation and storytelling techniques used, (2) age appropriateness of the story chosen and (3) developmental value of the activity
11 Evaluation of your role in the presentation
12 Description of ways in which the presentation could be extended at a future date
13 Conclusion
14 Recommendations
15 References
16 Appendices

Guidelines

Title Page

The title page will normally show your name and PPS number. It will give details of the module title and the title of your assignment, e.g. Early Childhood Education and Play (5N1773): Skills demonstration – Storytelling.

Table of Contents

Provide a list of contents with page numbers. This will be done at the very end, when you know exactly what is in your assignment and on which page each section appears.

Introduction: Aim, Objectives and Rationale

You must state your general aim, i.e. what it is you are hoping to achieve in your assignment. Your aim could be: 'To choose an interesting, age-appropriate story for a group of children in my workplace setting and to read it in a fun and interesting way using effective storytelling techniques'.

Break down the aim of your assignment into smaller parts or objectives. Examples of objectives could be to:

- Research and choose a story that is interesting, fun and age-appropriate for the children in my work experience setting
- Make suitable props to use while storytelling in order to enhance the children's interest and enjoyment.

You must provide a rationale for this presentation. Describe the story you have chosen, together with any props or storytelling aids. You should explain in this section why you made the choices you did. What is it about your chosen book or story that makes it suitable for this activity? (See Chapter 9 for guidance.)

Record of Consultation with an Adult in a Supervisory Role

Describe how you consulted with your work placement supervisor before carrying out the activity. This could take the form of minutes of a meeting between you and the supervisor. You should prepare for the meeting by having a number of potential ideas to show them. In the minutes, you could describe how you showed your supervisor the brief and explained the nature of the assignment to them. You should minute the details of the discussion that followed and any results or decisions that followed the discussion. When you have the minutes typed or written up properly, you could ask your supervisor to sign them as proof of consultation.

Details of Anticipated Developmental Benefits of the Presentation

Detail how you feel the presentation should benefit children developmentally. Most students start with physical development (fine- and gross-motor skills), then move on to intellectual, language, emotional and social (PILES). It is good to have a paragraph on each. Begin each paragraph with a brief definition of the area of development you are focusing on and then describe how you feel the activity could benefit that particular area.

Explanation of How Your Chosen Activity Fits with the Themes, Aims and Learning Goals of Aistear

For completion of this part of your assignment, read the section of this book that deals with Aistear's themes (see Chapter 11). You can also download a copy of the Aistear booklet 'Principles and Themes' online (http://www.ncca.biz/Aistear/).

It is important that you consider all four Aistear themes: Wellbeing, Identity and Belonging, Communicating, and Exploring and Thinking. You must look at the aims and learning goals for each theme and explain how your presentation could be used to promote them.

Details of Resources, Materials and/or Equipment Required to Carry Out the Presentation

List all the resources, materials and/or equipment required to carry out the storytelling. Examples include: seating, books, story boards, puppets, backdrops, story sacks, story boxes, masks and dress-up clothes. Where possible, take photographs of what you used and include them in this section to aid your description.

Details of Planning and Implementation of the Presentation

Here you can make a numbered list of what you need to do before the presentation (planning) and during the presentation (implementation).

Details of Storytelling Techniques you intend to use to Enhance the Presentation

Read Chapter 9 of this book for ideas on storytelling techniques. When you have decided on your story, techniques and props, describe them here.

Evaluation of the Presentation in terms of (1) Success of Planning, Implementation and Storytelling Techniques used, (2) Age Appropriateness of the Story Chosen and (3) Developmental Value of the Activity

In this section, explain what went well or not so well with regards to the planning and implementation of your storytelling activity.

- How successful were your storytelling techniques?
- How do you know?
- Do you think the book was age appropriate?
- Were the children interested to the end?
- Did they engage with the story? How?
- How do you think the activity benefited the children? Explain.
- What did you do well?
- What would you change next time?

Evaluation of Your Role in the Presentation
- Did you set up well for the activity?
- How did you ensure all children could see the story clearly?
- Were you nervous?
- Did this come across?
- Do you think you projected your voice well?
- Did you use your voice to make the story more interesting and lively?
- Did you put on voices for different characters?
- How did you encourage the children to interact or become involved in the storytelling?

Description of Ways in Which the Presentation Could Be Extended at a Future Date
Describe any extension activities that could be inspired by your presentation. List a range of activities that could be inspired by the storytelling.

Conclusion
Summarise the main points of your assignment. Restate what you set out to do at the beginning of your assignment. Give an account of how you carried out your presentation and then briefly restate your findings.

Recommendations
Consider how the activity could be improved upon in the future.
- Could you use a more suitable book?
- Could you perform the story in a more confident way?
- Could you encourage the children to engage more with the story next time?

References
Correctly list all sources of information used in the assignment e.g. books, internet articles, etc.

Appendices
Supply any additional information that is relevant to your work.

Appendix 1: Sample Aistear Theme

The following is an extract from *Aistear: The Early Childhood Curriculum Framework* (2009: 25–8). This section covers the theme of *Identity and Belonging* and lists its *aims*, *learning goals* and *sample learning opportunities*.

Theme: Identity and Belonging

The theme of *Identity and Belonging* is about children developing a positive sense of who they are and feeling that they are valued and respected as part of a family and community.

From birth, children develop a sense of who they are. Relationships with family members, other adults and children, friends and members of their community play a key role in building their identities. Children's sense of who they are is shaped by their characteristics, their behaviour and their understanding of themselves, their family and others. Belonging is about having a secure relationship with or a connection with a particular group of people. When children feel a sense of belonging and sense of pride in their families, their peers and their communities, they can be emotionally strong, self-assured and able to deal with challenges and difficulties. This creates an important foundation for their learning and development.

Giving children messages of respect, love, approval and encouragement enables them to develop a positive sense of who they are and a feeling that they have an important contribution to make wherever they are. Positive messages about their families, backgrounds, cultures, beliefs and languages help children to develop pride in who they are. These messages also give them confidence to voice their views and opinions, to make choices and to help shape their own learning.

By embracing difference, by exploring their own attitudes in relation to equality and diversity and by realising that their attitudes and values influence children, adults can develop the insights, self-awareness and skills that are needed to help children develop a strong sense of identity and belonging. This helps to ensure that all children are respected and valued and that they can recognise and deal with discrimination and prejudice.

Identity and belonging	
Aims	**Learning goals**
Aim 1: Children will have strong self-identities and will feel respected and affirmed as unique individuals with their own life stories.	In partnership with the adult, children will: • build respectful relationships with others • appreciate the features that make a person special and unique (name, size, hair, hand and footprint, gender, birthday) • understand that as individuals they are separate from others with their own needs, interests and abilities • have a sense of 'who they are' and be able to describe their backgrounds, strengths and abilities • feel valued and see themselves and their interests reflected in the environment • express their own ideas, preferences and needs, and have these responded to with respect and consistency.
Aim 2: Children will have a sense of group identity where links with their family and community are acknowledged and extended.	In partnership with the adult, children will: • feel that they have a place and a right to belong to the group • know that members of their family and community are positively acknowledged and welcomed • be able to share personal experiences about their own families and cultures, and come to know that there is a diversity of family structures, cultures and backgrounds • understand and take part in routines, customs, festivals and celebrations • see themselves as part of a wider community and know about their local area, including some of its places, features and people • understand the different roles of people in the community.
Aim 3: Children will be able to express their rights and show an understanding and regard for the identity, rights and views of others.	In partnership with the adult, children will: • express their views and help make decisions in matters that affect them • understand the rules and the boundaries of acceptable behaviour • interact, work co-operatively and help others • be aware of and respect others' needs, rights, feelings, culture, language, background and religious beliefs • have a sense of social justice and recognise and deal with unfair behaviour • demonstrate the skills of co-operation, responsibility, negotiation and conflict resolution.
Aim 4: Children will see themselves as capable learners.	In partnership with the adult, children will: • develop a broad range of abilities and interests • show an awareness of their own unique strengths, abilities and learning styles, and be willing to share their skills and knowledge with others • show increasing confidence and self-assurance in directing their own learning • demonstrate dispositions like curiosity, persistence and responsibility • experience learning opportunities that are based on personal interests, and linked to their home, community and culture • be motivated, and begin to think about and recognise their own progress and achievements.

Sample Learning Opportunities

Babies

The adult:

- ■ Closely observes babies, knows their **personalities** well, respects and responds to their **individual needs and preferences** and builds on **care practices** from home:
  - ◆ knows babies' natural rhythms, supports sleeping and feeding routines and provides favourite comfort objects, e.g. blanket, teddy, soothes
  - ◆ places photographs of parents near the sleeping area and knows at least a few words in the babies' home language when that language is neither English nor Irish
  - ◆ responds appropriately to babies' feelings, e.g. soothes them when upset, builds on their curiosity, provides positive physical contact such as cuddling, hugging and holding on the lap

- ■ Supports babies' emerging **sense of identity**:
  - ◆ helps babies understand and use their physical capabilities, e.g. encouraging them to clap hands, to reach, to smile, to wave, to point and to talk using gurgles and sounds
  - ◆ helps babies to distinguish themselves from others, e.g. says the baby's name and the names of family members, looks at and points to photographs
  - ◆ provides opportunities for babies to be with, to watch and to listen to other children
  - ◆ provides low level mirrors and reflective toys, such as activity cubes with safety mirrors attached, and describes what babies see to enable them to recognise their own reflection
  - ◆ displays photos of babies and their work in the setting
  - ◆ shows the daily routine through photographs, makes portfolios of babies' constructions and paintings as they grow
  - ◆ helps babies to identify body parts by pointing to, touching, and naming them, e.g. pointing to toes, wriggling fingers, tapping heads, touching ears

- ■ Provides opportunities for **older siblings**, **peers** and **babies** to see one another and to be together at different times during the day, optimising opportunities that will enable them to interact and communicate:
  - ◆ plans activities and events when babies, siblings, and/or older children can be together, e.g. meal times, song-time, before going home
  - ◆ ensures babies and siblings have time outside to play together regularly

- ■ Provides babies with experiences of the **outside world**:
  - ◆ brings babies outside to explore and observe on a regular basis
  - ◆ gives babies opportunities to see the outdoors, e.g. positions babies near low level windows where they have a view outside when they are inside

- provides babies with natural items, pictures and books about nature, e.g. the weather, animals and things that happen outside such as farming, travel, or buildings
- plans visits to places in the local community such as a park, a library, a playground, a market
- brings babies to the local parent-and-baby or parent-and-toddler group.

Appendix 2: Referencing

If you are quoting directly from a source (e.g. a textbook), you must quote the text accurately, word for word. Enclose the quote within quotation marks.

If you are quoting a small amount of text, you can blend the original quotation into your own text, marking it off with quotation marks. For example:

> In my observation, TC took four short steps from the activity table to the bean bag. This is usual for this age group, since 'when infants learn to walk, they typically take small steps because of their limited balance control and strength' (Santrock 2009: 158).

If you are quoting a larger amount of text, it should be presented as a paragraph on its own. It should be *indented* in order for it to stand out; because of this, it does not need quotation marks.

If you do not quote a sentence in full, you must indicate this with the use of an *ellipsis*. For example:

> The motor accomplishments of the first year bring increasing independence, allowing infants to explore their environment more extensively and to initiate interactions with others more readily… (Santrock 2009: 159).

If you want to mention an author's idea as part of your sentence, but you do not want to use their words exactly, this is called a *citation*. This means that you acknowledge (cite) the author in your main text and give a full reference for their work at the end of your essay. For example:

> Santrock (2009) believes that because infants have limited balance control and strength, they typically take small steps while learning to walk.

If you want to cite a book that was written by many authors, it might be easiest to use *et al.* in the main text and give a full citation (that includes all of the authors) in the references at the end of your essay. For example:

> Parental participation leads to higher adult expectations and increased parental confidence and aspirations (Schweinhart et al. 2005).

Ensure that you quote and cite correctly throughout your essay. Then, at the end of your essay, you must provide a section called References. It is here that you give full publication details for any work you have quoted or cited. Again, it is worthwhile to examine published books on the subject of ECEC, so that you can see how references are displayed.

An example of a reference for a *book* is:

Healy, J. and Spencer, M. (2008) *Surviving your Placement in Health and Social Care.* UK: Open University Press.

An example of a reference for a *book with a compiling editor* is:

Fink, J. (ed.) (2004), *Care: Personal Lives and Social Policy.* Bristol: The Open University/ The Policy Press.

An example of a reference for an essay in a *journal* is:

Anglin, J. (1992), 'How Staff Develop', *FICE Bulletin*, 6, 18–24.

It is also important to give proper references for any relevant material you view on the internet.

Within your essay, you might want to refer the reader to a useful website. If so, give the website address in full. For example:

La Leche League of Ireland gives useful information on their website: www.lalecheleagueireland.com.

If you cite online material in the main body of your essay, give a full citation in the references at the end of your essay. Ensure that you include the date on which you accessed the online material. For example:

SESS (Special Education Support Service) 'Differentiation in the Classroom for Students with Special Educational Needs' (online) <www.sess.ie/resources/teaching-methods-and-organisation> accessed 13 June 2011.

There are many different referencing systems and it is worthwhile spending time in getting to know one suitable for your ECEC essays. The best way to do this is to look at published books in the area of ECEC. Take note of how references are used in these books. Pay attention to the use of commas, full stops, brackets and italics; they are important.

References and Further Reading

Aries, P. (1988) *Centuries of Childhood: A Social History of Family Life*. New York: Random House.

Beaver, M., Brewster, J., Jones, P., Lesley Keene, A., Neaum, S., Tallack, J., Green, S., Sheppard, H. and Walker, M. (2001) *Babies and Young Children: Diploma in Childcare and Education*. Cheltenham: Nelson Thornes.

Bruce, T. (2009) *Early Childhood: A Guide for Students* (2nd edn.). London: Sage.

Bruce, T. (2012) *Early Childhood Practice: Froebel Today*. London: Sage.

Burghardt, G. M. (1984), 'On the Origins of Play', in P. K. Smith (ed.), *Play in Animals and Humans*. Oxford: Basil Blackwell.

CECDE (Centre for Early Childhood Development and Education) (2006) *Síolta: The National Quality Framework for Early Childhood Education*. Dublin: CECDE.

Cohen, D. (2006) *The Development of Play* (3rd edn.). East Sussex: Routledge.

Daly, M., Byers, E. and Taylor, W. (2004) *Early Years Management in Practice*. Oxford: Heinemann.

Frost, J. L. (2010) *A History of Children's Play and Play Environments: Toward a Contemporary Child-Saving Movement*. New York: Routledge.

Hainstock, E. (1986) *The Essential Montessori*. New York: Penguin Group.

Hughes, B. and Melville, S. (1996) *A Playworker's Taxonomy of Play*. London: Playlink.

Jasper, M. (2003) *Beginning Reflective Practice*. Cheltenham: Nelson Thornes.

Lilley, I.M. (1967) *Friedrich Froebel: A Selection From His Writings*. Cambridge: Cambridge University Press.

Lindon, J. (2002) *Childcare and Early Years Education*. London: Cengage Learning Vocational.

Minsky, R. (1996) *Psychoanalysis and Gender*. London: Routledge.

Montessori, M. (1972) *Discovery of the Child*. New York: Ballantine Books.

Montessori, M. (1988) *The Absorbent Mind*. Oxford: Clio Press.

Murray, C. and Urban, M. (2012) *Diversity and Equality in Early Childhood*. Dublin: Gill & Macmillan.

NCCA (National Council for Curriculum and Assessment) (2009) *Aistear: The Early Childhood Curriculum Framework*. Dublin: NCCA.

Nicol, J.and Taplin, J. (2012) *Understanding the Steiner Waldorf Approach*. New York: Routledge.

Orme, N. (2001) *Medieval Children*. New Haven: Yale University Press.

Tassoni, P., Beith, K., Bulman, K. and Eldridge, H. (2007) *CACHE Level 3: Child Care and Education* (4th edn.). London: Heinemann.

Winnicott, D.W. (1972) *Holding and Interpretation: Fragment of an Analysis.* New York: Grove Press.

Online Resources

Aistear

<www.ncca.biz/Aistear>

Barnados

<www.barnardos.ie/assets/files/information-pack/Diversity_IP.pdf>: Diversity information pack.

Belbin Associates

<www.belbin.com/content/page/6133/Belbin(uk)-2011-TeamRolesInANutshell.pdf>: Team roles, according to Belbin.

Centre for Early Childhood Development and Education (CECDE)

<www.cecde.ie/gaeilge/pdf/Questions%20of%20Quality/Murray.pdf>: Éist project.

Childminding Ireland

<http://www.childmindingireland.ie>

Children's Rights Alliance

<www.childrensrights.ie/resources/18th-anniversary-ireland-ratifying-un-convention>: Ireland and the UNCRC.

Citizens Information

<www.citizensinformation.ie/en/>: The role of the Public Health Nurse.

Community Playthings

<www.communityplaythings.co.uk/learning-library/articles/creating-indoor-environments-for-young-children>: Creating indoor environments for young children.

Daily Montessori

<www.dailymontessori.com/sensitive-periods>: Sensitive periods.

Department of Children and Youth Affairs

<www.dcya.gov.ie/documents/childcare/diversity_and_equality.pdf>: Diversity and equality guidelines.

<www.dcya.gov.ie/viewdoc.asp?fn=/documents/childcare/CityCountyChildcareCommittee.htm>: City and County Childcare Committees (CCCs).

Department of Health and Children

<www.dohc.ie/legislation/statutory_instruments/pdf/si20060604.pdf?direct=1>: Pre-school Regulations 2006.

<www.dohc.ie/publications/children_first.html>: Children First: National Guidelines for the Protection and Welfare of Children.

< www.dohc.ie/publications/our_duty_to_care.html>: Our Duty to Care: The Principles of Good Practice for the Protection of Children and Young People.

<www.dohc.ie/publications/pdf/HPU_pre-school_guidelines.pdf?direct=1 <accessed>: Food and nutrition guidelines for pre-school children.

Department of Justice and Equality

<http://www.justice.ie/en/JELR/EqualStatusActsConsldtd_00_04.pdf/Files/EqualStatusActsConsldtd_00_04.pdf>: Equal Status Acts

<www.justice.ie/en/JELR/modelframework.pdf/Files/modelframework.pdf>: Developing Childcare in Ireland.

Diversity in Early Childhood Education and Training (DECET)

<www.decet.org/fileadmin/decet-media/publications/Diversity-and-Social-Inclusion.pdf>: Diversity and social inclusion.

Early Childhood Ireland

Forbairt Naíonraí Teoranta

<http://www.naionrai.ie>

Froebel USA

< www.froebelgifts.com>: Froebel gifts.

Health Service Executive (HSE)

<www.hse.ie/eng/>

<www.healthpromotion.ie/hp-files/docs/HPM00406.pdf>: Infection in schools.

HighScope Educational Research Foundation

<http://www.highscope.org>

Irish Steiner Kindergarten Association

<www.steinerireland.org>

Meningitis Trust

<www.meningitis-trust.org>

National Association for the Education of Young Children

<www.naeyc.org/store/files/store/TOC/254.pdf>: Anti-bias education.

National Childminding Association, UK (NCMA)

<www.ncma.org.uk/pdf/being_reflective.pdf>: Being self-reflective.

Office of the Attorney General

<www.irishstatutebook.ie/1981/en/si/0390.html>: Infectious Diseases Regulations.

<www.irishstatutebook.ie/1991/en/act/pub/0017/index.html>: Childcare Act 1991.

<www.irishstatutebook.ie/1998/en/act/pub/0030/index.html>: Parental Leave Act 1998.

<www.irishstatutebook.ie/1998/en/act/pub/0049/index.html>: Protections for Persons Reporting Child Abuse Act 1998.

<http://www.irishstatutebook.ie/2005/en/act/pub/0010/>: Safety, Health and Welfare at Work Act 2005.

Oireachtas

<www.oireachtas.ie/documents/bills28/acts/2004/A3004.pdf>: Education for Persons with Special Educational Needs Act 2004.

Organisation for Economic Co-operation and Development (OECD)

<www.oecd.org/education/preschoolandschool/34431749.pdf>: Background report of thematic review of ECEC in Ireland.

Síolta

<www.siolta.ie/media/pdfs/Research%20Djgest%20-%20Communication.pdf>

St Nicholas Montessori Society of Ireland

<http://www.montessoriireland.ie>

Steiner Waldorf Schools Fellowship

<http://www.steinerwaldorf.org.uk/downloads/earlyyears/EY_Foundation_Stage_Guide.pdf>: Steiner Waldorf guide to ECEC.

UNICEF

<http://www.unicef.org/crc/index_30177.html>: UNCRC.

Others

<www.blog.montessoriforeveryone.com/how-to-evaluate-the-progress-of-a-montessori-child.html>: How to evaluate the progress of a Montessori child.

<www.friedrichfroebel.com/elements.html>: Elements of a Froebelian education.

<www.montessori.org.au/montessori/biography.html>: Biography of Maria Montessori

<www.suite101.com/article/baking-bread-in-the-waldorf-homeschool-a174919>: Baking with children in the Steiner Waldorf classroom.

< www.teambuildingportal.com/articles/systems/practical-use-belbin-theory>: Building teams using Belbin's theory.

<www.upstartcrowliterary.com/blog/?p=811>: Attributes that make a good children's book.

Index